WHAT HAPPENS WHEN YOU DIE

Robert Crookall

www.whitecrowbooks.com

What Happens When You Die

Original Copyright © 1972 by Robert Crookall.
First published by Colin Smythe Ltd.

Copyright © 2021 by Robert Crookall. All rights reserved.

Published in the United States of America and the United Kingdom by White Crow Books; an imprint of White Crow Productions Ltd, in association with Colin Smythe Ltd.

The moral right of Robert Crookall to be identified as the author of this work has been asserted in accordance with the Copyright, Design and Patents act 1988.

No part of this book may be reproduced, copied or used in any form or manner whatsoever without written permission, except in the case of brief quotations in reviews and critical articles.

For information, contact White Crow Books by
e-mail: info@whitecrowbooks.com.

Cover Design by Astrid@Astridpaints.com
Interior design by Velin@Perseus-Design.com

Paperback: ISBN: 978-1-78677-161-2
eBook: ISBN: 978-1-78677-162-9

Non-Fiction / Body, Mind & Spirit / Parapsychology / Afterlife & Reincarnation

www.whitecrowbooks.com

DEDICATED TO
my friend
G. R. SAMWAYS

By the same Author

The Study and Practice of Astral Projection. Aquarian Press, 1960. American Edition, University Books, Inc., New Hyde Park, New York, U.S.A., 1966.
More Astral Projections. Aquarian Press, 1964.
The Techniques of Astral Projection. Aquarian Press, 1964.
The Supreme Adventure. James Clarke & Co. Ltd., 1961.
Intimations of Immortality. James Clarke & Co. Ltd., 1965.
During Sleep. The Possibility of 'Co-operation'. Theosophical Publishing House (London), 1964.
The Next World – and the Next. Ghostly Garments. Theosophical Publishing House (London), 1966.
Events of the Threshold of the After-life. Darshana International, Moradabad, India, 1967.
The Mechanism of Astral Projection. ibid., 1968.
The Interpretation of Cosmic and Mystical Experiences. James Clarke, 1969.
The Jung-Jaffé View of Out-of-the-body Experiences. World Fellowship Press, 1970.
Out-of-the-body Experiences. A Fourth Analysis. University Books, Inc., N.Y., U.S.A., 1970.
A Case Book of Astral Projections. ibid., 1972.

CONTENTS

Introduction	vii
First Group of Cases: Vehicle of Vitality Only	1
First Group of Experiences: Soul Body Only	6
Second Group of Experiences: Part of Vehicle of Vitality + Soul Body	10
Third Group of Experiences: True Spiritual Body	13
Further Cases: Nos. 723-838	17
The Release and Return of Composite Doubles	118

The Succession of Events and Experiences in the Temporary Release of Composite Doubles, with Corroborative Data

A. Events in the First Stage of Release	124
B. Events in the Second Stage of Release	141

The Succession of Events in the Return of these Doubles

C. Events in the First Stage of Return	142
D. Events in the Second Stage of Return	143

The Succession of Experiences in the Temporary Release of Composite Doubles

I. Experiences in the First Stage of Release	143
J. Experiences in the Second Stage of Release	152
K. Experiences in the First Stage of Return	154
L. Experiences in the Second Stage of Return	154

Similar Succession of Events and Experiences Described by Communicators via Mediums

E. Events in the First Stage of Release	158
F. Events in the Second Stage of Release	161
G. Events in the First Stage of Return	162
H. Events in the Second Stage of Return	163
M. Experiences in the First Stage of Release	163
N. Experiences in the Second Stage of Release	166
O. Experiences in the First Statge of 'Return'	167
P. Experiences in the Second Stage of 'Return'	168
Summary of Events in Temporary Releases (A, B, C, D)	171

Summary of Events in Permanent Releases (E, F, G, H) -	171
Summary of Experiences in Temporary Releases (I, J, K, L) -	172
Summary of Experiences in Permanent Releases (M, N, O, P) -	172
Correspondence Between Micro-cosm and Macro-cosm -	177
Effects of Out-of-the-Body Experiences on Those Who had Them -	178
Review of Terms Used -	181
List of Cases in this Volume -	187
References -	190
Acknowledgements -	194
Subject Index to Cases in this Volume -	195

INTRODUCTION

During the last twelve years I have published almost as many books giving examples of certain human experiences that are superficially incredible, yet which I believe, as strongly as do the experients, are both true and of the first importance to mankind in general.

In each book I give evidence for each point made and the links in the chain of reasoning are manifestly reliable. By now, in books published and unpublished, I have over a thousand cases all pointing to two main conclusions, first that man is a multiple being and secondly that part of him —that which gives him character, namely the soul—is immortal.

The present volume, *What Happens at Death*, is a sequel to *The Supreme Adventure*, (James Clarke, 1961) and *Events on the Threshold of the After Life* (Darshana International, 1967). The former was based on "Communications". In the latter volume the the evidence was chiefly from observers of death. In the present work I describe in far greater detail what actually happens to a person when he dies, and the evidence being derived not only from the still-living, but also from the dead through mediumistic communications. All the evidence from these diverse sources is consistent, and to paraphrase Archbishop Whately's words, when there has been no collaboration between many witnesses whose evidence nevertheless agrees, then their reports can be considered valid.

I hope that the presentation of this evidence to the general public will remove the fear of death as a terrifying happening which people so dislike even talking about, that it is almost universally considered to be in "bad taste". This book replaces unreasoning fear with knowledge of what actually happens at the moment of death and after and of the strict spiritual laws involved. Death is no more than a transition, a passing, as it were, through a door from one room to another; although those left behind are unable to see into the next room, those who have gone ahead are closer in spirit than before. The fact is that death is a minor incident, a well-ordered and beneficent process, which is to be accepted with gratitude and peace.

Robert Crookall

"I SEE PSYCHOLOGY becoming the queen of the humanities . . . It is equipped for giving timely and practical aid to men . . . Science is morally neutral; the new humanities are morally committed. This is the field most attractive to human ability of every kind."—*Professor Arnold Toynbee.*

"Thousands are craving for a basis of belief which shall rest, not on tradition or authority or evidence, but on the ascertained facts of human experience."—*Dean Inge.*

"The only road to a fuller grasp of Reality is the exploration of super-normal perception."—*Dr. Albert Schweitzer.*

"Psychical research may have much to teach us about our mysterious selves. We should not rule out the possibility that the next great advance in our knowledge will come in this part of the field. Theologians cannot long remain indifferent."—*Dr. W. R. Matthews.*

"It is probably no exaggeration to say that we know less about the nature of man than about the solar system. The primary need is for an intensification of research into the nature of man himself . . . No other course is safe for the future of the human race."—*Dr. Rochester Berkley.*

"A careful and honest enquiry into psychic phenomena will yield often richer treasures for the well-being of man than physics, chemistry and biology have given, vast though those treasures are."—*Dr. Leslie Weatherhead.*

"Psychical research represents not only a body of important scientific truth but also the germ of a Cosmic philosophy which can be built on these facts and on these alone—a philosophy enabling us to formulate a rational interpretation of the Universe, clarifying and illuminating the meaning and destiny of life."—*Dr. Hereward Carrington.*

"It is through following the facts called psychic that the greatest scientific conquest of the coming generation will be achieved."—*Professor William James.*

"We accept the evidence as given by quite a limited number of men whose word we trust because, in the main, they all agree, and because their statements enable us to co-ordinate a large number of facts."—*G. C. Barnard, M.Sc.*

"When many coincide in their testimony (where no previous concert can have taken place), the probability resulting from this concurrence does not rest on the supposed veracity of each considered separately, but on the improbability of such agreement taking place by chance . . . For the chances would be infinite against their all agreeing in the same falsehood."—*Archbishop Richard Whately.*

"The man who announces his intention of waiting until a single conclusive bit of evidence turns up is really not open to conviction and, if he be a logician, he knows it. For modern logic has made it plain that single facts can never be 'proved' except by their coherence in a system: but, as all facts come singly, anyone who dismisses them one by one is destroying the conditions under which the conviction of new truth could ever arise in his mind."—*Professor F. C. S. Schiller.*

"Read not to contradict and confute, nor to believe and take for granted, but to weigh and consider."—*Bacon.*

FIRST GROUP OF CASES (VEHICLE OF VITALITY ONLY): NOT PERSONAL EXPERIENCES (VEHICLE OF VITALITY IS NOT AN INSTRUMENT OF PERCEPTION)

DR. NANDOR FODOR[1] dealt with these phenomena under the heading "the double, or etheric counterpart, of the physical body", regarding it as a working hypothesis that solves many of the problems of psychical research. He said, "The Roman Catholic Church admits it under the name of 'bilocation'. St. Anthony of Padua, preaching in the Church of St. Pierre du Queyroix at Limoges, 1226, suddenly remembered that he was due at that hour at a service in a monastery at the other end of the town. He drew his hood over his head and knelt down for some minutes ... At that moment the Saint was seen by the assembled monks to step forth from his stall in the Monastery Chapel, read the appointed passage in the office, and immediately disappeared. Similar stories are recorded of St. Severus of Ravenna, St. Ambrose and St. Clement of Rome. The best known case is dated September 17, 1774: Alphonse de Liguori, imprisoned at Arezzo, remained quiet in his cell and took no nourishment. Five days later he awoke in the morning and said that he had been at the death-bed of Pope Clement XIV. His statement was confirmed—he was seen in attendance by the bedside of the dying Pope." Fodor noted certain experimental work which tends to support such superficially incredible claims, the first being due to Col. Rochas (1837-1914) and the second to Dr. H. Durville (who used mesmeric "passes" to release the double of various subjects): It was *more or less luminous* and was united with the subject's body by *a little cord at the navel or the bregma or the epigastrium* (cf. p.129) ... its objectivity was proved by the glowing-up in brilliance of a calcium sulphide screen when it was bidden to approach it. *The sensory organs of the subject were seated in the released double. At close approach, it produced a sensation of cold and was humid to the touch*" (cf. p.124).

Dr. J. Lhermitte (*The British Medical Journal*, 1951, p.431) cited many instances in which "the etheric counterpart" or "vehicle of vitality" was seen. Aristotle told of a man who, when walking, often saw his released double approach him. Wigan and Mechea mentioned people who were followed by their released doubles. The idea also occurs in the writings of Peter Schemyl, Hans Anderson, Jean Paul Richter, Alfred de Musset, Ferdinand Raimand, Gabrielle d'Annunzio, Oscar Wilde, Edgar Allen Poe, Steinbeck and Robert Hitchens. Lhermitte cited one of his own cases: a girl, when ill, released her "astral" body, leaving her physical body lying on the bed.

A friend of Dorothy Grenside[2] awoke to see not only her husband asleep (with his double released), but also his released double which stood near the window. She shook her husband, whereupon the double rushed towards his body and disappeared into it. He awoke at once, but knew nothing whatever of what had transpired. (Mrs. Margetts, Case No. 779, and Mrs. A. Johnson, Case No. 827, are identical to this.)

A lady, "D.T.W.", sent the following query to Mr. Evan Powell, J.P., and it was published, together with his reply, in *Psychic News* (February 4th, 1956): "In a 'dream' I saw a man in deep distress lying on a bed, and standing by the bedside was his 'double'. I said to the standing one, 'You must help him: you must not leave him like that!' My husband had been far from well and, in the morning, he told me of an alarming 'turn' in the night; he would have called out but did not do so because he knew that I was so tired. Was he out of the body, and did I see it in my 'dream'?"

H. Prevost Battersby[3] described the released "double" of J. Deighton Patmore as being seen over a period of about a year: the phenomenon occurred when he was *worried*. He was charged with "cutting" friends in the street, since the (non-intelligent) "double" "looked right through them" (Compare Szaly Case No. 772). W. T. Stead[4] reported the case of Mrs. "A" whose released "double", which looked *"haggard and ghastly"*, was seen (collectively) in church while her physical body was *ill in bed*.

Edmund Gurney, F. W. H. Myers and F. Podmore[5] mentioned the case of the Reverend Mr. "H" whose "double" was seen collectively. It looked *"melancholy"* and *"gazed fixedly"*. They also cited Mrs. Searle whose husband saw her "double" in a mirror. Its face was *"white and bloodless"*.

When Walter de la Mare[6] was *unwell*, his "double" was seen at a distance from his physical body. *It looked ill.* His sister, thinking it was de la Mare's physical body, supposed that he had fainted.

Susan B. Pendleton "saw" the head and shoulders of an

acquaintance. It looked *"very weary"*. At the time, the man himself was in a distant town. Soon afterwards Mrs. Pendleton met him and learned that when she had "seen" his "double", he himself was *"worn out"*.[7]

The *Sunday Dispatch*, August 3rd, 1958, reprinted several cases of this type from an American medical journal. A Mrs. "A", after the funeral of her husband and when she was *under great emotional stress*, "saw in front of her a woman of about her own age [her own released 'double']. She lifted her right hand to switch on the light: the 'stranger' did the same with her left hand. Their hands met and Mrs. 'A' felt her right hand grow cold." She "felt empty of feeling". The stranger "wore" a replica of her own clothes [the doubles of her own garments—see the writer's *The Next World—and The Next*, 1966]. She suddenly stared in the "stranger's" face —she was staring at herself! Her "double" "was more alive and warm then herself" [physical body]. She said, "It is me —split and divided!"

An apprentice similarly said, "My 'double' suddenly takes two or three steps forward and walks out of me. Soon it becomes the real me. I [physical body] have to follow him ['double']." Much like Mrs. "A", he observed, "I [vacated physical body] feel like the empty shell after the chick has hatched".

W. E. Abbott[8] had no knowledge of psychic matters. His case was published in the *Sydney Telegraph* (November 20th, 1924). When reading, he rose to light the gas. He said, *"I felt dizzy [=vehicle of vitality loosening]. My sight failed for a moment [=the 'blackout' or momentary coma while the 'double' actually separated from the body]*. The next moment I was standing looking down at 'an old man' falling down . . . until he was lying on the floor against the wall. 'His' back was turned to me. Then my sight failed again [=a second 'blackout' as the 'double' re-entered the body] and I became conscious that I was lying huddled up against the wall . . . I was not dazed or confused . . . I did not realise that the 'old man' whom I saw was myself until I had recovered consciousness in my own body." Abbott declared, "I was out of my physical body: I was in another, similar form . . . I had the experience that there was another body and another consciousness. It has altered my former opinions."

Dr. J. Kerner[9], a famous German physician, as early as 1829, published a highly significant case, that of one of his patients, Frau Hauffe, an uneducated lady of the highest character. Frau Hauffe stated that, over a period of about three days, she saw "only a ball of light" [=her own, largely-released vehicle of vitality] attached to her body by "luminous threads": on several occasions she also saw both (a) her [largely-released] vehicle of vitality which was sat on a stool, and (b) her [largely vacated] physical body which lay in bed. At one period her "double" was almost completely released (and, of course, she was on the verge of dying); she then "existed only through the emanations [vital forces] of others—someone had to hold her hand, and that person felt depleted of vitality. Dr. Kerner described Frau Hauffe as "more than half dead". On one occasion, when his patient claimed to see her own released 'double' and said where the latter was, the doctor tried to test her statement by interposing himself between the two: she stated that he had made her feel as if "cut off from her Soul". What we call the "vehicle of vitality" she called "the nerve soul", since she felt it in her nerves. She observed (a) that "the Soul is united to the body by the nerve spirit", i.e., that *this electromagnetic, "semi-physical" portion of man's total physical body acts as a "bridge" between the Soul and the physical self, implying that the Soul Body, not the physical body, is man's primary body.* She repeated this: *"During life, the nerve soul forms the bond that unites the Soul with the body"*; (b) that the nerve soul leaves the physical body at death, leaving it more slowly than the Soul (which "must wait for it"—and in the moments or hours of "waiting" the dying person often sees friends who, having pre-deceased him, come to welcome him—compare Sir William Barrett's *Death Bed Visions*, Methuen, 1926 and Dr. Karlis Osis, Parapsychological Monographs, No. 3, 1961); (c) that after death, until the nerve soul is shed, the discarnate Soul is in the "mid-region" [mid-way between the physical world and the "super-physical" Paradise realm, i.e., in Hades or Sheol— just as man's vehicle of vitality is "mid-way" between his physical body and his "super-physical" Soul Body]; (d) that she saw certain "ghosts" (discarnate Souls who have retained, for an unduly long period, the vehicle of viltality) and, significantly, she claimed to see these with her physical eyes—if she closed her eyes, or turned her head, she could no longer see them; (e) that the (spiritually) "darkest ghosts" [=the most material, the most dense, nerve spirits] had the strongest voices and the greatest ability to make noises, a statement that agrees with the suggestion that a number of Dr. K. Raudive's taped "voices" (*Breakthrough*, Colin Smythe, 1971), come from "earthbound" Souls who were victims of pogroms, etc. —killed in the prime of life; (f) that such "ghosts" seek the help of those mortals who see them: they often plead, "Pray for me!"; (g) that if the nerve soul is not quite physical, it is "at least organic—our muscles are dead without it".

Mrs. Eileen J. Garrett[10] stated: "In a *relaxed and passive* state one day, looking before me, I saw the shadowy replica of myself . . . I rose and tried to approach that other self, and, as I did so, it lost its outline, drew back towards me, and fell into place as my own protective surrounding [=aura or vehicle of vitality] . . . *I . . . later came to know that such projections were not uncommon occurrences. They take place when the objective mind is completely relaxed. In time I came to understand that, in everyone's case, in states of sleep, intoxication or illness, the protective envelope [vehicle of vitality] moves out from the physical body.* I learned of the positive importance of the 'surround' as a protection to the physical body, receiving and condensing the impacts of sound, light and movement, and diminishing their violence." [Mediumistic people are more than ordinarily sensitive to sounds, etc.] Mrs. Garrett continued with the following highly significant observation: "I learned to use this capacity to divide consciousness, finding that *I could make this protective covering into a mirror, in which I could see myself at any time. Whenever I wished to assure myself that my appearance was as I wished, I need never look in a mirror, but viewed myself by means of this projection . . .*" She could not have done this if her "double" were purely imaginary and based merely on her mental images: this "double" was objective (though not physical).

In an earlier book, Mrs. Garrett[11] had distinguished between the "surround" [=vehicle of vitality] and "a second body" [=the Soul Body]. She said, "Throughout my whole life I have been aware of the facts that everyone possesses a second Body, not to be confused with the *'surround'*, . . . *an energy-body, a magnetic area associated with the physical corpus,* an area in which the immaterial forces of the cosmos, the solar system, the planet, and one's own immediate environment are normally transformed into the life and being of the individual . . ."

FIRST GROUP OF EXPERIENCES (SOUL BODY ONLY —AN INSTRUMENT OF PERCEPTION AT "SUPER-PHYSICAL" LEVELS WITH TELEPATHY, ETC.)

IT IS EVIDENT that someone who was well known to St. Paul underwent the release of the Soul Body from the physical body, though the details given are meagre. The Apostle (II Cor. xii, 2) mentioned a man who had been "caught up as far as the third 'heaven' ", i.e., as far as Paradise, the Soul Body of the physical world. He heard unrepeatable words spoken.

Perhaps the most complete and convincing case of this type is that of William Gerhardi, M.A., B.Litt., the well-known author. In a note prefacing his book, *Resurrection*[12], Gerhardi insisted that the experiences which he described therein were genuine ones. They obviously cannot be explained on the basis that this "double" was imaginary, a body-image, and they show that its appearance does not necessarily indicate illness.

Outside his physical body, in his "double", Gerhardi said, "I had stretched out my hand to press to switch off the lamp . . . but found myself ['double'] suspended in mid-air. I was fully awake . . . and said to myself, 'Fancy *that!* Now would you have believed it! Now this *is* something to tell! And this is *not a dream!*' Then I was seized and placed on my feet. I stood there, the same living being . . . If the whole world united in telling me that it was a dream, I would remain unconvinced.

"I was in the body of my resurrection. 'So that's what it is like! How utterly unforeseen!' I staggered to the door. I felt the handle, but could not turn it. Then, turning, *I became aware of a strange appendage. At the back of me was a coil of light. It was like a luminous garden-hose. It illuminated the face on the pillow, as if attached to the face of the sleeper.* The sleeper was myself [physical body].

"Who would have thought that I had a spare body at my disposal adapted to the new conditions! But I was not dead; my physical body was sleeping peacefully, while I was apparently on my feet and as good as before. 'Now how will I get out?' I thought . . . At the same moment the door passed through me, or I through the door. I was in the corridor, dark, but illumined by *a subdued light which seemed to emanate from my body ['double']*. The next instant I had entered my bathroom, affecting from habit to switch on the light, but unable to press it down.

"*There was this uncanny tape of light* [*the 'silver cord'*] *between us like the umbilical cord, by which the body on the bed was kept breathing* . . . 'Now, be scientific!' I said. 'This is one chance in a million! You must convince yourself so that nothing later will make you think it was merely a dream!' All this I said to myself while going round and collecting such evidence as: that window is open; that curtain is drawn; this is the new towel-heater . . . *I noticed a familiar outline of myself in the looking-glass* . . .

"'What evidence? What more evidence?' I kept asking myself, as I passed from room to room. Here I noted which windows were shut, then I tried, and failed, to open the linen cupboard. Then I noted the time . . . I flew through the front door and hovered in the air, feeling an extraordinary lightness of heart. Now I could fly anywhere, to New York, etc., to visit a friend, if I liked, and it wouldn't take me a moment. *But I feared that something might happen to sever the link with my sleeping body* . . .

"What was I going to do now? 'Proof,' I said, I wanted irrefutable proof which would convince me and others when I came back into my body . . . Whom could I visit? And at that moment the thought occurred to me: let me visit my friend Max Fisher at Hastings. Again I flew off . . . Suddenly, I was stepping over an open patch of grass . . . *I thought, 'How do I know I am not dreaming this?' And the answer, 'Look for the lighted cord behind you'. I looked round. It was there, but very thin* . . .

"Then, *with a jerk which shook me* [=*re-entering body*] . . . I opened my eyes. I was in my bedroom . . . Not a detail of my experience had been lost to my mind and there was quite another quality about it all, that of reality, which removed it from the mere memory of a dream . . . We had a duplicate body all there and ready for use, the almost indistinguishable double of our natural body . . . It seemed that, for the first stage of survival at any rate, we already had a body, stored away, it is true, like a diver's suit, but nevertheless neatly folded in our everyday bodies, always at hand in case of death or for special use . . . I got up, and went through the rooms, checking the mental notes I had made about which windows were closed or open, which curtains drawn; and the evidence in all cases proved correct."

Gerhardi reasoned as follows: "If my body of flesh could project this other more tenuous body, while I could behold my flesh stretched out as if in death . . . then this subtler body, adapted to the subtler uses of another plane, was also but a suit or vehicle, to be in turn, perhaps, discarded for another [the True Spiritual Body] . . . Gone was the notion that death was eternal rest . . . Gone was the notion that the Soul was like a little fleecy cloud. *That twin [Soul] Body was real enough.* Perhaps it was rash to think that conditions beyond the grave were entirely different from ours. The surprise might be that they were the same . . ."

The well-authenticated "reciprocal" case of Mr. and Mrs. Jansen was reported in *Journal* American S.P.R., 1923, by Dr. Gerda Walther. Mr. Jansen was away from home (on the Isle of Bornholm) on business, his whereabouts being unknown to his wife. The latter mentally "looked for him, though in vain, in all the various towns which he usually visited". She then concentrated on, i.e. directed her attention towards, her husband (instead of possible towns) and suddenly she had a "vision" of him going along an alley and into a house which was unknown to her. Mr. Jansen entered a room, undressed and went to bed. Mrs. Jansen felt comforted and fell asleep. The next day she wrote to her husband (addressing the letter to Copenhagen) and told him of her "vision". That evening Jansen had been in Randers, a town that his wife had never seen. After a short walk down an alley, he returned to his hotel and went to bed. Suddenly he saw the figure of his wife standing beside his bed. The description which Mrs. Jansen gave of the alley and the hotel corresponded to where he had been that night.

Dr. Walther considered this to be "bilocation" (i.e., the "double" being in one locality and the body in another) and not merely telepathy, since Mrs. Jansen was thinking of her husband and of what he was doing, while he was thinking of her (and not making a mental picture of himself walking about), i.e., they did not take up what was in each other's minds.

Mrs. Thomas Doan[13] of Long Beach, California, obviously had no prior knowledge of these matters. She wrote, "I wonder if any of your readers have experienced the dreams, or visions, which I have and if they could explain them. For years I have experienced a peculiar sensation when asleep. When sound asleep, I suddenly become completely numb and have a feeling like electricity in my body. I try to move and can't. I also feel the presence of someone beside my bed. I get petrified and cannot speak. On one occasion . . . I could see myself (physical body) lying in bed and at the same time I (the 'double') was lying across a pair of bare shoulders and spinning as a wrestler spins another wrestler . . . Once I dreamed that I (in the 'double'), was trying to float away from my body. I saw myself in bed [=physical body] with *a smoky string [=the 'silver cord'] connecting the two of me. Then I snapped back into my body* . . . I wish to find out, if possible, if I am dreaming or if the visions I see are actually there."

Mrs. L. "Ringwood" sent the following account to the present writer: "In 1917 I had a great friend who was a wireless operator in the Royal Navy. One night I could see myself [physical body] in bed. Another body [the 'double'] seemed to rise out of my chest. *It was attached to the body on the bed by a silver streak of light* [=the 'silver cord']. I floated out of the open window and over gardens and fields. Then I went over strange country and at length over the sea until I was on a ship, close to my friend as he sat with the ear-phones on. *The silver streak of light was there. It had stretched as I floated. I returned as I went, the silver streak of light drawing me back until the second body returned to the one on the bed. I woke with a start* . . ."

In answer to my question, Mrs. "Ringwood" stated that she had not heard of astral travel or the "silver cord" before having had this experience. Her description of the "cord" agrees with that given by Muldoon and others—it was "about the thickness of a rope clothes-line". On various occasions she met her parents and her son (who had all "passed on").

Mr. E. G. Williams had an experience at the age of twenty-six, at which time, he informed me *(in litt.,)* he had no interest in psychic matters. His account is as follows. "Lying in bed, I suddenly became aware that there were two 'me's' . . . Suddenly I found that one of 'me' [the 'double'] was walking across the floor of the hospital ward towards the door. On reaching the door, I turned and looked and saw the other 'me' [=the physical body] apparently asleep. *The two 'me's were joined by a white cord [=the 'silver cord'] like a piece of thin string* . . . I saw a beautiful blue opaque mist . . . I sensed that if I passed into the mist [=Hades conditions] I should never return. It was not a frightening thought: in fact, the peace and tranquillity that the mist offered seemed very inviting—so I just stood looking. I have no record of returning to my physical body, but suddenly I was there . . . I often ask myself, 'Was I standing at the gateway of death?'."

J. W. Stuart-Young[14] said, "It is as though the 'astral body' floated above the physical. It invariably *turns upon its back, even should the sleeper be upon his stomach. When it has risen to some 5 or 6 feet, floating freely, but always attached to the 'silver cord', the 'astral body' begins gradually to tilt forward, feet towards the ground. By degrees it reaches the perpendicular position.* It is then able to become aware of its surroundings, to see the physical shell upon the bed, etc. . . . *The 'silver cord' never disappeared . . . At times it was like a clothes-line for diameter, and at other times as fragile as a silken thread.* If I touched it intentionally . . . presto! I was back on my verandah. I felt myself pushed upwards and *backwards: I became supine immediately over my sleeping body* (compare the descriptions of the "return" independently given by Muldoon, Mr. "H", etc.). I repercussed with such a shock that I awakened with an involuntary cry of fear."

SECOND GROUP OF EXPERIENCES (PART OF VEHICLE OF VITALITY PLUS SOUL BODY AN ENVEILED INSTRUMENT OF PERCEPTION: SUB-NORMAL LEVEL AT FIRST)

PROFESSOR S. Ralph Harlow[15] described how his sister, Anna, "could be seated at her desk, across the room from the phonograph, and the machine would begin to play". He continued, "Yet it had not been switched on, and its playing-arm had been left not on the recording but on its rest. Somehow the switch became engaged and the arm moved to the record." Many times her husband attempted to discover some rational explanation—the vibration of someone walking through the house, a child gleefully playing a trick on his mother, faulty mechanism in the phonograph. But he failed. "Once six of us were sitting before the fire . . . no one was in the next room, but the phonograph was there, and it began to play. It was a repetition of what had happened many times before. Again we checked and found no normal explanation."

Psychic News, May 12th, 1956, carried an account of the experiences of Emil Lattinger of Graz: on each occasion, when *asleep*, he "dreamed", and on each occasion other people claimed to have seen "him" (or, more properly, his "double"). In 1926, on the first occasion, a woman who was waiting for a tram saw his "double", which then vanished: she fainted. Lattinger, from his "double", saw this incident, the arrival of an ambulance, etc. The Graz daily paper published a narrative headlined, "The Quest for the Vanishing Young Man". Lattinger "visited" his friends in his "double": *he used his "double" to pull an old-fashioned bell.* (Compare the dying Alfred de Musset.) The account ends as follows: "In all his experiences he felt that he was still attached to his own body, lying in his bedroom, by means of *a continuously-extending cord [the 'silver cord']*.

Evan Powell was a well-known English "physical" medium (i.e., on our interpretation, in possession of a loose vehicle of vitality). When he made reference to certain astral projections he had had, I wrote to him, asking if he had read any books about projection or whether others had told him about it prior to the experiences? He replied, "No books; not from others: the experiences came as a surprise (58 years ago)". Powell further said, "I was aided [by 'deliverers'] on these journeys. I visited both earth and astral scenes . . . *The physical body ceased to have a pull on the released 'double' after about 10-12 yards.*" [Compare the American, S. J. Muldoon, who started a metronome and must also have had a loose vehicle of vitality: he described the distance as varying, according to the state of his physical health, from 8 to 15 feet.] *We suggest that, up to the point described—10-12 yards with Powell, 8-15 feet with Muldoon—the "doubles" remained close to the body because they included part of the vehicle of vitality (and were composite), but if the projector persisted, this "semi-physical" substance separated, leaving the Soul Body only (a simple "double"), and this was quite free from body-pull. The process is highly significant, since it clearly corresponds to the second "death" that is described by discarnate souls as occurring, in natural deaths, some three days after physical death. This points to "doubles" that are objective and not mere body-images.* It cannot be explained away on the basis of impersonation, telepathy, dramatisation, archetypal symbols, etc. Powell stated, "*I saw my own silver cord: it was very much like a light, luminous, flexible rod, about the thickness of one's thumb and attached to the solar plexus*". [*This point of attachment of the "cord" is also highly significant—see the* present writer's book, *Events on the Threshold of the Afterlife*: when, as with "physical" mediums, part of the vehicle of vitality leaves the body, the extension ("silver cord") connects at about the solar plexus, but when, as with non-mediumistic people, the Soul Body only quits the physical body, it is usually via the head and the extension ("silver cord") connects with the head].

The case of Mrs. Eileen Landau was published in *Journal S.P.R.*[16]. She had told her husband, the scientist Lucian Landau, that she had visited his bedroom during the night (minus her physical body) to check his pulse. He asked her to repeat the visit the following night and on this occasion to bring with her a small object, namely, his diary (weighing 38 grammes). Landau woke at dawn to see *"the figure of Eileen"* with a face that was *"extremely pale"* in his room. This "double" was "clearly visible, quite opaque, and looking like a living person but for the *extreme pallor* of the face".

S. J. Muldoon[17] first projected at the age of twelve years, thereafter having hundreds of such experiences. He supposed that he had a natural tendency to project but did not realise that it was because his vehicle of vitality (the electromagnetic "bridge" between the Soul Body and the physical) was loosely associated with the physical body—hence his health was very poor. (The physical body dies, ceasing to be vitalised, when the whole of the vehicle of vitality is projected from it.)

At first Muldoon saw "a foggish light" around him (his vision being obscured by the released portion of his vehicle of vitality). He observed, "Just as the 'astral' body [in his case a composite double, consisting of vehicle of vitality plus Soul Body], leaves the physical, the consciousness grows dim for an instant, then comes back again", i.e., there is a "blackout" in consciousness, because during their separation, neither the physical body nor the released double can be used as an instrument of consciousness.

The fact that his Soul Body was enshrouded by part of his vehicle of vitality (which corresponds to the "semi-physical" aura of the earth, i.e., Hades) obliged Muldoon to first contact Hades, and occasionally he encountered "hinderers", i.e., "earthbound" Souls: one tried to attack him. He realised that a person is "earthbound" on account of his "psychic condition". He observed that when his newly-released double (vehicle of vitality plus Soul Body) was within "the range of cord activity", it lay in a horizontal position above the body, and any movements it made were identical to those made by the body. (This is not surprising, since the vehicle of vitality is essentially the electro-magnetic portion of the total physical body.) He noted the presence of dual consciousness in connexion with such (composite) doubles—if the physical body were touched, it was felt also in the released double and, conversely, if the released double were touched, it was felt also in the body. Muldoon studied the extension between his temporarily vacated body and his temporarily released "double" which has so often been likened to a silver cord: it was like a spider's web. The re-entry of this (composite i.e., relatively dense) double into his body caused a "jerk" or a "jolt", i.e., a repercussion.

On many occasions Muldoon's originally composite "double" passed through the equivalent of the second "death": he observed, "There is a spot, just out of coincidence (with the physical body), in which, as the double passes upwards through it [shedding the vehicle of vitality and thus becoming a simple "double"—Soul Body only], consciousness seems to fade out to some extent" [this is a second "blackout"; the first occurred when the composite "double" was separating from the physical body; the second occurred when the vehicle of vitality separated from the Soul Body, and for the same reason—neither was momentarily available as an instrument of consciousness. Now there were no (ectoplasmic) "fogs", no moving of physical objects (e.g., metronomes), no supernormal raps, no identical movements, no moments of dual consciousness, etc. Consciousness tended to be super-normal.].

In the first stage of projection, return to the body could be caused by a physical sound: in the second stage it was chiefly caused by emotions (often by fear).

THIRD GROUP OF EXPERIENCES (TRUE SPIRITUAL BODY—AN INSTRUMENT OF PERCEPTION AT TRANSCENDENT OR SPIRITUAL LEVEL, WITH AWARENESS OF GOD

WHEN CONSCIOUSNESS operates through the True Spiritual "Body" men have direct awareness of God. Such experiences were cited and discussed by the present writer in *The Interpretation of Cosmic and Mystical Experiences,* James Clarke, 1969: Dr. Winslow Hall felt "a conscious connexion with all

CORRESPONDENCES

MAN THE MICROCOSM			THE MACROCOSM (UNIVERSE)
Hierarchy of bodies	Hierarchy of "selves"	Hierarchy of levels of consciousness	Hierarchy of "worlds", "spheres"
TRANSCENDENT, TRUE, SPIRITUAL "BODY" (an infinite, eternal, changeless, formless radiation or emanation from a Centre: "KHU" (Egyptians), "AUGOEIDES" (Greeks), "PRIMAL FORM" (Jung), "CAUSAL BODY" (Hindus), "KARANA SARIRA" (do.), "THE COGNITIONAL VESTURE" (Upanishads)	"SPIRIT"; "REAL", "GREATER", "INNER", "HIGHER", ETERNAL SELF; HIGHER SOUL (Plato), OVER-SOUL (Emerson); UNIVERSAL SOUL; "RA" (Egyptians), ATMAN (Hindus), TRANSCENDENTAL EGO; CHRIST-IN-YOU (St. Paul); "BRANCH OF VINE" (John xv, 5) DIVINE SELF, "SEED", "SPARK"; INWARD (INDWELLING) "LIGHT" (John i, 9) THE MONAD CAUSAL SELF "THE SECOND MAN" (I Cor. xv, 47-9)	TRANSCENDENT, SPIRITUAL, MYSTICAL LEVEL OF CONSCIOUSNESS WITH MYSTICAL EXPERIENCES, i.e., DIRECT AWARENESS OF THE COSMIC CHRIST AND "THE FATHER"	SPIRITUAL WORLD — T INFINITE, ETERNAL, CHANGELESS, PERFECT WORLD OF BEING, THE TRANSCENDENT HEAVENS, REALM OF IDEAS (Plato (An infinite number of dimensions; highest, hence n potent "vibrations")
Three Temporary Bodies	Three Temporary "Selves"	Three Levels of Consciousness	Three Finite, Temporar Changeable Worlds—Becon Perfect and Real by Spiritual Aid
(1) "Super-physical" Soul Body, Pneumatic Body (Paul), "ah" (Egyptians), "asteroides" (Greeks), Astral Body (Hindus). (Ovoid in form, but, being ideo-plastic, can temporarily assume the physical form for purposes of recognition: can also be "materialised" by the accretion of ectoplasm.	BECOMING PERFECT AND REAL BY SPIRITUAL AID (John xiv, 3; I Cor xv, 5) (1) Soul, "Lower" Soul (Plotinus), Psyche (Greeks)	(1) "Super-physical" level of consciousness, i.e. with telepathy, clairvoyance, foreknowledge.	(I Cor. xi, 26) (1) Soul World, Paradise (Persians), Third "heaven" (Paul), Garden of Eden (Jews) Elysium (Greeks), Islands of Blest (Plato) Summerland Devachan (Hindus) (intermediate number of "vibrations")
(2) "semi-physical" and "semi-mental" vital "body", vehicle of vitality, "etheric" double, linga sharira (Hindus), bardo body (Tibet), kra (Ghanians), mogwee (Australians), breath of life (Gen. ii), larva (Romans), wraith (Scottish), ka (Egyptians), body of Osiris (Egyptians), body of Jason (Greeks), moon body, eidolon (Greeks), similacrum (ditto), unbra (ditto). (human form: "the form of the body"—Scholastics)	(2) "Sub-conscious" self	(2) Sub-normal level of consciousness, with dreams, fantasies and hallucinations, also instinctive impulses and the emotions that accompany instinctive behaviour.	(2) "Semi-physical" and "semi-mental" Hades (Greeks), Sheol (Jews), Limbo (Romans), Inferno (ditto), Astral light (Occultists), World of similitudes (Sufis World of formation (Kabbal swarga (Sufis), kama loca (Hindus), tuenela (Finns), irklla (Babylonians), greyworlds (clairvoyants), land of mists (ditto), "water", "a river", "river Jordan" (Jews), "river Styx" (Greeks). (intermediate "vibrations")
(3) physical, body, chemical body, animal body (Paul)	(3) "lesser", "outer", temporary self; personality; phenomenal, empirical, existential, ego. Kama Manas (Hindus) "the first man" (I Cor. xv, 47-9)	(3) "normal" consciousness (with reason and instinct)	(3) physical world (three dimensions; lowest, r sluggish "vibrations")

THE CLASSIFICATION OF OUT-OF-THE-BODY EXPERIENCES

Psychologists have long felt that some reality and objectivity lies behind these fairly common experiences: but they failed to demonstrate the fact because they failed to achieve a satisfactory classification: (a) different doubles released from physical bodies may have different properties and (b) different kinds of people may release different kinds of double. Our classification is given below (v. of v. = vehicle of vitality; S.B. = Soul Body).

Province		Mode of Release*	(I) Release of Double Natural*	(II) Release of Double Enforced*
rue religion— lfless love, uth, beauty, pressed wards others selfless rvice.		MORAL TYPE OF PERSON CONCERNED	People of high moral and spiritual development.	Anyone—people of high, low and intermediate type.
		STAGES IN RELEASE OF DOUBLE	A single stage only (Soul Body only)	Two stages, first involving vehicle of vitality and second Soul Body.
		NATURE OF DOUBLE RELEASED	Simple-Soul Body only.	Composite (v. of v.—the "bridge"—plus Soul Body)
		EXPERIENCES VIA THESE RELEASED DOUBLES	Many psychic experiences (telepathy, etc.) seeing "dead", etc.	Fewer psychic experiences, fewer saw dead.
		ENVIRONMENT CONTACTED VIA THESE DOUBLES	Bright Paradise conditions (the Soul Body of the earth)	Either earth or dim Hades conditions (including the "etheric" doubles of all physical objects—Hades represents the vehicle of vitality of the earth and is therefore earth-like).
hree Types of nvestigation				
) "Mental" ienomena of ychical search, i.e., lepathy, airvoyance, reknowledge		Bodily Type of person concerned	(IA) v. of v. Tight (non-mediumistic)	(IB) v. of v. Loose (mediumistic)
		STAGES IN RELEASE	As above (very few cases) Single: un-enshrouded Soul Body; Psychic experiences and Paradise realm.	Most natural cases Two stages (v. of v., then Soul Body), i.e., double composite — Hades contacted, as with (II); Then v. of v. shed & S.B. un-enshrouded, Paradise glimpsed as in (C):
) "Physical" ienomena of ychical search, i.e., per-normal ovements (PK), ;hts (incipient aterialisations) aterialisations, rect voices, ports.		STAGES IN RETURN	Single	Then return in two stages — S.B. re-joins v. of v., re-forming composite double, contacting Hades. This re-enters body.
) sciences— ysics, iemistry, tronomy, ology, etc.				

* see R. Crookall, *The Study and Practice of Astral Projection*, University Books Inc., N.Y., U.S.A., 1966; *More Astral Projections*, Aquarian Press, 1964; *The Techniques of Astral Projection*, 1964.
† see R. Crookall, *Intimations of Immortality*, James Clarke, 1965; *Out-of-the-body Experiences*, University Books Inc., N.Y., U.S.A.; 1970; *A Case Book of Astral Projections*, ibid., 1972.

things—union with the All", Dr. Raynor Johnson's correspondent was "one with the Eternal, merged in the I AM", William James's informant felt "face to face with God", J. H. Leuba's "in the presence of God", Dr. R. H. Ward realised, "God is here—He is in everything", John Addington Symonds that "the Kingdom of God is within" and so on. These are "mystical" or true "Spiritual" experiences.

We suggest a helpful analogy. When total light is passed through a prism it appears as various colours, (a) violet, the shortest "waves", (b) blue, (c) yellow and (d) red, the longest "waves".

When total consciousness passes through man's total body, it appears as various levels of consciousness (a) as Spiritual or mystical consciousness, with awareness of God, when passing through the true Spiritual "Body" which has an infinite number of "vibrations", (b) as psychic or Soul consciousness, with awareness of other, including discarnate, Souls, when passing through the Soul Body, and (c) "normal" consciousness, with reason, scientific investigation, etc., when passing through the physical body.

In addition to thus acting as instruments of consciousness on their appropriate levels, the denser and therefore less reactive bodies necessarily envelop or enshroud the higher and therefore more reactive bodies—the physical body enveils both the Soul Body and the Spiritual Body while the Soul Body enveils the Spiritual Body. Hence, during our physical embodiment we mortals, at best, obtain only partial and fleeting glimpses of the "higher" spheres—via the Soul Body, of Paradise, with its discarnate Souls, and via the Spiritual "Body" of Heaven, and of God (I Cor. xiii, 12).

A complication can occur in connexion with the electro-magnetic portion of the physical body—the "vehicle of vitality", via which the body received cosmic vital forces: with some persons, and under certain conditions (e.g., when drugged by soporifics, alcohol or anaesthetics) a significant portion of this bodily feature separates from the physical body to which it belongs, enshrouding the Soul Body and giving a "sub-normal" level of consciousness (with hullucinations and fantasies): the "sphere" contacted is the Hades of the Romans.

FURTHER CASES

In *The Study and Practice of Astral Projection* we gave 160 cases, in *Still More Astral Projections* 222 cases, in *Astral Projection and Survival* 162 cases and in *A Case Book of Astral Projection* 178 cases.

Case No. 723—A doctor of medicine
A medical man wrote from a highly-respected hospital:
"I read with much interest your article on astral projection in the July issue of *Fate* magazine, 1970.

"A young man named George who was a member of my Church when I was a Presbyterian Minister (before I studied medicine) was a very good hypnotic subject [= had a somewhat loose vehicle of vitality] . . . Once I hypnotised him with the specific object of exploring astral projection. I told him that he could leave his body and visit back home in the U.S.A. (We were in Alaska.) This he was able to do, and to see the town where his parents lived. [See other examples of this "travelling clairvoyance" below.] His parents had moved home since he had left them and he had never visited the house they now lived in.

"He went to the house and to the front door, but just went right through it. Room by room he described the contents and could even read a letter lying open on a dresser—but he could not pick it up and turn it over. Later letters confirmed the accuracy of his visit." The doctor concluded:
"Your work is very interesting and you may have found a key to some of the puzzling things we do not know."

Case No. 724—Mrs. M. Claxton
Mrs. Claxton wrote as follows to Canon J. D. Pearce-Higgins:
"I am wondering if you can give me any possible explanation of the following. For my own part I don't know whether I should not tell anyone of such things. I suppose they must happen for some purpose.

"I very rarely dream dreams but when I do, I know the difference between a 'dream' and another kind of experience. I stress this in case you think it was a dream.

"The other night I was going to sleep quite relaxed. The next thing I remember is that I was standing (although I was not conscious of having a body at any time) in space and

I looked around and found that it was night. There was a lovely atmosphere and I was enjoying it . . . The next thing was that the night had disappeared and it was light. Then I felt the most glorious uplifting feeling, the true bliss described so many times in books you read written by mystics . . . but it became too much and I felt that if it lasted much longer I could not bear it. *Then suddenly everything fell clean away from me and I was so free I could not believe it. I was freed from some binding something [the vehicle of vitality, which hitherto had enshrouded the Soul Body] which had previously held me down. This was followed by a great thump in my chest [=repercussion] and I was lying in bed awake.*

"I can only think that I died for a time. I feel almost sure of it. We all at some time or another come across people who are afraid to die and I just wondered if it might be of help at any time for anyone to be able to say how wonderful it is and something to look forward to and nothing to be afraid of at all. What do you think? Have you ever heard of anything happening to other people like it?"

Case No. 725—Dr. D. M. A. Leggett's first case

Dr. Leggett, Vice Chancellor of the University of Surrey, published this case, representing an experience told him by a friend: "I was wounded and in hospital. Though I had lost consciousness, I remember looking *down* on the body of someone who was severely wounded and whose wound had opened. I remember thinking that if the bleeding continued unchecked, the person concerned would rapidly bleed to death. Then—but not till then—I realised that the person at whose body I [released 'double'] was looking was myself [physical body]. I then willed the 'me' who was in bed to press the bell and summon the nurse. This I did and nurse arrived in the nick of time." [The released "double" carried little consciousness since the soldier was nearly dead and much of the released vehicle of vitality enshrouded the Soul Body.]

Case No. 726—Dr. Leggett's second case

A dentist told Dr. Leggett: "A patient, on coming round after being given 'gas', said that he had had the experience of looking *down* at 'himself' from a point near the ceiling while I extracted his tooth.

"Seeing my reaction of disbelief, the patient said, 'And to prove it, I tell you that on the top of that cupboard there are two pennies'. As the cupboard was tall and I was busy,

I did nothing at the time and forgot all about my patient and what he had said.

"Some months later, when I remembered the incident, I climbed up to see what, if anything, was on top of the cupboard: there were, in fact, two pennies." [This knowledge, by the patient, was "doubtless" obtained by observing from his released "double": but it might, theoretically, be due to pure clairvoyance: however, the fact that he claimed to *"look down"* (as in innumerable projections) leaves little doubt that it was a projection.]

Case No. 727—Mrs. M. C. Wilke

Mrs. Wilke wrote: *"It has been my pleasure to read your article on Astral Projection and it was quite enlightening. Too often people who have had this experience attribute it to a dream caused by anaesthesia and are afraid to relate it to anyone for fear of scorn, ridicule or being made to feel they are insane. Now after reading your article I feel free to relate my experiences.*

"While going through surgery I saw the doctors and nurses hovering over my body yet I was floating out of the window. I remember saying, 'Well, they can't hurt me now' and I laughed as I looked down at them and saw my body lying there."

Case No. 728—Mary L. H. Evans's case

Mary L. H. Evans told of a woman who "died" in hospital and *found herself walking in sunshine towards a gate leading to a most lovely landscape, which filled her with eager joy. At the 'gate' she saw her first husband awaiting her;* but as she drew near to join him, she saw and felt (rather than heard) him say to her, "No. Not yet. Go back." She realised that it was for the sake of the sub-normal daughter, and she obeyed him, striving to hold on to her physical life again—her fear still was to have to leave the daughter unable to fend for herself in the world. It was a relief to her to be able to tell the story to me, who fully believed it. Her other acquaintances would not have done so.

"I have personally experienced the choice of leaving or returning to my work in the world during a crisis of illness, and think it is probably fairly common."

Case No. 729—William Blake (1757-1827)

Wyatt Rawson drew attention to several of Blake's psychic experiences.

(1) When his brother died, Blake saw his released spirit "ascend heavenwards" and he provided illustrations to Blair's

Grave depicting "*the released second body lying horizontally a foot or two above the corpse*". Mr. Rawson observed, "This, as we learn from Dr. Crookall's books, is the normal way in which the 'double' is released".

(2) On at least one occasion Blake saw beneath him his own body and those of his wife and sister.

(3) In a letter to Hayley, on the death of his son, Blake wrote, "I know that *our deceased friends are more really with us than when they were apparent to our mortal part* ... I lost a brother, and with his spirit I converse daily in the spirit".

Case No. 730—Richard Jefferies

Jefferies made two references to being out of the body[18]. Thus:

"Travelling in an instant across the distant sea, I saw, as if with actual vision, the palms and coconut trees of the extreme South ... as clear as the plain beneath.

"I looked at the hills ... In a moment all that was behind me. The house, etc., seemed to disappear and leave me alone. Involuntarily I drew a long breath, then I breathed slowly. My inner consciousness [Soul] went up through the illumined sky and I was lost in a moment of exaltation."

Case No. 731—Freda G. H. Laycock

This lady went to bed. She observed, "My body became numb and rigid [because the vehicle of vitality had, to a large extent, left it—incidentally disconnecting the Soul Body from it]. I became aware that I had left my body ...

"I was deeply conscious and appeared to be wandering in a long distance of darkness [because the released vehicle of vitality enshrouded the Soul Body] ... Then light [that of Paradise] was seen at the end of *a long tunnel* [=shedding the enshrouding vehicle of vitality=the second 'death'] and ineffable music and a living presence. I felt my whole being was about to be merged into this bliss when I returned to my body and was conscious of *a thud in my chest* [repercussion as the vehicle of vitality re-engaged with the body]." She asked, "Is this what all mortals must endure while crossing the border?"

Case No. 732—Catherine M. Washburn Westall

Mrs. Westall wrote from New York:

"One night in October, 1970, I was suddenly awakened by the sound of a small explosion in my room. I felt no presence and no fear. Our doors to the corridor were locked.

All was quiet. I thought of the empty glass tumbler on my chest of drawers and wondered why it should explode. It was open end up when I put it there. I didn't light the light to see—too sleepy, so I went back to sleep.

"In the morning, before my husband or anyone else had come in, I looked out, and there was the glass, shattered to slivers at the side of my bed, in the middle of the floor, some six to eight feet from the chest of drawers. If it had merely fallen, it would surely have broken when it hit the bare floor. It simply could not have rolled to eight feet and then broken with such violence into all those pieces. No slivers were near the chest. It must have been shot through the air to the middle of the floor where it broke on contact.

"I have had no repetition and no light on what it meant. There have been no deaths or disasters in my personal environs near that date. I never had a poltergeist before. If your readers can throw any light on this subject, I shall be happy to hear from them.

"When I recounted this experience to a friend, she was at once struck by its similarity to one narrated by S. Ralph Harlow[15]. In the course of a conversation, Harlow spoke of his sister, who had recently died. When he spoke her name, the heavy glass inkwell was sundered, with the sound of a report of a pistol, although none was there of course.

"Are there many cases which involve an explosion? If so, what explodes?—and why? More baffling still—how?"

The physical effect of shattering glass, in both cases, was doubtless due to electro-magnetic forces [from the vehicle of vitality] exteriorized from the body. The phenomenon is, of course, of the "poltergeist" type.

Case No. 733—Harwood Thompson's friend

This man was anaesthetised for an operation. He said, "*All of a sudden,* I found myself standing outside my body in the operating theatre. I could see my body on the table, and there seemed to be some sort of a 'flap' going on.

"Then the matron rushed out and returned with a glass ampule. She broke the top of it and jammed the ampule against my arm. The next thing I knew was when I woke up in bed. I told the matron what I had seen. She said, 'That's impossible—you were completely under the anaesthetic!'."

Case No. 734—Mr. Thompson

Thompson's daughter was away from home nursing wounded soldiers. He was anxious about her and wondered if he could "travel" and find out. "It conjured up a picture of my daughter and concentrated my mind on her. After a time I fell asleep and the next thing I knew it was morning. By the next day's post I had a letter from my daughter—'Is Daddy all right? I had such a strange experience last night: I fell asleep and *all of a sudden* I heard Daddy call me. I woke up and there was Daddy standing at the foot of the bed. Then he vanished.'" This was a case in which Mr. Thompson *directed his attention* and his Soul Body, released in sleep, travelled to that place.

Case No. 735—Mr. Thompson's second experiment
"Two years later, when our daughter was in the Air Force, I tried the experiment again. I had a vague idea of what the mansion where she was stationed looked like, so conjured up a picture in my mind and mentally tried to explore the grounds and then to find her.

"When I repeated the experiment several nights in succession, we had a letter from my daughter asking, 'Is Daddy trying his experiments again? Every night lately *all of a sudden there is a cold wind* [? *ectoplasm from Mr. Thompson's vehicle of vitality*] *blowing round my bed.'*"

Case No. 736—Dr. Joost A. M. Meerloo
Dr. Meerloo, when a boy of six years, fell on his head and became unconscious of the physical world. He "awoke" to find a big man probing his skin with needles. He said, "Years later, when studying medicine, I realised that the doctor had been giving me a routine neurological 'going-over'. *But at the time . . . I felt the goodwill and friendliness behind his formal manner* [=*although physically unconscious, the boy had a telepathic experience*—compare, e.g., Lord Geddes' doctor-friend[19], who "saw" his doctor "think"; Mrs. Jeffrey[20] observed, "You hear what people are saying to each other and what they are thinking at the same time—it is amusing, for they do not say what they think!" Mrs. Garrett, in New York, left her body and visited Newfoundland, conducting experiments with a doctor. She stated, "The doctor walked to his book-case in his room. Before he reached it I knew that he was thinking of a certain book: this was telepathy. He took it down and opened it . . . I was able to receive, from his mind, the telepathic impression of what he read." Percy Cole[21], anaesthetised, "saw the doctor's thoughts—he was afraid I might slip through his fingers".] His new sensitivity has continued throughout his life.

Dr. Meerloo stated, "To only a few friends did I dare mention my awareness of the intrusion of other people's feelings into mine". He has a *"compulsion to identify with someone who was ill and this especially when that other person emanates an intimation of danger . . . Usually it triggers off the need to do something."* [Compare Zoë Richmond[22], who, in England, described another doctor's urges to help. "There is . . . a curious sense of the necessity to obey an impression . . . the impression seems to convey an intention of loosening the distress of impending trouble . . . It is difficult to see where the source of this intention lay, unless the doctor's general relationship to people and willingness to serve them caused a special sensitivity to such warnings." Dr. Gertrude Schmedler[23] similarly said, in U.S.A., that "Openness to the world and to oneself" influences the occurrence of psychic experiences: in telepathy the agent tends to be characterised by openness, the recipient by warmth and need for human contact. In point of fact, Dr. Meerloo stated, "I am open".]

The origin of Dr. Meerloo's E.S.P. in a fall on the head calls to mind the supposed origin of the ("physical") mediumship of the Italian, Eusapia Paladino[24]—she had a peculiar depression of her parietal bone caused by an accident when a child. This area gave off a kind of "breeze" (? ectoplasm). Mollie Fancher, an American, when a girl, had two serious accidents: she exhibited, among other psychical phenomena, the special type of "astral" projection which is called travelling clairvoyance, i.e., seeing at a distance and reporting back through the (partially vacated) physical body[25].

Case No. 737—Harold Owen
Owen's experience[26] occurred when he was eight years old. He said, "I became petrified [=cataleptic, because his vehicle of vitality was, to a considerable extent, projected from his body], standing on the stairs with one foot off the ground.

"An unseen thing was there [his extruded vehicle of vitality had enabled him and the 'thing' to be aware of each other], something menacing, utterly unphysical and . . . so terribly dangerous that I felt with clear and absolute knowledge that here was something . . . realised with a clarity and a vision brought to me by a new sense [the extruded vehicle of vitality providing a 'bridge' between the two] I had not before possessed. It was as if I had plunged out of this world [into the Hades world that surrounds it] and I literally saw [*from the projected 'double'*] my own body poised with one foot on the landing . . ."

Case No. 738—Attila von Szalay
Raymond Bayless[27] satisfied himself of the genuineness of the phenomena—paranormal photographs, raps, lights and voices, and astral projections—of Mr. von Szalay, who is evidently strongly mediumistic. Since childhood, he has projected hundreds of times (which is not surprising).

Ninety-eight per cent of the projections were on earth, but sometimes he enters the Hades realm—a gloomy, twilight realm, i.e., when his "double" is composite. On one occasion, when gliding along, he suddenly "blacked out", momentarily losing consciousness, i.e., the enveiling vehicle of vitality was shed from his originally composite "double" and he now had a "helper" and saw "an exquisite landscape"—that of Paradise. But this was only a glimpse and not a full entrance into Paradise conditions. It was as though he was outside in darkness [Hades] looking into the scene [Paradise]. The people who inhabited this beautiful realm were "radiant with light"—*they, or rather their unenshrouded Soul Bodies, "seemed to be made of light"*. The trees and grass also were radiant with light.

The above are, of course, typical descriptions of the dim Hades realm and the bright Paradise spheres. There is no reasonable doubt that the deponent has "been there"—contacting two objective, non-physical environments via two objective, non-physical bodies, i.e., first a "double" that was composite and later one that was simple, consisting of the Soul Body only. Mrs. von Szalay's first-hand descriptions are given under No. 772.

Case No. 739—Miss S. Ridgway
Miss Ridgway had two projections. In the first, 15 years ago, she was *exhausted* (which condition, in an effort to recuperate by obtaining cosmic vitality, releases part of the vehicle of vitality) and slept. She said, "I became conscious but was *absolutely paralysed*—my body refused to obey my mental commands. I ['double'] seemed to be up *near the ceiling*. I wasn't able to see myself on the bed—or anything. I just "felt" I was there (not *imagined*)." (The released Soul Body was evidently very considerably enshrouded by the released vehicle of vitality.)

Her second projection occurred six months ago. "I became conscious, in the middle of the night, that I ['double'] was standing by the wall in my bedroom. Immediately I thought, 'Oh, marvellous! I've got outside my body! I'll see if I can get across the Seven Seas!' *Mentally concentrating, I found myself going over the sea. Everything was very grey* [Soul Body much enshrouded by vehicle of vitality, therefore contacting Hades conditions]. I couldn't keep up the necessary concentration and, *in a flash, I was back in my body.*"

Case No. 740—Eva Burton's "communicator"

"After a person has died, when his psychic body [= vehicle of vitality plus his Soul Body] have gone out of his physical body, *there is still a fine thread of electric vibration* [the 'silver cord'-extension] *connecting the three bodies just as a child is still connected by a cord of his mother, until this cord is cut* . . . It takes at least a day, and usually two, to develop the power to cut this thread. *Until it is cut, the physical body has feelings* [= there is possibility of dual consciousness—awareness both of this world and the next]."

Case No. 741—St. Augustine

St. Augustine told of a doctor who doubted survival: he had a "dream" in which he met a man who took him to a "city" where there was beautiful music [= Paradise conditions]. Later, in another "dream", he again met this man, who said, "Do you know me?" "Very well," the doctor replied. "How?" asked the man. The doctor described all he had been shown on his previous visit. The man assured him that he would survive death, seeing and hearing in a similar manner—"Do not doubt that there is a life after the present one."

Case No. 742—Mrs. I. Guhasy

Mrs. Guhasy, originally from Puerto-Rico, wrote (*in litt.*,) from Great Falls, Montana, U.S.A., as follows: "I have some real trouble and thought you might help me.

"I started to have these experiences about seven years ago. The first few times I didn't know what it was. *I was taking a nap when all of a sudden I tried to get up and couldn't* [= catalepsy because a significant portion of the 'semi-physical' electro-magnetic vehicle of vitality—the 'bridge' via which we control our bodies—was projected]. Here I was, aware of noises. I was able to see my kids but, at the same time could not open my eyes. I struggled to wake up and finally was able to do so. This occurred, on and off, for two years: it always happened *when I took a nap in the afternoon. One day I saw my body just lying in bed, and, at the same time, I knew that was not the real me.*

"Sometimes somebody would come into the room and

that would cause me to get scared and I would go into my body too fast, and that would make a strange noise ['click', 'plop', etc., due to repercussion].

"After a long time I became used to these experiences and I didn't think much of them. Sometimes I would wonder why, but I never tried to find out. I must say at this point that *I have had mediumistic experiences* [which are due to a loose and projectable vehicle of vitality], but nothing too deep: I have gone into a trance, or something like it, but I have never been able to lose consciousness.

"Now comes the second part of my story. About eighteen months ago I became very aware when I went out of my body. By then I knew a little bit more about it and, for the first time, was really able to realise what was happening. *Then I had a 'dream' in which I saw myself* ['double'] *come out of my body and float around the room. Then, for the first time, I went out of my room.* I tried to walk, but couldn't. It was very strange. This kept happening and I kind of took it for granted: for one thing, *it was not unpleasant*, though by this time I was really anxious to find out why this was happening to me so often.

"Then, last summer, I had some real good ones. I went out of the house and just floated around. It was a very nice feeling and I became conscious that I could float far away— to another city or so. *But something happened each time I became more aware of coming out of my body. I got this sick feeling all over me like some strong vibrations like electricity* [= *the 'vibraitons', 'tingle', etc., due to the rapidly-vibrating vehicle of vitality leaving the slowly-vibrating physical body*]. It didn't feel good at all. I started getting scared of that feeling and the thought that somebody could touch me while I was like that was terrifying.

"All my experiences were natural—they just happened. I was never able to control them at all. In the last four times my heart was beating real hard. *I had awful cramps in the stomach* [? *solar plexus*] and the next day I was very weak. I have come to dread the thing, yet there is nothing I can do to stop it for good. Please could you help me? What can I do? I hope you don't think I'm crazy. I am very normal otherwise, but I can't talk about this subject to anyone. No one would believe me, anyway.

"I hope that you can suggest some good books on the subject. In fact, I have never read anything on that except your article [in *Fate* Magazine, 1971] and a book by Susy Smith."

I suggested to the writer—whose experiences were obviously genuine—that she had a somewhat loose vehicle of vitality (on which account she was a potential medium), that she would be be wise (a) to avoid increasing that tendency by deliberate passivity (especially by attending seances, using ouija-boards or engaging in "automatic" writing); (b) to decrease it by positive thoughts and feelings connected with the physical world and among people, that she should deliberately and perseveringly improve the physical health by (a) proper meals (well-balanced, i.e., always including proteins such as meat, eggs, cheese, milk and vitamins obtainable from fresh fruits and vegetables); (b) proper relaxation and rest; (c) avoiding sedatives, including sleeping pills, drugs and alcohol. All who show signs of a loose vehicle should overcome it by these means.

Case No. 743—Dr. R. W. Laidlaw's patient
Dr. Laidlaw told of one of his patients, a mother, who began: "I haven't wanted to tell anyone about this because it seems so utterly strange—but it did happen ... I [released 'double'] was *suddenly* about twenty feet up in the air, *looking down on myself* [*physical body*] sitting on the bench. I could see myself and the children in detail and the landscape as ordinarily seen ... then, *suddenly* I was back in my own body again." The doctor observed, "Here was something which was brand-new, somewhat disquieting, and yet completely real to my patient. It made a lot of difference to her when I told her that this wasn't the first time that this sort of experience had happened and that books were written about it."

Case No. 744—Mrs. D. King
Mr. King, of Leyland, near Preston, wrote (*in litt.,*): "I hope you don't mind my writing to you. I have written a similar letter to the Society for Psychical Research but received no reply. I must stress that the following information is completely true ...

"I have read your *Techniques of Astral Projection,* Aquarian Press, 1964, and tried various methods of producing projections without any success.

"My wife was not interested in the subject, so I hardly discussed it with her. Occasionally, while I was relaxing on the bed (trying to 'get out' of my body) she would also try it. On May 16th, 1971, my wife told me she had projected around the bedroom and seen herself and me lying on the bed. She said our bodies [released 'doubles'] had a golden 'aura' about one inch thick around them, while our physical bodies appeared dull. The rest of the colours in the room appeared to be very bright.

"After that date, she became enthusiastic about the subject and achieved a projection on June 4th, 1971. She described: 'I floated through the wall dividing the front and back bedrooms and observed, from the back bedroom window, *a round ball, grey in colour, stationary over the roof-tops* [? *a "spirit-light", i.e., an incipient materialisation*—see the writer's book, *The Jung-Jaffé View of Out-of-the-Body experiences*[29] and Cases No. 745, 767, 768]. I got the impression of being watched by it. I then returned to my body.

"In her next success, June 27, 1971, she described: 'I floated to the same position as before and again saw the 'globe'. I tried to approach the object and returned to my bed.'

"My wife, previous to her first projection, had never heard of an 'aura', or that things would appear brighter. Neither had she read any books on it. She probably had heard me talk of the 'silver cord' (which she saw) but, apart from that, she just wasn't interested. So the knowledge couldn't have come from her sub-conscious. Is it safe to practise it? I feel my wife may have progressed if she hadn't lost interest."

On October 24th, 1971, Mrs. King wrote: "I write in response to your request for information re the 'silver cord'. *It appeared as a shimmering silver line, about 1/8th inch thick, attached to my stomach, just above the navel* [=*solar plexus—she has the mediumistic bodily constitution—compare Cases No. 742, 748*]."

Case No. 745—Steven Recchia

Recchia, eighteen years old, said (*in litt.,*): "Yesterday I purchased two books on astral projection—your *Out-of-the-Body Experiences. A Fourth Analysis*, 1970 and Robert Monroe's *Journeys Out of the Body*, Doubleday, 1971 (our Case No. 749). Of the two, I have read your Preface. I have also read *Don Juan* and *Autobiography of a Yoga*. I read these books after my experience.

"In July, 1969, I was living in Greenwich Village. I have lived in New York all my life. I had tickets for a concert. About two hours before the show I had taken some LSD— I had taken it maybe fifty times before because it made me feel peaceful.

"But, when it started coming on that Saturday night, I felt very strange. I started hearing voices of the people around me but none were speaking. When I left my house and started down the stairs I heard people talking in the apartments I walked by. It was super-amplified voices. I never went inside the show. I saw flames coming out of the concert hall and the sky turned red. I thought we were under nuclear attack. I started walking, *then blackness [a 'blackout' as the vehicle of vitality was shed from the hitherto composite double, i.e., as it passed through the second 'death'] followed by the appearance of four or five light bodies [='spirit lights',* cf. Cases No. 744, 767, 768]. *I can't describe their size. Their shape was sort of oval. I was not aware of any physical being. We communicated. There are no words for it [=telepathy]. I saw my entire life flash by me [=the first, non-emotional, non-responsible review of the past life as the vehicle of vitality is stripped from the body].*

"I said, 'I want to go back!' [*=directed attention towards body*]. *But I was back before I said it.* I might add that, wherever I was, it was timeless . . .

"I would like to leave my body again, but without drugs. I can't understand why I wanted to come back. Write and tell me what you think. I declare that everything I have written is true."

I advised the writer to (1) leave drugs alone, (2) study the subject, (3) welcome any experiences that come unsought, (4)*not deliberately to seek them.*

Case No. 746—Robert Brocato

Brocato (*in litt.,* November 5, 1970) told me of projections he had had during the last two years. He is a Master of Science and his investigations suggested that "Potentially good projection subjects can be detected by analysing a person's sleeping habits and mode of dreaming". He considers that about 3% of Europeans can easily project if they tried. "*Bodily metabolism* not only dictates whether one will be a projector, but also reveals, through *the mode of dreaming which the metabolism allows,* if one is in the condition in which he might be a projector. The metabolism can be changed by *diet,* etc. [including certain drugs].

"I do not try to 'force' projections but I do try to provide *the conditions* by which a projection will occur."

Case No. 747—W. H. Bradley

Mr. Bradley observed (*in litt.,*): "I have been an inveterate astral traveller since childhood. When I recently picked up a back issue of *Fate* for September, 1970, I read your article on astral projection and wondered if one of your theories, while probably correct enough in its essence, is not subject to exception. I refer to the theory that, when the astral [body] goes gadding off in its more solid form [with much of the vehicle of vitality] it finds itself restricted from passage through walls.

"In two instances that I was able to verify later, I was seen in my 'astral' form. One involved a 'trip' from Hawaii to Mexico. A letter from a lady I visited in that manner begged me not to do it again. I had scared her. What convinces me that I take a rather solid form at times is another, recent, incident. *I take afternoon naps, and these seem almost invariably to result in involuntary 'astral' journeys.* On one such occasion I found myself in a garden in what I took to be China. There was a brick wall and a willow-tree. Working in the garden was an old Chinese. I noted his deeply-lined face and the fact that several of his front teeth were missing. *I returned to my body (in British Columbia) with a slight jolting sensation that usually accompanies the rejoining of my astral and physical bodies* [N.B.—especially when the 'astral' body includes much of the vehicle of vitality = reunion causes repercussion]. I opened my eyes and immediately closed them again. I still saw the face of the elderly Chinese gentleman . . . Now I am familiar with the phenomenon of the retained retinal image but, to the best of my knowledge, this is restricted to the physical body. [The phenomenon was due to the 'semi-physical' nature of the vehicle of vitality]. It seems to me that I must have had a pretty substantial portion of myself with me at that time. [This type of phenomenon connects the denser astral projections with witchcraft.]

"The Colorados Indians of Ecuador, S.A., have a drug they take from the root of the bajuca vine: it produces trance. Returning from a 'trip', an Indian told us of a dock fire at Callas, Peru, giving details. That evening I heard the news on the radio in Santo Domingo."

Case No. 748—Peter van Muyden

Van Muyden, of Traverse City, Michigan, said (*in litt.,*): "I have had many out-of-the-body experiences and only one time have I succeeded with proof of many witnesses. I want to be sure and not just accept psychic things on a weak basis. My last experience I wrote up and partly told to two doctors. I say 'partly'—I am afraid to be ridiculed . . .

"I am sinde [*sic*] three years an American citizen and have still loads of trouble to write a decent English letter, so please accept my apologies for this.

"On March 19, 1971. I broke my ankle. I was put on the operating-table. On April 4 I was very depressed, feeling that my death was near. On the 5th I felt much better and did leg-lifts as my doctor had told me. *Suddenly there was an explosion in my chest* [? *solar plexus*]. *The room went out of focus* [='blackout' *in consciousness as the double separated from the body*] *and, before I knew, I was out of my body in a golden-yellowish vapour, standing by the window, about two metres from my body* . . . *Then I was sucked back, as by a vacuum, in my body*. This repeated three times . . . The doctor told me to relax, as if he thought I was just imagining the attack. An E.C.G., however, showed the heart-attack. Lesley, a friend came and noticed that I was out of breath. I told her that I had had this condition since my operation.

"On the Monday the doctor asked me if I felt like fainting after the attack? I answered, 'No—like dying!' He asked, 'How do you know what dying feels like?' I told him that I was out of my body and he stopped asking questions. I know for sure he thought I was a nut.

"On Friday, April 9, at 2 a.m., I found myself sitting up in bed, my right arm pushing against my left arm. I fainted. When I came through, I saw a doctor by my bedside and asked him who he was? He told me he was Dr. 'S', replacing Dr. 'H'. I must have fainted again and woke up when I was put on a stretcher with loads of people around me. *Suddenly everything went out of focus* [='blackout' *in consciousness as the 'double' separated from the body*] *and I was floating face to face with my physical body. I looked at myself without any emotion* [=*regarded the physical body with indifference*]. *When we came at the room with the oxygen unit, I was gliding from the stretcher and the 'other me'* [*released 'double'*] *stayed on the theshold and was watching the technicians around my physical body.*

"*The most beautiful 'dream' or experience I ever had began with the feeling that I had travelled at an enormous speed and was suddenly in a beautiful peaceful park* [=*Paradise conditions*]. *I had a feeling that I had entered the park after I had left a kind of building, a station* [='gate', 'a door', *a 'barrier', etc.*, see *Jung's Cases No. 754, 760, 762, 778, i.e. after passing through the second 'death', shedding the vehicle of vitality from the originally composite 'double', thus leaving Hades and entering Paradise—which numerous 'communicators' say happened to them some three days after their physical deaths]. There was an enormous lake surrounded by high trees and a beautiful blue sky. I felt happy and peaceful.* I was surprised, alone but not lonely.

"The lake had seven bright-coloured plankiers [docks?] *I rested on the first 'dock'. The 'water' was very dark and, on the surface, a slow-moving vapour. There was complete silence. While I could not see anybody I had a strong feeling that I was surrounded by lots of people who went through me and I through them.* [This was doubtless a glimpse backwards of Hades.]

"When I arrived on the yellow dock, I felt someone was at my right hand but could not see him. I asked (I think without using my voice)—i.e., by telepathy, 'Who are you?' and *I heard a warm, metal, tinkling voice* [a description which suggests those obtained apparently super-normally by Dr. K. Raudive, recorded on magnetic tapes, and described in *Breakthrough*, published in 1970 by Colin Smythe], 'I am your guide: I am appointed to take care of you'. I asked, 'Am I dead?' He replied, 'You mean physically dead?—No!'

"We walked over a bridge to the last, seventh green dock and sat down. I asked, 'Where am I?' He answered (in a voice full of love), 'In a mental sphere—you could call it a waiting-room [numerous 'communicators' use this term when describing a sphere that is intermediate between earth and Paradise, a sphere in which newly-dead Souls wait for a time before moving on to their more permanent place in the after-death spheres, the 'many mansions']. In front of us was an enormous building with big doors. He called it 'Gate'—'We are waiting for the decision—they are deciding if you have to live longer or stay with us.' I asked, 'Why cannot I see you?' He laughingly said, 'Look at yourself!' *I looked down where I expected my body but could not see anything other than a silvery cord—sometimes it looked light-blue—attached to where my navel had to be* [i.e., the solar plexus —typical of 'doubles' that contain much of the vehicle of vitality—compare Mrs. D. King, Case No. 744]. *I looked to the left where it went and saw . . . myself lying in the oxygen-tent in the hospital. After a while, I heard my guide say, 'You have to go back and live!' I felt as if sucked away, as by a vacuum, at first slowly, then at enormous speed . . . and looked into the face of the nurse."* [It is surely significant that Case No. 789 and many others used the word "sucked" back to describe the pull of the released "double" by the vacated body—compare *The Supreme Adventure*, 1961, p.175, *The Study and Practice of Astral Projection*, 1961,

Cases No. 52, 105, and *More Astral Projections*, 1964, Cases No. 287, 291, 360, 368. It is one of many answers to those who have suggested—without adducing evidence—that all descriptions of the "silver cord" by astral projectors, etc., had been copied from Ecclesiastes: Mr. van Muyden has only recently learned English.]

Case No. 749—Robert Monroe
Monroe devoted a book (*Journeys Out of the Body*[30]) to his projections. Like Muldoon, he evidently has a loose vehicle of vitality: as his "double" was loosening further and getting free from his body he felt "vibrations" or "tingles", rather like "an electric shock" and felt cramp at the solar plexus, then he heard "a hissing sound" in his head and felt "cold winds", all electro-magnetic (or ectoplasmic) phenomena, due to forces in the vehicle of vitality. He found that rhythmic breathing aided the projections, metals were inimical to them. Eventually, a "semi-physical" substance which resembled "grey mist" or "grey chiffon" left his body and occasionally he felt as if passing through water.

The newly-released (and composite) "double" had "semi-physical" properties—when he pinched a person's physical body, the person concerned not only felt an effect but the pinch left red marks on the skin. Also, as with Muldoon, this (composite) double made movements that were identical with those of its physical counterpart.

The environment contacted via the composite "double" was the dim "semi-physical" Hades aura of the earth, with some "hinderers", again as with Muldoon.

As with Muldoon and most (but not quite all) other mediumistically-constituted projectors, Monroe's (originally composite) "double" passed through the equivalent of the second "death" of "communicators"—he learned "the trick" of passing through the early, dim (Hades) conditions (by shedding the vehicle of vitality that enshrouded the Soul Body) and contacted Paradise conditions (which, instead of "hinderers" contained "helpers"). All essential details given by Mr. Monroe are identical with those of Muldoon and others.

Case No. 750—Kelvin Stevens
Stevens, aged seventeen, wrote (*in litt.,*) from Manchester on August 5, 1971:
"In *Fate* Magazine, December, 1970, you asked for reports of O.B.E.'s I have had more than seven over the past

year or so and after each projection I have wrote [sic] down all the detailes [sic]. All were inforced [sic] and all at night.

"This is my best O.B.E., which I had on August 11, 1970. It was a fully conscious projection. I had gone to bed and was thinking about projection. I lay on my back, closed my eyes and thought of moving up, out of my body. *Right away I felt a slight tingling all over my body* [=*vehicle of vitality separating—compare Monroe, Case No. 749, and many others*]. I then thought of moving up again and I felt a wonderful warm vibration go through me like shivers going up my spine. I now was rising and floating away from my body. I went to the end of the bed and *hovered in the air*. I new [sic] that I was out of my body and felt very light, free, uneffected [sic] by gravity. *I was fully conscious—in fact, more than usual. I felt what it was like to be really alive.* I was very excited and wanted to get out of my bedroom and fly away. *Then I thought I would fall—and did so.* I thought I would hurt myself, but did not. Instead, a blackness came [the 'blackout' in consciousness which occurred when the released 'double' was re-associating with the body—just as it often occurs when they are separating at the commencement of a projection: these experiences, of course, indicate an objective double and not one that was merely imagined as is supposed by many students of these matters]. *I felt a slight tingling* [the same sensation as when the electro-magnetic vehicle of vitality was leaving the body] *and, with that, I was back in my body. The reason why I did not fly away from my bedroom was because I did not believe I could go through my bedroom wall—while out, I still think, etc., as if I was still in my physical body. My believe* [sic] *that I could not get through the wall made it all the more solid.*

"Hear [sic] is another O.B.E. which I had on May 10, 1970: I went to bed and fell asleep, thinking of getting out of my body. At about 2 a.m. I found that another body was moving out of my physical body. I [released 'double'] then stood on my bed and could see my room, the same as it looked when in my body. I was completely conscious and I new [sic] I was out of my body. I then floated back into my body. But I found that I was still loose. So I again pushed myself out and stood on my bed again. *Each time I came out of my body I could feel a tingling* [sic] *vibrating sensation. I then thought of moving to* [=directed the attention towards] *the window—and, right away, I did. I seemed to move towards it without walking. I wanted to go through the window but* could not [*glass is one of the anti-psychic things, reason obscure*]. Instead I felt the cold window-pain [sic] on my ['double's'] face. I looked through it and could see clouds. After a few seconds I moved away and found myself standing at the end of my sister's bed. Then I started to fall and seemed to be hanging on to something. I found I was hanging over the side of my bed—out of my body still but with my ['double's'] feet where my physical stomach was. Eventuelly [sic], however, I got back into my body and fell asleep. This is the only O.B.E. where I have felt or touched myself [physical body]: I could feel my [physical] leg with my other one ['double's']: it felt nearly the same as when in my body.

"I had another projection on January 22, 1970. I whent [sic] to bed thinking of astral projection and soon fell asleep. And I started to dream about projection. But I was truly conscious and new [sic] it was not a real dream. I remember awakening and *a feeling of vibration and a tingerling* [sic] ... *I seemed to be in my body but unable to move* [*not fully aligned*] ... *I was moving up and, at the same time, I could feel my blankets pressing down on top of me* [= *dual consciousness—awareness of both 'double' and body*]. *I whent* [sic] *to the end of my bed. I then opened the bedroom door* [= *dense 'double'*] *and went into the front room where I saw my Mum and Dad. All the time I could feel the terrible surging sensations going through my body. The more faster* [sic] *I moved, the worse the vibration was. It was like being slowely* [sic] *electricuted* [sic].

"*I shouted for help to my Mum and Dad but of course they did not hear me. I looked into a mirror and saw my face* [*dense 'double'*] *but was drawn away as if by a wind and I felt the terrible sensation again.*

"I then found myself flying over fields. It was a wonderful feeling, but I was scared I might fall and I found myself standing on a road. I then found myself back at home and started to fall, spinning round and down to my physical body, which, at the time, I could not see. But I could see the room and my bed (it seemed spinning round). I then saw my cupboard which was also spinning round, and *it was fleecy* [compare Muldoon and others]. But I new [sic] I was in my body and my heart beat slower. I could feel my heart beat in my head of the astral body throughout the projection [again compare Muldoon, etc.].

"October 18, 1969. I woke up, stayed where I was and went back to sleep thinking of moving out of my body. I found myself facing this and moved towards my bedroom window. I went through the window which was open. I new [*sic*] I was out of my body but was not fully conscious, but conscious anathgh [*sic*] to no [*sic*] what I was doing. I stood on the roof, and *felt an odd tingling on the bottom of my feet, like a tingerling* [*sic*]. I could see everything as usual. I moved away without walking, feeling very light and at peace. I looked towards some distent [*sic*] buildings and thought, 'I can go anywhere in the world!' I was drawn back to my body. Every projection I have had seems to agree with what was written by Muldoon.

"July 3, 1969. I went to bed and concentrated on projection. I must have fell [*sic*] asleep and became conscious to hear and feel the now familiar vibration which went through my whole body when I moved. My body was num [*sic*] and I could not move [catalepsy because the 'bridge'—the vehicle of vitality—was broken]. Then I was about six feet away from my body. *I thought of spinning round. Right away, I did so, head over heels.* I went round, faster and faster, unable to stop. Terrible vibrations surged through me. *After a few seconds I thought of going somewhere outside— Blackpool tower. Right away I saw it* [=*mere direction of the attention produced the requisite movement*]. Then I drifted away and found myself in a crowd of people. Their faces had no expression. They were all walking the same way—towards me. They seemed to pass right through me. Then I was back in my bedroom, about six feet from my body—floating upright and found myself back in my body. I could not feel it and could not move. I tried to open my eyes, which I did, and saw the bedroom. *Realising that I was not in my body properly, I thought of trying to do something when I seemed to come out of my body and then to enter it again, with a thud and, I think, a jerk* [=*repercussion*]. I could then move.

"I had been reading that night about projection and went to bed with the intention of doing it. I became conscious from a dream and *saw a person in front of me* [*released 'double'*]. *I then realised it was me.* I was moving towards it. Its eyes were closed and its mouth open and my whole body [released 'double] seemed to glow. When I was near it, I seemed to hit it, and then *suddenly woke up in my body with a jerk* [=*repercussion*].

"August 16, 1970. I went to bed and fell asleep to wake up, about 2 a.m., finding my body incapacitated [catalepsy, because much of vehicle of vitality released]. I was lying on my back and new [*sic*] I could get out of my body while in this incapacitated condition. So I made the attempt. I came out of my body on my right side and at the same time going half-way through the wall next to my bed. I saw my physical body, the bed, etc. *I carried on out of my body, turning anti-clockwise, still on the same level, lying horizontally, until my astral feet were at my physical body feet.*

"I then went into a standing position. I stood for a minute and felt myself spinning round. *I went towards the light-switch and tried to turn it on, but the light never came on, even though I felt it.*

"Every word I have told you is true. My O.B.E.'s were not dreams. *I no [sic] that I will live after my physical body dies because I have had my personal proof; after being out of my body. The body is not me.*"

Case No. 751—T. Cain
"I am 56 years old and had my first experience at 17," said Mr. Cain, of Blackburn (*in litt.,*). "It was a *spontaneous* release, in fact, *I knew nothing of such things* . . . though I had had clairvoyant experiences from the age of nine.

"I was lying in bed, and became aware of *a noise something like a dynamo* [compare the 'tingle', etc., heard by Monroe, Case No. 749, Stevens, Case No. 750 and many others]. It started with a low-pitched whine and increased. At the same time I felt something ['double'] rising upward with a rhythmic movement and my body seemed to be falling [= *dual consciousness*, i.e., awareness of both the 'double' and the body—see *The Study and Practice of Astral Projection*, 1961, Cases No. 13, 19, 31, 39, 58, 61, 64, 78, 105, 142 and *The Supreme Adventure*[31], 1961,] with the same rhythmic motion. Eventually I found myself [released 'double'] floating above my body on the bed. I felt wonderfully free. I passed through the walls into the garden—somehow a 'garden' but not my garden, the roses were larger than any on earth [= Paradise conditions]. Then I saw monks marching in an endless stream and a voice said, 'Do not be afraid. We need you for our work.' This began to fade and *I felt myself rushing through the air at a terrific speed down a white line* [? *the* 'silver cord'—extension—cf. Cases No. 449, 767, etc.], through the walls and into my body. How dull it seemed after such beauty!

"My next experience was *enforced* owing to an accident when 20 years of age. One minute I was conscious and the next oblivious to things physical. I was speeding down *a dark tunnel towards a golden light.* [Compare *The Study and Practice of Astral Projection,* Cases No. 9, 13, 18, 65, 78, 87, 116, 123 and *More Astral Projections,* Cases No. 170, 254, 277, 301, 346, 361.] On arriving, I entered the most beautiful place I have ever seen [Paradise again] but, as I tried to go further, I was drawn back. I fought, but of no avail and awoke on the ground.

"I had no more experiences until June, 1962. Then one night, in bed, I *suddenly felt a severe electric shock: my whole body seemed to be vibrating* [='tingle']. Then I was floating in a vast deep-purple void. Then I returned.

"Similar experiences have come in June, 1963, and each year around June or July until October, 1970, when I had a partial release from the waist downwards. *On this occasion* [*doubtless when the released 'double' included part of the vehicle of vitality, whereas on the previous occasions it consisted of the Soul Body only*] *I was psychically attacked* [*by 'hinderers'*]. It was only by calling on my Spiritual helpers that I freed myself from this influence which almost strangled me.

"When these shocks come now, I know about three seconds beforehand. At first I thought I was having mild 'strokes' and consulted a nerve specialist. After a thorough two-hour examination, he pronounced me physically fit.

"Perhaps you could give me some explanation of these happenings. I would be deeply grateful if you could."

Case No. 752—Eric Laliberté

Mr. Laliberté, a Canadian, wrote (*in litt.,*): "I am twenty-five years old. I have experienced projection after retiring—woke up and found that my consciousness was in the middle of the room. I could hear my parents playing cards downstairs. *I wished myself back in my body and woke up.* The experience was so real, I knew it had happened. I have experienced it at other times but none so vivid as that time.

"I once had a 'dream' of green lawns and trees so vibrant as to be beyond description [? Paradise conditions]. It was ecstasy and it lingered for quite a while."

Case No. 753—Mrs. J. Wade

Mrs. Wade wrote (*in litt.,*): "Thank you for your interesting article in *Fate* Magazine, July, 1970.

"One night I went to bed. I must have fallen asleep promptly because a bedside lamp was left on. Some time later, I awoke. I said to myself, 'I wonder what time it is?' My left arm rose and turned so that I could see the face of my watch on my wrist: the time was 11.10 p.m. I suddenly realised that *I could not move: I was cataleptic [because much of the vehicle of vitality, the 'bridge' between the Soul Body and the physical was outside, projected from the latter]. I was lying on my back [compare Muldoon, etc.]*

"Eventually I managed to get my left arm from under the bedclothes. I tried to look at the face of my watch. To do this, I had to turn my body and lean towards the light—my watch is not luminous. The time was 11.12 p.m. It must have been my 'astral' arm that I first saw, but how is the watch (and the time) explained? *Is everything duplicated in the 'astral'?* [The answer is 'Yes'—see *The Mechanisms of Astral Projection*[32], with 'communications' concerning this[33], the observations of clairvoyants[34], Dr. Raynor Johnson's hypothesis and Professor Hornell Hart's hypothesis[35]. The Kahunas of Hawaii—who could neither read nor write and had no contact with Western culture, also stated that all physical things, including men, animals, plants and minerals, have 'shadowy bodies' which survive the death of their physical counterparts.]

"Another evening I was doing some embroidery. The work was very intricate and I was concentrating intensely. Suddenly I was out of my body and projected backwards. Astonished, I stared at myself working on the embroidery. I saw stooping shoulders and untidy hair. It was not flattering. I was soon 'back'."

Case No. 754—Dr. C. G. Jung's case

This case of the pseudo-death of a woman, described by Jung, is abbreviated.

"A woman patient lost much blood. The nurse asked her, 'Do you want anything before I go for supper?' The patient tried to answer but could not move her lips. *She felt as if sinking through the bed* [=her consciousness, in the partially-released Soul Body, was with the physical body: in many cases it is with the partially-released 'double'; in a few cases it is in both, i.e., there is a dual consciousness: see *The Supreme Adventure*, p.115 for falling-sensation and pp.14, 15 and 20 for rising-sensation. In *The Study and Practice of Astral Projection*, Redgwell, Case No. 26, described both sensations, while others, Cases No. 60, 65, felt falling, and many, Cases No. 48, 53, 57, 59, 60, 65 and 68 felt rising. In *More Astral Projections* Major Priorleau, Case No. 315 felt rising only.]

"She saw the nurse hurry and take her pulse. Then she [released 'double'] was looking down from about the ceiling, seeing her body, deathly pale and with its eyes closed, and the nurse and doctor. The latter 'lost his head'. *She knew that, behind her, was a glorious park-like landscape with the brightest colours and an emerald-green meadow [=Paradise]. A 'gate' [=barrier, compare Cases No. 748, 760, 762, 778, she was still attached by the 'silver cord' to her body] was between her and the beautiful landscape.* She said, 'I knew that this was the "gate" to another world and that if I turned back to my body I would not die!' [Compare the 'communicator' of Cora L. V. Tappan, an uneducated lady whose 'communications' were published by J. Burns in 1875; 'Each death is a mere "gateway", a "door" through which the Soul is admitted into the "spiritual"—Paradise—world', and she later gave a first-hand description, by Judge Edmonds, of his "passing". In the course of dying, he had stood in "a vestibule—like a massive 'gateway' between the real land of spirit—Paradise—and the atmosphere of earth."]

"The next day she made a remark to the nurse about the 'hysterical' behaviour of the doctor. Only when she described in detail all that had transpired during her coma did the nurse admit the correctness of her descriptions."

Case No. 755—Mrs. S. Schoenberger

Mrs. Schoenberger wrote (*in litt.,*): "Three years ago . . . I went to sleep and my finer body rose up from the waist while my physical body lay almost flat, in bed. Then I was standing next to my bed. *I wanted to move away from my body and into the living-room* [=directed attention] *and glided through a closed door into the living-room. My 'astral' body was illuminated . . . I could see my black cat in his finer body. I scared him. I had been worried about* [=directed attention towards] *him before going to sleep.*

"Finally I decided to go back to my body. As soon as I thought about it [=directed attention] I was back in my body. It was an exhilarating experience.

"My eleven-year-old daughter has seen me in my 'Soul' Body twice. She saw *a smoky figure* leaving the bedroom.

"A few months later she saw a 'woman' in a white gown at her door. She concluded it was me. On each of these occasions I had the feeling of leaving the body.

"Four years ago, my sister was killed in a car crash. That night—before I knew she had died—*I saw a smoky figure take form before my eyes: it gradually formed* [as it withdrew ectoplasm from the observer] *and then gradually de-materialised.* I learned of her death the next day."

Case No. 756—An anaesthetised man
Phoebe Payne told of "a materialist" who discovered that he had a Soul when given nitrous oxide for the extraction of teeth. Like so many others when anaesthetised (see, e.g., *The Study and Practice of Astral Projection,* 1961, Cases No. 120-145 and *More Astral Projections,* 1964, Cases No. 347-367), he found "himself", i.e., his released "double", standing in a far corner of the dentist's surgery, looking at his body sitting in the chair. He saw both the anaesthetist and the dentist; he felt each tooth pulled out (but no pain). He knew that, although separated from his body, he himself (in the released "double") was alive and thinking.

"On returning to consciousness in his body, he mystified the two men by telling them what they had said to each other while he was deep under 'gas'."

Case No. 757—The Kahunas of Hawaii
The Kahunas (priests) of Hawaii have been mentioned under Case No. 753. According to Max Freedom Long, they explained the difference between clairvoyance and "astral" travel, i.e., astral projection, on the basis of the amount of the vehicle of vitality (which they called "the low shadowy body"—i.e., ultra-physical—body, as distinguished from "the middle shadowy body"—the Soul Body, midway between the physical and the Spiritual Body) by the amount of the vehicle of vitality projected from the physical body: if only a little is projected, consciousness remains in the physical body; if much is projected, "the centre of consciousness necessarily . . . becomes actually present at the distant place which is visited".

They also described the "silver cord"—extension which forms in the latter condition: it is *"a thickish thread of shadowy substance"* connecting the released "double" to the vacated body.

Case No. 758—J. H. Brown (further projections)
Brown (who was mentioned as our Case No. 73 in 1961) gave several projections in *Light*[36] which developed from normal dreams.

"I dreamed that I was in my mother's home, some twelve miles away, and quite suddenly I became fully conscious, realising that actually I was astrally projected. I saw my mother in the kitchen and she looked very ill. Within a few minutes I felt myself drawn backwards into the air, returning to the physical organism and normal consciousness. On the following morning I received a telephone call from a neighbour of my mother's, to say that they feared she had had a stroke on the previous day; which I found to be the case when I went over to my old home. Subsequent analysis and one or two judicious questions forced me to the conclusion that when my mother was taken ill, her first thought was to let me know; this thought registered on my mind (unconsciously) and finally became sufficiently strong to call me to her side when my physical organism was at rest.

"Another astral projection experience arising out of a normal dream was the following, proof of which came within twelve hours. I was dreaming that I was in my office building when the door suddenly opened and two men came in, one leading the other, who appeared to be very ill. This unusual experience, plus the fact that the sick man was coloured, led me to realise that I was dreaming. Immediately I became aware that I was astrally projected, and consciousness became increasingly clear. The one who was leading the sick man then spoke to me, saying: 'This is a West African and he is very ill. He is being brought to you for healing treatment and is suffering from some form of brain disorder . . . I will now leave him in your care . . .' The African seemed in a very bad state and could not speak, appearing to be dazed, as if unaware of what I said to him, and I had to hold him in my arms to prevent his falling to the ground. Gradually consciousness left me and I drifted back into normal sleep, ultimately to return to what, for the sake of differentiation, I will call "physical" consciousness. The following morning I received a letter from West Africa, in which a father asked for help on behalf of his son, who had suddenly been struck deaf and dumb and was in a dazed condition. In my answer I gave the father a detailed description of the man I had seen during my experience of the previous night, and I subsequently received his reply in which he confirmed that I had accurately described his son. From this I came to the conclusion that the patient and I had been brought together on an astral level.

"This awakening to full consciousness during sleep state has to be experienced to be really appreciated, and I have found it impossible to convey to others the difference between this and dream consciousness. I can only say that when a realisation of the fact that I was out of the physical body literally burst upon me, a sensation of freedom always predominated, together with which I had a sense of power quite foreign to my normal spiritual energy. As to whether I feel

really happy or not, depends entirely upon the surroundings in which I find myself. Sometimes I awaken to consciousness in an atmosphere of light and beauty, and I am able to move freely through the air with but a slight effort of will [=Paradise conditions]. On other occasions I seem to be struggling through a thick fog, where all is dark and foreboding [=Hades conditions]. Under the latter conditions, movement is extremely difficult and demands a tremendous effort, during which I am supremely conscious of the weight of my 'etheric' body. These experiences I can only liken to the efforts of a diver far below the surface of the ocean, as he struggles to move forward against the pressure of *water*."
Case No. 759—Mrs. F. W. Strine

This and the following cases, here abbreviated, were kindly sent to me by Jo Filardo of New York.

"An old woman acquaintance became very ill. One day she felt her 'spirit' ['double'] leaving her body. She looked back at the hospital room where she saw her body lying on the bed, the doctor shaking his head and her husband weeping.

"She got to 'heaven' [Paradise] and met an 'angel' [helper]. Then she saw a young man and said, 'Why, Tom, I didn't know you were up here!' He answered, 'I didn't know you were up here, either!' She said, 'I have just come'. 'So have I!' he replied. [There are several cases cited by Sir William Barrett[37]: a dying person claimed to see relatives who had 'passed on', and then said, (e.g.) 'Why, there's Martha! You didn't tell me she had died!' In point of fact, Martha had died unexpectedly and it had not been thought prudent to disclose the fact.]

"Suddenly the 'angel' said to the sick woman, 'You are going back to earth for a while!' She replied, 'But I have just come!' For a moment she was disappointed for, she said, 'heaven' [Paradise] was the most beautiful place. *Then she thought of [=directed her attention to] her husband and child and suddenly was back in her body.*

"A little later news came that Tom had died in an automobile accident."
Case No. 760—Clara Burke

Clara, a young woman, after a long illness and an operation, developed pneumonia and "passed into a death coma" [=almost all of the vehicle of vitality left the body]. "But," she declared, "I was conscious of everything said in my bedroom.

"Suddenly I—my consciousness [*in the released 'double'*],

that part of me which really lives, thinks and is spiritual— seemed to rise and hover over my body.

"My connexion with my physical body seemed to be like an invisible, fragile thread of life [*the 'silver cord'—extension between the released 'double' and the vacated body*]. That part of me that seemed to try to separate itself from the body [= the 'double'] appeared to be a weightless manifestation. I saw my body on the bed and the nurses putting hot turpentine on my chest. My mind, which for a long time had been sluggish because of my physical suffering, became keen and active. *No matter what my body appeared to be suffering, 'I' was not conscious of it.*

"I thought, 'I did not think death was like this!' That which I was experiencing was a great relief to me. During many months of illness I had dreaded dying. I had made enquiries of visiting clergymen, etc., and found that everyone had only vague ideas about it . . . Now I was intensely interested. I was an active member of a Philadelphia Presbyterian Church.

"*My memory unfolded like a scroll* [*compare Case No. 813*], *everything I had done, from infancy to that time, came before me* [= *the first review of the past life, due to the stripping away, or projection, of the vehicle of vitality, with its memory-traces, from the body, as recorded in* The Supreme Adventure[38] (*from people who, having died, later communicated*) *and* [39] (*from people who, like the present deponent, suffered pseudo-death from grave illness, from others who fell from great heights, others who were partially suffocated by fumes or by drowning, others who underwent accidents or who took drugs such as opium*) *and recorded in astral projection in* The Study and Practice of Astral Projection *and in* More Astral Projections.]

"Suddenly a voice greeted me with great joy, 'Oh, that's Clara!' I thought it was the voice of my 'departed' grandmother. It said, 'It is not Clara's time yet!'

"When I regained physical consciousness the nurse told me that she had several times thought I had died."

Case No. 761—The Rev. Dr. A. D. Sandborn

"A young woman, a member of Dr. Sandborn's Church, was seriously ill. Her family, as well as Dr. Sandborn, were at her bedside where she was bolstered up in a nearly-sitting posture. She seemed to see a glorious city for she said, 'As soon as they open the "gate" [cf. Cases No. 745, 748, 751, 767, 768], I will go in. They will be here very soon now.'

Suddenly she had a happy, eager expression. 'There! There! They ["deliverers"—see *The Supreme Adventure*[40]] are coming now and I shall go!'

"Then she sank back: 'They have let little Mamie in ahead of me!' Later, 'There! They are opening the "gate" for me! Now I shall go in!' Again, however, she sank back disappointed. 'They have let Grandpa in ahead of me—but next time I will go in for sure.' She seemed to see nothing but the beautiful city.

"Dr. Sandborn left the house. Later he heard that she had died. He enquired about 'Mamie' and 'Grandpa': the former was a little girl who, having lived with them for some time, had moved to another town; the latter was an old friend who had also moved to a distance. Enquiries elicited the fact that both had died on the morning when the dying girl had claimed to see them."

Case No. 762—Mrs. Julia Roupp

Mrs. Roupp, the wife of a Minister, became very ill, needing a thyroid operation, and was given a local anaesthetic. She gave the following description:

"*Suddenly, to my amazement, I was looking down at myself and the group around the operating table from a short distance just above their heads. The nurse was saying, 'Doctor, her pulse is going!' Then I started through what seemed to be a long, dark passageway* [='tunnel', i.e., the 'double' was in course of separating from the body]. *As I went along, I thought calmly, 'This must be what they call "dying". I began to wonder how long the "journey" would last when I emerged into a wide space of light. My body* [released 'double'] *felt light and free and seemed to be . . . looking into an enormous convex window. I knew it was not glass, for I could easily have stepped through to the other side— I was looking through a 'window' into one bright spot of 'heaven'* [actually Paradise]. *I longed to join a merry crowd of children. The air had a brilliant clarity. There were both fragrant blossoms and ripe fruit on the trees.*

"I became aware of a Presence. My heart yearned to become part of this beauty, but somehow I could not bring myself to go through the 'window' [=complete the act of dying]. *An invisible, tenacious restraint* [? the 'silver cord'-extension, compare Case No. 767] *pulled me back each time I leaned forward with that intention . . . All I needed to do was to step through the 'window' to be part of what I saw* [i.e., Paradise] *. . . I seemed to recede farther and farther* *away from that 'window'* [*compare Cases No. 748, 754, etc.— others call it a 'gate', a 'door'—see below*].

"*After another long journey through the passage-way* [= *the re-entrance of the released 'double' into the vacated body*], *I returned to my body. Reluctantly* [*as is characteristic of out-of-the-body experiences*] *I entered it through what seemed to be the natural 'door', the former soft spot on the top of my head, asking myself, 'Why must I return? Do I have to come back?'*

"One of the nurses exclaimed, 'She's coming to!' *This painful return was almost unacceptable, but I was aware that the dying of the physical body is not a calamity. It is a natural transformation into another phase of living, where one can go on joyfully progressing, if ready.*

"I believe [*as did Swedenborg, Dr. R. B. Hout and many others who had out-of-the-body experiences*] there is a comparison to be drawn between the 'birth' of the spirit [the release of the 'double'] and childbirth . . . One begins in the next world where one leaves off in this. This gives a meaning to suffering and to one's everyday relationships. My brief glimpse [of Paradise] through the 'window' of 'heaven' was a flash of revelation about the meaning of life itself."

Case No. 763—Albert Payson Terhune

Terhune's sister Alice gave notes of an article by A. P. Terhune and his own projection, due to ether, for an operation. As he was regaining consciousness he "saw" two attending nurses who pointed to the back of his head at a scar which was there. He later spoke to the nurses who verified his out-of-the-body vision of their actions.

Case No. 764—Jerold Mogerl

Mr. Mogerl, of Yorktown, Sask., U.S.A., wrote: "I read your article in *Fate* magazine. I feel that I experience astral projection similar to Sigrid Kaeyer. Also I see my 'double' . . . I sort of disliked this. *One person* [*own released 'double'*] *I always see wears a cap such as I do.* [Compare the present writer's *The Next World—and the Next*, T.P.H., 1970— 'semi-physical doubles', which are the counterparts of our physical bodies, wear the counterparts of our actual clothes.] He appears to know what I think. He walks quickly, as I do. Could this be astral projection?"

Case No. 765—H. Davies

Mr. Davies wrote seeking "an instructor" in projection. (I replied that, so far from instructing people how to project,

I discountenance deliberate projections in all my books.) He said:

"While lying down, performing relaxation techniques and meditating for an hour, my *body goes numb* [=*catalepsy*] *with a feeling of pins and needles* [*'tingles'*—compare Cases No. 742, 750, 751, 793, 797, 804].

"By taking a deep breath about every five minutes and letting the air out quickly, and at the same time concentrating on my body sinking deeper and deeper into the bedclothes [the converse of the 'double' projecting from, and rising above, the body], my body relaxes even more, making it more numb with this feeling of 'pins and needles'.

"When I relaxed very deeply, I suddenly felt my consciousness pass into another dimension. In this condition, I could hear *a deep hissing noise* [compare Case No. 749].

"On several occasions, after retiring for the night, I found myself in a kind of trance, half-awake and half-asleep [= the hypnogogic state]. My body was totally paralysed, though I was conscious of my surroundings. On these occasions a roar or a low-frequency vibration goes through my whole body. If I breathe deeply it intensifies, but if I look about the room and get more awake it passes off altogether.

"In September, 1966, I was asleep and 'dreamed' I was standing in my mother's home. Everything was in colour—*not vivid colours, but dull and misty from within myself* [=*part of the vehicle of vitality enshrouded the Soul Body*]. *I heard a roar or buzzing noise* [*tingle*] *and then snapped back into my body*. I had no feeling in my body, but after half a minute could move again. The average dream is a distortion of facts but the details in this one were exceptionally clear—I am 100% sure that this was an out-of-the-body experience."

Case No. 766—Gordon W. Creighton

Mr. Creighton is an M.A., F.R.A.S., F.B.I.S., a member of the S.P.R., and a retired Officer of H.M. Diplomatic Service. He wrote (*in litt.,*) as follows:

"For many years I was stationed in China . . . The strain and ill-health must have been the cause of my only experience of astral projection.

"Very ill and exhausted, in 1941, I was on my way to Australia to recuperate. I had to fly over the Japanese lines and this meant travelling 'very light'. I took with me two suits—a darker-grey one for colder weather and a white palm-beach type of suit for hot days.

"One night I was still in poor health, and greatly keyed-up by the knowledge that 'Pearl Harbour' was coming any day. I was asleep in my cabin, the night very hot. About 2 a.m. I found myself ['*double*'] *wearing my white palm-beach suit* [compare Case No. 764 and note similar instances in *The Next World—and the Next*, T.P.H.], walking down the deserted corridor towards my cabin. Turning into the cabin, I beheld *myself* [*physical body*] *lying there in the bunk wearing my dark-grey suit*.

"The shock of seeing myself must have produced *a gigantic 'repercussion' as my 'double' shot down into my body*. I awoke sweating with heart palpitating."

Mr. Creighton, 33 when he had this experience, 62 now, considers that, in this experience, the two types of clothes seen were symbols—that the white suit symbolised his 'Spirit' [Soul] Body and the dark one his physical body. I, however, consider that the white suit was the 'double' of his actual white suit ("donned" because of the heat) while the dark suit was the actual dark suit. He has "no doubt" that in sleep one is slightly out of coincidence.

Case No. 767—Mrs. Olga Adler

Mrs. Adler, of Brooklyn, N.Y., wrote (*in litt.*,): "I read your article in *Fate* magazine, 1970, and thought, 'Here is another understanding for my story' . . . Ever since it happened to me I've hugged it to myself and am hoping it would happen again now that I know what it is and am no longer afraid.

"It happened in the summer of 1960. I had read the story of Edgar Cayce but had not yet touched on the subject of astral projection: so I was not exactly prepared for my experience.

"I was in the middle of a disastrous marriage. My husband was threatening me and our two-year-old daughter. One night I was especially worn out and went to bed with a death-wish in my mind. My husband was already asleep when I got to bed. I was mulling over the day's events when *a wave of coldness* [*due to the release of the vehicle of vitality*] *began at my feet and slowly swept over me*. [*This is a common description of the complete, and therefore permanent, release of the vehicle of vitality at death—see* The Supreme Adventure, *1961.*] *Suddenly I was completely immobile* [= *cataleptic because much of the vehicle of vitality was projected*]. *It was as if I had become mysteriously paralysed.*

"Then I had the sensation of falling [*compare Case No.*

20] and of being very dizzy [ditto]. I ['double'] seemed to whirl round in a spiral with sparkling lights, like fireworks, before my eyes [compare ditto]. There was a buzzing and a crackling noise inside my head [compare Case No. 749, etc.].

"I knew I was awake and not dreaming and I reasoned with myself that one of two things was happening to me: either my mind had become unhinged from worry, and I was going mad [compare Mrs. Eileen J. Garrett, etc.] or I was about to die [compare Case No. 761, and many others who had projections which included much of the vehicle of vitality].

"I must have 'blacked out' for a moment, because the next thing I knew was that the dizziness [loosening the vehicle of vitality] and falling [finally projecting it] was over and I was hovering or floating up near the ceiling. I was very frightened: I thought I was dead.

"Instead of the usual darkness of the room, it now seemed to be a sort of half-light [because the released vehicle of vitality enshrouded the Soul Body—compare Muldoon, etc.], something like a dim, indirect glow. Everything was perfectly visible.

"I saw my husband and baby. Somehow I could not bring myself to look down at my own bed because, if my body were lying there, I didn't want to see it. I looked up instead and, strangely enough, the roof was no longer there—I could see outdoors: my vision had somehow expanded and sharpened [because that of the Soul Body was being used]. Everything was clear and beautiful. I was still frightened, but that did not stop me enjoying the situation. It was such a joyful weightless feeling: I felt completely free for the first time. I saw the trees, etc., and heard the traffic noises.

"As I rose higher in the air I looked below and saw into my bedroom and there was my body sprawled face-down on the bed. There it was and there was no pretending—I was quite sure I had died.

"Suddenly I was travelling at tremendous speed out into space. Now there was no more fear, only exhilaration and freedom, and *never a thought of what I had left behind* [=indifference, when out of the physical body]. I [released 'double'] was clothed in something whitish and my flesh ['double'] looked as solid and real as if I was still alive [=as does a physical body]. I had now completely accepted the fact that I was dead and was enjoying every marvellous minute.

"As I flew onward, I heard music—a sort of musical

humming. If there is such a thing as 'celestial music', or 'music of the spheres', I heard it then.

"*Suddenly I was surrounded by tiny sparkling pin-points of light that floated in space* [='spirit-lights', i.e., incipient materialisations of the Soul Bodies of discarnate helpers—see Cases No. 744, 745, 768 and the writer's The Jung-Jaffé View of Out-of-the-body Experiences[41]]. *It was like passing through a field of millions of fire-flies, only they were much brighter. I tried to touch them but they eluded me.*

"All this time, I [in the Soul Body and therefore Paradise conditions] was travelling at high speed towards a light in the sky towards Heaven. It was not the sun. I felt that when I reached that bright spot I would be with God. It made me happy.

"*Suddenly thoughts came to me of my baby back on earth* [direction of the attention] *and I began to fall back as though I were being reeled-in on a tremendously long fishing-line* [? the 'silver cord'-extension, compare Cases No. 449, 751, 762].

"*I returned with incredible speed and must have 'blacked out' again for an instant because the next thing I knew I landed in my bed with a tremendous repercussion: the bed actually bounced when I fell into my body. Instantly I felt heavy and clumsy.*

"I fell asleep. When I awoke the remembrance of this experience was very vivid—not vague and muddled as a dream would be. To this day I remember all the details clearly and accurately.

"Then, quite a bit later, I read an account of an astral projection in a book and recognised my experience for what it was. Until then, I thought of it as 'the night I died'. When it's my 'time to go' I will not be frightened now."

Case No. 768—W. H. Butler

Mr. Butler, of Boston, Mass., also recorded having seen "spirit lights" while out of his body. He wrote on January 16, 1970 (*in litt.,*): "Since I last wrote (November 3rd) my index shows: simple travel (catalepsy) on October 1, November 10, December 2 and January 4 and travel with projection October 7, November 4, December 2. Borderland experiences also occur: one wakes in sleep—there is no dream on—only the grey wall [=Hades conditions due to the vehicle of vitality enshrouding the Soul Body]: *when, by willing, one succeeds in penetrating the grey* [=in passing through the second 'death'] *one is suddenly, instantly through the grey in a living world of colour, persons and intelligent conversation* [= *Paradise*] . . .

"I am certain that the strange 'worlds' I move in at night are *real worlds* and the (unknown) people and the 'doubles' (of known people) are *real*.

"Answering your enquiry, 'Have you read Muldoon, 1929?' the answer is that I had projected months before reading any book on the subject. I have encountered 'spiritual' people, both in normal [physical] form and as *'clusters of light'* [= *'spirit lights'*, i.e., incipient materialisations].

"The beginning of catalepsy—what I call 'full trance'—can be with the *solar plexus* or with general body 'tours', in legs, etc.

"I have had little repercussion: I usually just find myself back (*suddenly, reluctantly*).

"I have made a couple of bad exits projections—off centre—and been put back immediately for a fresh try. Only once did I have any follow-up to same [to 'bad' exit]—pains, in elbows and shoulder throughout the day. *In these days I just go out and in horizontally*, with no developments.

"I became fascinated with the different ways in which 'I' appeared—sometimes naked, sometimes dressed in my own 'clothes' that I was not wearing in bed, sometimes as I was actually dressed, sometimes in 'clothes' I did not own, sometimes in 'spiritual' garments of great beauty. Sometimes I could create my own 'garments' by will and concentration. [Compare the writer's *The Next World—and the Next*, T.P.H., 1968.]

"The *'clicks'*, on re-entering the body, which some describe occur with as *great jolts*. They are sometimes very severe.

"I consider myself on a very elementary level in all these things . . ."

Case No. 769—W. D. Wuttenee—a Cru Indian

This gentleman, a Cru Indian from Saskatchewan (and a soldier) wrote (*in litt.,*):

"I was always a 'fan' of Abraham Lincoln. For many nights before I went to sleep, I would take a thick book of his life . . .

"One night I went to bed wearing a pair of pyjamas (which was something I never did for they would roll up my legs to my discomfort). Well, this evening I read a book as usual and, as usual, felt part of the emotions Lincoln must have felt.

"During the night I woke up to find a heavy weight across my chest. Suddenly I realised that my arm was 'asleep' and lying across my chest. However, I was not particularly worried and went to remove it with my other hand: then I found my other arm was similarly handicapped . . . When I went to sit up I realised my legs were both 'asleep' and then I realised I could not move [=catalepsy].

"Then I noticed that the ceiling of my room was not there and, perhaps 15 feet above me, was a dark hooded figure who extended his arms, gently put his hands under my knees and arms and picked me up.

"*The next thing I noticed was I was up above my room —about 40 feet—looking down at my body* . . .

"Then I was standing in Washington, D.C., in the street (Johnsons) where Lincoln died. I was there only ten seconds. The next thing I was in my own room, looking down on my lifeless body. *Suddenly I was slowly fitted back into my body.* [Similar descriptions are cited in More Astral Projections, 1964, p.134: one man said that re-entry into the body was like entering *a bag*, and several said *a glove*. It is surely significant that similar symbols were used to describe getting out of the body—*a sack, a tight bathing-suit, a glove*, etc. See also Cases No. 770, 774.]

"*The conclusion I came to was because I felt so emotionally involved with Lincoln* [= directed attention to Lincoln] *I was allowed to go, for a few seconds, into his era.*"

Case No. 770—Mrs. N. Robinson

This lady wrote (*in litt.,*) from Manchester:

"It is very rare to meet anyone with the same experiences as myself. I have had such experiences for about fifteen years. On many occasions I had no remembrance of what I saw or felt, but only of returning to the body. (Mrs. Elizabeth Gaythorpe[44] has made a special study of returns.)

"The first time I was really frightened of going to sleep for six weeks—and always slept sitting-up in bed. *I felt myself* [Soul Body] *being drawn through the top of my head* [compare cases cited in The Study and Practice of Astral Projection[42] and More Astral Projections[43]]. I struggled to 'stay put' when I was half-way out. The pull was terrific— I went swiftly on my back. I stayed in that position all through my trip. I got the pull-back as I was being drawn back about three feet from the floor. I wanted to see over the hedges which were on either side of me.

"Although I had never heard of 'astral projection', I

instinctively knew that I was out of my body and returning. As I thought [=directed attention], I rose about three feet, enabling me to see over the hedges. I saw children playing.

"I went very swiftly then and seemed to pass foot-first through the top of my head. I felt a tightening at my solar plexus [compare Cases No. 742, 744, 748, 768] and then slid easily in, as though I was liquid filling a mould [compare Cases No. 758, 762, 769, 770, 771, 774 and those who likened re-entry into the body to entering a bag, a glove, etc.]

"I have had many pleasant experiences since then, and seen gardens of flowers, many 'out of season' [Paradise conditions]—earth-roses are heavy-looking to me.

"I once found my body . . . being guarded, as it were, by *evil-looking creatures* [*'hinderers'*, compare Case 521] and fought to return. It was a most terrifying experience. These are not dreams.

"The last time was different as I sensed someone was with me and told me to turn my head [a 'helper']. (I always glide upright, after the first experience when I was on my back) and I saw, as though I was looking through a porthole, myself, asleep in bed, looking tired and with my hair down over one side of my face. I thought, 'This time, I'm dead!' . . . I came back with someone [a 'helper'] with me all the time—staying slightly behind me.

"At first when I found myself returning, I used to go round corners of paths, etc. [=habit] till I realised I had no need: now I cut corners as I arrive home [=direction of attention].

"I glide up and down stairs and am always slightly above the floor. *I have seen the* [*'silver'*] *cord.*

"Thank you for giving your address in the article. I have so long needed to tell these experiences to someone who would know what I was talking about. It has worried me for years."

Case No. 771—Mrs. Peggy Miller
"I venture to share my one projection to date. It changed the whole course of my life. During 1950 I worked in a bank. The Manager, a devout Christian, was keen on his staff attending Church. But I would have none of it. We had long arguments about religion. I knew nothing of psychic phenomena and could not accept the Bible as anything but a myth.

"One night I sat reading a light novel in bed. I must have fallen asleep, for *I found myself* [released 'double'] *staring at myself [body] still reading in bed.* I was 3-4 feet from the bed. I noted the ugly contour of my nose from an angle I had never seen it—just behind the left shoulder.

"A 'ballerina' entered the bedroom and began to dance: I knew the 'dancer' was death; should she touch the bed, my body would die. I had no fear for myself ouside the body [i.e., for the released 'double'] but was anxious for my body. It did not occur to me that this was an unnatural state of affairs.

"Suddenly the 'dancer' touched the bed. I moved towards the body. To my amazement, I found it wasn't me but Mrs. 'Johnson' who was dead. I awoke my husband shouting 'Thank God! It's Mrs. "Johnson", not me!'

"My husband knew no Mrs. 'Johnson'. Neither did I, except as the name of a bank customer. I had never met her. She had not visited the bank during my employment there. My ledger was S-Z and her account was kept by another employee. So I had no contact with Mrs. 'Johnson', except that a week previously a letter from her husband had arrived at the bank stating that he and his wife were sailing to Ceylon to visit their son.

"I dismissed the unpleasant 'dream' from my mind. Two days later a cablegram arrived at the bank to say that Mrs. 'Johnson' had died on the night of my 'dream'.

"The bank manager was very interested in my story. It is doubtful if my experience can now be corroborated, but I do assure you that it is absolutely true."

Case No. 772—Attila von Szalay

This case was sent to me by my friend Raymond Bayless, author of *The Other Side of Death* (University Books, Inc., N.Y.)

(Tape Recording)
November, 1970

"Note: I first met Mr. von Szalay in the last part of 1948 and from that date to the present (1970) he has discussed his projection experiences many times and his accounts have never varied in the least.— R. Bayless.

"I had my first conscious astral projection when I was about seventeen years of age. I went to a dentist and took nitrous oxide for anaesthesia. I waited to become unconscious but I found myself about twenty feet from my body talking to a young person. I saw the dentist pulling my tooth. I did not recognise the accompanying spirit to whom I was talking.

There were, then, three present; the dentist, a nurse and myself. I could feel my tooth being pulled but the pain felt muted. Dual consciousness was present.

"*In hundreds of projections I saw the 'cord' only once. I could always feel it throbbing and pulling at the back of my neck.*

"From this time, as a young man, I would consciously project. I could never see my astral body but just had the feeling of a floating consciousness.

"About 1941 I was practising rhythmic breathing and suddenly found myself cataleptic. *Four spirit helpers aided me to project from my body.* Two were at my ankles and two were at my shoulders. One spirit at my right shoulder said, 'He still sticks here' and pointed at my heart area and when he did I felt a vibration. He then said, 'He's all right now' and the four figures vanished. *The room appeared smoky and cloudy. [Compare Case No. 20, etc.] I turned back and saw my physical body. From this time on I was able to leave my body freely. I always used breathing to project.*"

(Upon questioning, von Szalay estimated at this point in the interview that to the present he has had a least 500 spontaneous projections.)

"In 1941, using the rhythmic breathing technique, I found myself over a battlefield and saw soldiers pointing in my direction. I seemed to be at about 300 feet elevation. When I returned to my body I could see through the floor and apparently sank below the floor, rose up above my body, and then settled down into my body. I began to practise induced projection in earnest. *I noticed that repercussion only happened during spontaneous projections.*

"On one occasion when projected and fully conscious, I decided to experiment. First, I went halfway through a wall and *felt the pull of the astral cord*. I also decided that I did not want the occupant on the other side of the wall to see me. I returned to my dark room and picked up a glass, turned on the water faucet, and drank the water. Everything seemed perfectly normal. I then picked up my tooth-brush and put it into the glass for evidence that these events had really happened, and then returned to my body. I got up and went to the sink and saw that my tooth-brush was not in the glass. (At this point I questioned Mr. von Szalay carefully regarding this odd point and its obvious implications.) I believe that all is illusion. The tooth-brush, the glass, etc., were all 'astral' counterparts and existed in an astral world. This projection was my third controlled projection.

"I will now describe my fourth controlled projection. I was bothered by rats in my studio. About one in the morning I heard a scraping, rose from bed with a flashlight, and saw a rat. Returning to bed, I projected into the air. I literally chased the rat around the room, and in desperation it ran between two sheets of glass by a wall to hide. I returned to my body intending to check these events but fell asleep. The following morning I found a dead rat pressed between the glass and also found fur on the edges of the glass.

"My spontaneous projections continued and I also induced projections almost daily. On occasion I projected to the street and went down the boulevard (Hollywood Boulevard).

"On one occasion I went up the boulevard, etc., and went back of a dress shop. I stood in the alley and saw women sewing. To attract attention I pounded on the wall and saw a woman look out of the window and then throw up her hands and dash back into the store. *I was then pulled back through the air into my body and repercussed badly.* I returned later (physically) to the shop and found that the woman had been taken home. Later, the alley was blocked up with bricks and I wonder if it was due to a fear of 'burglars'. I estimate that 98% of the time during my projection I saw the normal boulevard (Hollywood Boulevard) and surroundings. The rest of the time I saw a twilight state as at dusk. I saw buildings, cars, etc., but oddly I saw no street lights. *I felt that it was another world [Hades] even though it was much like this world. It was dark and gloomy.* Its general feeling was not elevating. It was populated by normal-appearing people.

"I have seen three states; the normal, everyday, physical state, the dusky world [Hades] and the Paradise state.

"I have seen hundreds of people but did not actually know if they were dead (surviving spirits). I never saw my relatives, which was very strange, and never saw anyone I knew.

"I was once in 1938 resting on the Santa Monica beach and lying on my stomach in the sand with my head placed in my arm so that I had actually cut off my air supply. I decided to experiment and concentrated on the ajna chakra and found it difficult to breathe. *I saw a little ball of pink light, which rolled up. There appeared a huge, dark tunnel and at its end was a brilliant light.* This light obscured the normal landscape. I felt a desire to go into the tunnel but realised that I was suffocating and rose from my prone position. When I did this *I repercussed at the solar plexus.*

"About November 2, 1952 I went to a dentist and took pentothal. I then found myself out of my body and in a studio looking at a group of men watching about one dozen colour TV monitor sets. This was the first time that I had ever seen colour television. I recovered from the anaesthetic and did feel pain from the tooth surgery. [Mr. von Szalay told me about his experience that afternoon.] One week later I picked up a newspaper dated November 3, 1952, if I remember correctly—the day after the operation—and an article told for the first time in history N.B.C. had showed a close-circuit colour television programme to executives at the studio at the corner of Sunset and Vine in Hollywood.

"On January 10, 1954 *I made an attempt to astrally visit Mr. Bayless at his home.* I did my usual breathing exercises, etc., and found myself in a room which was not known to me but I did not see Mr. Bayless. I saw a pair of glass doors, went through them thinking that he might be having dinner in the dining area. I entered the living room but lost consciousness and returned to my studio. [I can in part verify Mr. von Szalay's experience. At 6.15 p.m. at my home in West Los Angeles, eleven miles from his studio on McCradden Place and Hollywood Boulevard in Hollywood, I was tying my shoe laces while sitting on a studio couch. I saw something flicker in front of me and thinking it was my cat I paid little attention but again I saw something move in front of me. I looked to the end of the couch, saw that my cat was sitting there, and looked back and saw a fantastic, slipped rectangular shadow about the height of a man floating about one foot from the floor in front of me. I received the definite impression that it was an aware entity and as I looked it 'turned' and rushed at a great speed through two glass doors which were open, reached the living room and disappeared. I immediately glanced at the clock and saw that it was 6.15 p.m. I then drove to the studio of Mr. von Szalay, knocked at his door, and when he answered I said, 'Guess what happened to me'. He spontaneously replied, 'You saw me!' In the ensuing conversation he told me that he had just previously projected to my house in an attempt to show himself to me so as to prove that astral projection is a reality, could not see me, and went into the living room attempting to reach the dining room, where he thought I might be, but lost 'control' and returned to his studio. I can, therefore, verify that he spontaneously stated 'You saw me!' without any leading statements on my part. In all the years that I had known him, he had never before made such a remark to me and I regard this statement as good verification of his experience.]

"At least ten times during my life people have said that they have seen me during projections. These experiences began in about 1931, when I was away from my home for five or six months. I would find myself on State Street, Schenectady, New York, in a perfectly normal environment, but had no sense of having a body—I seemed to be just a floating consciousness. I at first thought that these experiences were dreams but one day *I received a letter from my wife which indignantly accused me of coming to town but not seeing her and child.* [Compare the Deighton Patmore case, *p.1.*] My wife wrote that her brother's wife, Myra, claimed that she saw me on Hollywood Boulevard—I was in New York City and my wife and child were about 180 miles from me. I wrote to my wife saying that I had never left New York. [Myra eventually said that when she had 'seen' von Szalay, his actions did not seem normal.]

"When I started my conscious projections, a friend insisted that she had seen me in front of a window apparently shout. She thought that I had been drinking due to my actions weaving back and forth, etc. I thought that she had simply been hallucinated. [Von Szalay practically never drinks and most certainly does not become drunk.]

"A friend, Miss Helen Jackson, worked in the New Yorker restaurant in Hollywood during the late 1940's or early 1950's. I took her to work one evening and then went on to the theatre to see the picture 'Waterloo Bridge'. Suddenly I saw the front of the restaurant and I waved to Helen who could be seen. The theatre screen disappeared, by the by. I looked at my watch and saw that it was 9.20 p.m. After this I regained normal consciousness, left the theater and went to the restaurant. Miss Jackson said that she had seen me walking down the street, approach the front of the restaurant to tap on the window and tip my hat. I attempted to explain what had happened but she could not believe my explanation. [About fifteen years after this happening, I met Miss Jackson and she confirmed the entire story.]

"During the years 1957/1958 a friend, Miss Jean Lewis and her fiancée visited my studio and during this time suddenly remarked that she did not know that I liked French fried potatoes: I do not, and said so. She insisted that both she and her fiancée had definitely seen me in the Paris Inn near La Brea (Hollywood) and I denied that I had been there. She again insisted that I had been there and Major —

confirmed her statement. She then said that at the restaurant to which she had gone to see me, I was having a cup of coffee, and that *I seemed preoccupied.* As she left she looked back and this time could not see me. I questioned Miss Lewis about this incident and she repeated each detail exactly.

"I married in 1964 and all psychical phenomena and projections ceased. Later, after an unfortunate separation, my phenomena and projections began again."

Case No. 773—Ann Sinclair

Mrs. Sinclair, of Toronto, Canada, very ill, felt dizzy. She said, "I was floating near the ceiling—it was strange to watch my husband and friends down below and to hear what they said.

"Slowly I floated down and returned to my body on the couch with *a gentle thump."*

Case No. 774—Thomas M. Johanson

Mr. Johanson writes:

"There was only a period of about six months during the end of the year 1959 and the beginning of 1960 when I had these vivid experiences. Though I have, like most people, had vivid dreams, the experiences I had of astral projection were unmistakable and totally unlike any dream experience. I found that with astral projection the consciousness is on a completely different level. One *knows* it actually happened.

"My first experience was quite simple: I found myself standing by the bed looking down upon myself. I was mildly alarmed at the stillness of my body. I tried to reach down and touch it but my hands simply passed straight through. After that I just wandered about the room and went out into the passageway. Then I remembered no more until I woke up next morning. I remembered the experience with some excitement.

"The next occasion: like my father, I have always been something of an amateur inventor. I had conceived an idea for a new kind of table lamp. I had made the prototype, but for some unknown reason it would not work. I tried different methods but without success. One night I went to bed as usual and then sometime during the night I was out of the body and there standing before me was my father (he had passed on some years previous). *I always knew when I was out of the body, because I always experienced the passing out. With a dream there was never this experience.* He mentioned the lamp I had constructed and proceeded to tell what was wrong. The next morning I remembered every detail and later that day I worked on his instructions and immediately the lamp worked. Later I was able to market the lamp.

"In September, 1959, my fiancée died. Her mother had died whilst giving birth to her daughter. The child was immediately adopted by another woman. The child grew up believing the woman was her mother. In adult life she was told about her real mother. This information she only imparted to a few friends, myself included. One evening, some months after her death, I was sitting at home in an armchair when *suddenly I was out of the body. For a few seconds I saw my room with myself [body] in the chair. Then I was immediately in another room which I did not recognise. Standing before me was my fiancée and standing to one side of her was another lady whom I did not recognise, but I knew instinctively that she had a perfect right to be there.* I talked to my fiancée about certain happenings that day and then suddenly I said, 'I must return now right away!', and with that I found myself in my armchair and the man upstairs was hammering away. For a while I wondered who the other lady was and then gave it up. A few days later I sat with a professional medium and immediately she began to tell me about my fiancée and she ended by saying, 'By the way, *she is being taken care of by her real mother in spirit*'.

"On another occasion *I was out of the body and as usual facing the front door. Again the momentary 'blackout'* [the second 'death', i.e., shedding the vehicle of vitality and thus un-veiling the Soul Body] *and I found myself in a large room which seemed vaguely familiar*. In this room were standing my father, mother and young brother who was killed in the war. No one seemed to be very excited except myself. I kept saying, 'Do you realise I am here with *full* consciousness?' I knew exactly what was happening and where I was. During this time someone, unseen, was standing constantly behind me. This person (somehow) indicated that we should move on. I then found myself in a hospital type of ward. Rows of beds with people in them, and moving quietly among them were ladies who gave me the impression that they were Sisters of Mercy. *This was obviously a rest-home for those leaving the earth. Whilst in this 'ward' I actually witnessed a person dying on the earth and move into spirit. I saw this person collapse and then he came slowly towards this 'ward' where he was greeted by one of these ladies.*

"At the far end of this 'ward' there was a very large window and through this there streamed the most glorious sunlight. Outside this window there was a most wonderful garden, ablaze with glorious colour. Colour in 'spirit' [Paradise] is breathtaking. It is very different from colour on earth. It has a profound depth and a purity that is beyond description.

"I then went out to this garden and then I seemed to be lifted up into the air and *I seemed to speed through the air in a horizontal position*. Then I passed through the windows of my home directly towards my body on the bed. *The most wonderful experience was the actual fitting of the two bodies together.* [Compare the descriptions of fitting into a 'glove', etc.—Case No. 770—a Red Indian.] *It astonished me to realise how perfectly they matched* [*one was a replica, or double, of the other*].

"Whilst on some of these astral trips, I have seen parts of 'lower astral'. These were awful experiences which often filled me with revulsion and sadness. On one occasion I came back with such tremendous haste that a split second after opening my eyes *I saw an awful creature* [*a 'hinderer'—compare Cases No. 521, 770, etc.*] standing by my bed, but in a flash it was gone.

"I am not an imaginative person; in fact, I tend to be rather sceptical, but these experiences I know were real. I have dreamed many times, but I know the difference.

"Here are the answers to your questions: (1) 'Astral' cord: No, I did not feel this while travelling. (2) When projection took place I did not know about it or read about it. In fact I have never read a book on projection. (3) The travelling is quite natural. I did not feel amazed on being in an unnatural environment . . . it was all very natural."

Case No. 775—Harwood Thompson
Mr. Thompson wrote (November 19, 1970) from New Westminster, B.C., Canada: "On January 20, 1970 we received a letter from Wales of which I send you a Xerox copy. The lady writer is one of our dearest friends . . . She has occasionally received 'visions'. I was not aware of my astral travelling on this occasion, but I have tried several times unsuccessfully to make myself visible to this lady when I have been going to sleep.

"This time, allowing for the difference when she was watching the T.V. show, we in Canada, 6,000 miles away, were opening Christmas presents, among them presents from her, and naturally a flood of memories of the happy times we had spent in her home flashed through my mind. I have underlined the reference in the Xerox copy [below].

"We had a very nice Christmas; cards, etc., from all my friends. Holly from the garden, too—a huge log-fire and a very good T.V. programme. *About late afternoon I had a visitor, which was a surprise. It was Harwood Thompson. I wondered if anything had happened*: it lasted a second or two only. Did he think of St. Cadwan or Wales? I am still puzzled; perhaps he didn't know of the visit? I was amused, at the time, at a 'Cinderella' film on T.V.—so I was not asleep. Queer!"

Case No. 776—Mary Swainson

"When, I ask myself, have I been able to say, 'I do not merely believe, I *know*'? Only once. It was this experience which started me on the way of learning to 'see through' material appearances; to interpret them in terms of the fuller life. I was seventeen and at boarding school at the time of a severe 'flu epidemic. When my temperature rose to 105°, they moved me to a separate room for I was seriously ill. I remember the experience of delirium. I mention this because a part of me was aware of my state as being confused, and it was completely different from what happened next. *I then came out of my body, not only into clear consciousness, but into a more intense livingness than anything I had previously experienced. There was an awareness of expansion, of immense well-being and clarity, of joy and meaning. I remember thinking, 'If this is death, how wonderful, how easy, how natural'. Something seemed to say to me, 'This is very important; fix it'. So I looked down, finding myself lying still, horizontally, about six feet above my body on the bed. Below me, Matron was lighting the gas fire. I was aware of a tremendous magnetic pull to go on, for I was far more alive and well than in my physical body; but, although everything in me wanted to go, I knew I must not do so—yet.*

"The next thing I knew was that I was back in my physical body, feeling awful. Going out had been wonderful: expansion, awareness, light, life. But coming back was the opposite, and very unpleasant, like being constricted and limited into something heavy, cold, dark and painful.

"By the age of seventeen, and brought up in an orthodox clergyman's household, I had never heard or read of dying described in this way as a living experience. Later I did read descriptions similar to my own, and I realise now that I had not been actually aware of that 'cord' which many perceive as linking the two bodies. [There are several possible reasons for this.] Since the experience, however, I have never been afraid of dying. When suicidal patients seek death as a means of escape into oblivion, I often wonder what they will find; for death, as I nearly had it, is life to the Nth degree. And so I have always sought to understand this box-like existence in the context of that wholly simple and obvious awareness of what living can really be."

Case No. 777—Dr. Karl Novotny ("communicated")
"It was a lovely evening in Spring and I was spending Easter at my country home. I had not been really well for a considerable time, but was not confined to bed. So I agreed to go for a walk with some friends. As we started out, I felt very tired and thought perhaps I ought not to accompany them. However, I forced myself to go. Then I felt completely free and well. I went ahead and drew deep breaths of the fresh evening air, and was happier than I had been for a long time. How was it, I wondered, that suddenly I had no more difficulties, and was neither tired nor out of breath?

"I turned back to my companions and *found myself looking down at my own body on the ground*. My friends were in despair, calling for a doctor and trying to get a car to take me home. But I was well and felt no pains! I couldn't understand what had happened. I bent down and felt the heart of the body lying on the ground. Yes, it had ceased to beat—I was dead. But I was still alive! I spoke to my friends, but they neither saw nor answered me. I was most annoyed and left them. However, I kept on returning. To say the least it was upsetting to see my friends in tears and yet paying no attention to what I was saying. It was very upsetting, too, to look down at my dead body lying in front of me, while I felt in perfect health.

"And there was my dog, who kept whining pitifully, unable to decide to which of me he should go, for *he saw me in two places at once, standing up and lying on the ground*.

"When all the formalities were concluded and my body had been put into a coffin, I realised that I must be dead. But I wouldn't acknowledge the fact; for, like my teacher, Alfred Adler, I did not believe in an after-life. I visited my university colleagues: but they neither saw me nor returned my greeting. I felt most insulted. What should I do? I went up the hill to where Grete lives. She was sitting alone and appeared very unhappy. But she did not seem to hear me either.

"It was no use, I had to recognise the truth. When finally I did so, I saw my dear mother coming to meet me with open arms, telling me I had passed into the next world—not in words of course, since these belong only to the earth. Even so, I couldn't credit her statement and thought I must be dreaming. This belief continued for a long time. I fought against the truth and was most unhappy. Eventually, however, I accepted the suggestion of my spirit-guide, who pointed to the glorious realms to which I might aspire, if I gave up my foolish ideas and sought to make progress in the spirit world.

"It was not easy for me. It would have been much simpler if I had been convinced of the continuance of life after death; and had trusted to being helped across and joyfully received on the other side. There would then have been no dilemma, nor such a long transition period as those go through who do not trust their spirit-guide and consider earthly life as the most desirable existence. They may continue for many years bound in thought and feeling to the material world, thus slowing up their spiritual progress, although they can neither stop nor prevent it.

"In April, 1965, Dr. Karl Novotny, a well-loved Viennese psychiatrist, died of a heart attack at the age of 70. Two days before Grete Schröder, a former patient and a great friend of his, had dreamed of a figure that appeared to her and said: 'Novotny is dying'. That was all. The dream haunted her and a few days later she heard of his sudden death. She had never had anything to do with Spiritualism before, but was now persuaded to go and see 'Berta', a clairvoyant then visiting Vienna. At the first sitting 'Victor', the medium's control, announced the presence of Dr. Novotny, of whom Berta knew nothing. A short conversation ensued, which ended with a typical remark of the doctor's. Grete had asked him what he was doing now. He replied: 'Many people in this world come and ask for my advice, as many did on earth. But they never follow it. Like children released from school, they forget at once all they have learnt'.

"Grete continued contact with Dr. Novotny through Berta, and eventually suggested that he should use her hand to write what he had to say. This he agreed to do, and in October, 1966, a first attempt was made. Two days later short messages began to be received. Finally, in April, 1967, after regular daily practice, there commenced a series of communications in what was apparently Dr. Novotny's handwriting. These were issued in book form, *Mediale Schriften* ("Communications through a Medium") by Dr. Karl Novotny in 1968 by the Therese Krauss publishing house. It is from this book that the above is taken. Besides being translated from the German, it has also been curtailed and condensed."

Case No. 778—Mrs. "I. Beach"
This lady wrote in January, 1972, saying that she was 49 years old, a registered nurse with a medical husband. The latter "knows little of the psychic world"—and "those who hear not the music, think the dancers mad". She had just finished reading my *Out-of-the-Body Experiences,* University Books, N.Y., 1970, and considered that some of her own experiences "did not conform to the patterns there mentioned". "Perhaps," she suggested, "they are something else altogether". She had also read my *Study and Practice of Astral Projection,* 1961, and Muldoon's *Projection of the Astral Body,* 1929. "But," she repeated, "there are still many things which puzzle me. I have kept a written record of these experiences which began two years ago. I say 'began' inaccurately, but that is when I first recognised them as being psychic and when their quantity increased. I have had flying-'dreams' since childhood (compare Case No. 822). I wrote in a diary a 'dream' which occurred at the age of twenty. Here are excerpts (1942):

"Then I had a brilliant idea: I would fly back to Tours— I was trying to fly back to Tours, this time with a baby in my arms. Finally I got as high as the telephone-wires—and then got tangled up in them . . . The difference noticed in the past ten years has been the freedom from hampering frustrations. A typical pattern now is that of dancing, perhaps on a hillside or stairway, then taking some mighty swirl which carries me up into the air to a height of fifty or sixty feet. The mood is always one of exhilaration . . . The reality of the 'flying' has puzzled me all my life.

"Prior to the night of March 11, 1970 (which see later) I had not believed in immortality for some twenty-five years. One dream from the period I have remembered because of a unique feature—the intense glowing colours [=Paradise conditions], though ordinarily I 'dream' in 'every-day' colours. In this 'dream' I was being escorted through a garden-like land by a man of great beauty dressed in *flowing robes* (but no wings). I was convinced I had visited 'heaven'. With one possible exception (February 2, 1971) I have never been to a place quite like that.

"Before beginning a chronological account of the events that began in 1960 and culminated in a veritable barrage in 1970, I must recount the three other events of my earlier life that were probably astral projections.

"When I was about nine years old I went to the dentist to have a tooth extracted under nitrous oxide. Before the operation I had been looking out of the second-floor window at 'flying' squirrels among the trees: I wished that I could fly like them. While 'asleep' I 'dreamed' that I was out in the trees with them. They were unafraid of me.

"In 1941, at nineteen years, I was on a car-trip in Mexico and became car-sick. A pharmacist gave me a pill and we continued our journey. In about twenty minutes *I felt peculiar and then found I could not speak or move [catalepsy because much of the vehicle of vitality was projected from the body—it is the 'bridge' via which the Soul, using the Soul Body, controls the physical body]. The 'peculiar' feeling resembled being slightly drunk [also due to the projection of much of the vehicle of vitality] and also that experienced in some trance states [ditto]. I feel as if floating, light-headed and light-hearted with effervescence—as if millions of tiny bubbles [substance from the vehicle of vitality] were rising all through me.*

"*Then there must have been a period of unconsciousness* [= *the 'blackout' or 'tunnel'-effect as the double, here composite, separates from the body*] *because I was high,* 100 *feet or* 50, *up in the air, outside the car.* But the most amazing thing was the clarity with which I could see everything down below. It seemed as if I could see all of Mexico—for hundreds of miles . . . I seemed to have a sudden insight into the cause and cure of all evil, pain and sorrow in the world [=*a mystical experience*—our Third Group of Experiences in Introduction]. Then I wanted to hurry back to the world to use this marvellous new knowledge . . . I 'awoke' in the car.

"During the years I lived in Kansas City (1951-62) I was homesick for New Orleans, 800 miles away, and for my family there. My mother, in 1970, related the following episode from that period: *my mother awoke one morning and saw me [released double] standing in her bedroom. She asked, 'What are you doing here? But no—it can't be—I must be dreaming.' I answered, 'No, mother, it's not a dream: I am really here!' Then I came over to her, bent down and kissed her and then she woke up. I had vanished.*

"In the Spring of 1960 I had gone back to bed for a nap—alone in the house, except for my baby daughter, asleep in her room. Something awakened me and I thought, 'That must be the maid coming in'. Then I realised it was not her 'day'. *I started to get up but was quite paralysed [cataleptic].* Then I knew that someone was behind me who had an evil intent [= *a 'hinderer'*]. Suddenly everything was normal. I recount this—and other experiences of the kind which follow —because I was told, in February, 1972, that these paralysis episodes represented difficulty in returning to my body after an astral projection . . . But I would like your interpretation.

"Then this sort of thing started happening at night: I would suddenly wake up with the feeling of terror, paralysis and evil presence. I would eventually manage to call out and the 'spell' would be broken. This happened four or five times a year. I am sometimes afraid to go back to sleep [= to disconnect the vehicle of vitality].

"In 1967 two other incidents occurred during a paralysis state. On one occasion I felt that my mattress had been given a sharp blow from behind me, causing it to bounce. Several months later I saw the figure of a man, wearing no clothes, who seemed to be seething with rage.

"*A few years ago I was in a huge 'sewer': the walls were damp* [Hades conditions]. *I was wading through water in a vain search for a child who had been washed into the 'sewer' during a rainstorm* [= *an unsuccessful attempt to pass through the second 'death'—Paradise conditions were not entered*]. More recently, my baby had been flushed down a toilet into the 'sewer' which emptied into a 'river' [= Hades]. I knew I must go into the 'river' to find her [her own Soul Body, un-enveiled by substance from the vehicle of vitality— i.e., that she must pass through the second 'death']. I was afraid to enter the 'water'.

"Again—I was waiting in my car for the ferry to come and take me across a 'river' at twilight [Hades]. Suddenly the brakes slipped and the car rolled down the bank into the 'water'. I awoke terrified [= again failed to pass through the second 'death' and so to enter Paradise conditions].

"In March, 1970, two weeks after the onset of menses in my eleven-year-old daughter there was poltergeist phenomena [*due to excess-forces released from vehicle of vitality*]. They ranged from ink-stains, mattresses heaved, blankets were pulled, objects were moved, our names were called, touches, the shadow of a man, *green light* ['*spirit lights*', *i.e., incipient materialisations*] and attempts at 'possession'. By April I had guessed the probable identity of the disturber when his photograph was moved several times.

"On January 13, 1971, I saw him for the second time and there was a resumption of the poltergeist activity, though it was brief.

"In 1960 my husband's best friend died. He came to me, 800 miles away [= he directed his attention to her] as I was a latent medium [= provided the 'bridge' represented by the vehicle of vitality] and he could communicate with me. He could not do so until my daughter had reached puberty and provided the necessary 'psychic energy' [from her rapidly-developing vehicle of vitality—i.e., the daughter 'boosted' her mother's psychic power]. He is 'earthbound' [retaining his own vehicle of vitality for an unduly long period after death] because of his attraction to me.

"March 12, 1970: I dozed off again at 4.30 a.m., after having had the blanket pulled off. I went back to sleep, thinking, 'It's all imagination!' *I was awakened with the feeling of being invaded by something like electricity—a mild tingling* [the same 'tingle' as Monroe and others felt when *their own* vehicle of vitality left their bodies]. *'It'* [a would-be 'possessor'] *was trying to push me out of my own body and take control. 'It' was trying to make me raise my right arm and I have since thought it was an attempt to write with a pencil.*

"March 28, 1970: I woke with a tingling in my hands. Thinking it was the poltergeist [would-be 'possessor'] trying to 'take over' again. *I said to myself, 'Oh, no, you don't!', and the tingling* [attempt at 'possession'—the merging of his vehicle of vitality with hers, preparatory to his 'possession' of her body] *stopped immediately* . . .

"April 2, 1970: completely paralysed, with a sense of an evil presence ['hinderer'] behind me—felt a coldness on the back of my neck [withdrawal of ectoplasm from vehicle of vitality]. I prayed, 'Oh Lord, deliver me!', and immediately the 'force' was gone.

"January 3, 1971: the only reason for including this is *the possibility of the cord being a disguised reality.* I had a 'dream' and a frustrating journey back. My way was suddenly blocked by a house with a fenced-in yard. I climbed over the chain-link fence. I carried an electric blanket with me and *the cord (white) trailed behind me* [N.B.: Highly significant —see p. 119], *causing some difficulty* [= ? the 'silver cord' extension—many other projectors observed that it 'trailed behind' them—see More Astral Projections, 1964].

"April 27, 1970: a little old lady was walking with me in a department store. *We were about to go down [and pass through the second 'death'] when I saw a misty film in front of me [=substance from her own vehicle of vitality which enveiled her Soul Body and acted as a 'door', 'window' 'station', etc.—Cases No. 748, 754, 762, etc.] across the entrance—and I knew why not—because of 'ghosts' ['hinderers' in the corresponding Hades conditions].* I was snatched up into the air . . . I now know that the little lady was my mother.

"April 30: *I was in that helpless trance-like state with paralysis, but it was heavier than usual, as though I were trying to break through a thick fog [= trying, unsuccessfully, to pass through the second 'death', un-veiling the Soul Body and so leaving Hades and entering Paradise].*

"May 26: I was driving a car. It went off the pavement and plunged down an embankment. When I realised that death was inevitable, *I suddenly found myself [released double] floating in the air above the car.* Then I realised that, in my fright, I [whose vehicle of vitality is loose] had perhaps left my body too hastily; that if I had remained calm I would have had time to unfasten my seat-belt and escape.

"May 28, 1970: I awoke shortly after going to sleep in the 'trance' state—paralysed. I [released 'double'] was disorientated in regard to my bodily position in bed. I ['double'] lay with my head at the foot of the bed; my body was lying just the opposite. When, finally, I admitted this, I 'came to'.

"December, 1970: I awoke shortly after falling asleep with the feeling that *I was being lifted [by 'helpers'], then slowly lowered* . . .

"January 13, 1971: I went to bed, foregoing the night-light I had used, apprehending unpleasant experiences, since last Spring. I became cataleptic and realised someone was standing by my bed. But I was not frightened this time. *I was lying on my back. My left arm and hand felt very cold.* Then I saw the figure of a man walk out of the door. It was like a black shadow, but three-dimensional . . . *In this experience I seemed to be fighting through a fog [= trying, though failing, to pass through the second 'death'].*

"February 2, 1971: I 'dreamed' I had visited a friend who was a patient at the mental hospital. My friend was discharged, but I found myself coming back to the hospital to see 'S' [who was earthbound] to tell him to leave me alone and [to pass through the second 'death', to quit Hades and enter Paradise] i.e., to go on in the spirit world. I had notes of a speech with all the reasons why he should leave. Then I saw a shadowy figure coming towards me: it was 'S'. Then I saw *an exceedingly brilliant, blue-white light in the shape of a large oval, about ten feet long by six feet wide* [a *'spirit light'*, i.e., *an incipient materialisation of a discarnate Soul Body*]. It—or he—enveloped me. I now felt the familiar 'swarming of millions of particles' indicative of trance, only the movement was much faster than before. All else in the universe was total oblivion and darkness. *The emotions of one-ness, dissolving and bliss were over-whelming, indescribable* [*compare Yram*]. Then I 'blacked out, and woke up in the after-glow of that mystic welding.

"February 10: *I seemed to be in very dense fog or, more aptly, as though trying to surface from a deep dive into water. It felt as if I were trying to move my arm through thick toffee* [*trying to pass through the second 'death'—again unsuccessfully*].

"February 11, 1971: I fell asleep and 'woke' with the sensation that *I was slowly rising in a horizontal position towards the ceiling* . . . (Having read Dr. Crookall's *Astral Projection,* I feel sure that is the explanation of the above incident—and of the other during Christmas). I dozed off again and 'awoke' with the feeling that some sort of jointed cage-like affair was resting on my abdomen [compare 'hinderers' described by Yram in France, Monroe in U.S.A., etc.] I was frightened and came out of 'trance'.

"March 15, 1971: I dozed off and 'woke' feeling a pencil in my left hand. I felt sure that 'S' was standing by my bed. Later a friend told me, 'You should have got a pencil and paper—he wanted to write a message!'

"April 7, 1971: I floated upwards. I knew that 'S' was with me. We swirled in exhilarating loops and I kept repeating, 'I love you!' Then I returned to my body.

"April 10, 1971: I was floating off in space and became frightened. An 'angel' (?), wingless, came and brought me down to earth. There was a child with us: both were dressed in robes [Paradise conditions].

"April 20, 1971: I was paralysed and then *felt I was being engulfed, or wrapped up, like a cocoon, in a dense black, evil cloud* [also due to a 'hinderer'?]. *I prayed for help and immediately it vanished.*

"August 6, 1971: Enveloped in a cloud of glowing, vibrating force and light. It invaded me, so that I could not distinguish myself from it—and I knew it was 'S'. I could feel his presence strongly.

"August 31, 1971: I fell asleep, awakening in a 'trance'—tingling, vibration, etc., but, instead of the usual euphoria, I seemed in the presence of an unpleasant entity, possibly my recently-dead brother-in-law, a schizoid person. I was uneasy and recited the Lord's Prayer. It worked—both 'trance' and entity disappeared. A medium friend contacted 'S' and put my question to him: 'Is our attraction harmful to you?' 'I cannot go forward [cannot pass through the second 'death', shedding the vehicle of vitality, leaving Hades and entering Paradise]. I need help [to do this]. 'Are you "earthbound" because of me?' 'No! *It is because of me. Pray for me!*' [This is a very common request by Souls who are 'earthbound' and therefore delayed in Hades—see *The Supreme Adventure*[45]]. 'What are you doing now?' 'Making retribution'.

"December 28, 1971: I told B. [medium friend] that I had, several times, a peculiar feeling; *it was as though I were the ocean, and the moon was pulling everything in me [vehicle of vitality] towards it—of being drawn towards something like a magnet.* She said it was because I was a medium [= *because of her loose vehicle of vitality—statements that the moon draws loose vehicles of vitality out of gear with their respective physical bodies, increasing the mediumicity, have often been made—probably representing the origin of the word 'lunatic', some, though not of course all, those described as 'insane' being essentially mediumistic*]. James Hyslop, among the greatest of American psychical researchers[46], considered that "If we believe in telepathy, we believe in a process which makes possible the invasion of a personality by someone at a distance" and he elsewhere pointed out that if there are discarnate souls ("spirits") it cannot be only sane and helpful ones who contact and influence mortals. The greatest of American psychologists, Professor William James, considered that the medical profession should treat the ancient idea of obsession (in certain cases) as a hypothesis and that "it will have its innings again". He said, "One has to be 'scientific' indeed to be blind and ignorant enough not to suspect any such possibility". (The mistake is the either/or attitude: in ancient times the tendency was to regard all mental illness as obsession; in modern times it is to regard none as so caused.) Reference may also be made to Dr. Arthur Guirdham's *Obsession*, 1972.

In *The Newsletter of the Parapsychology Foundation*[47] it

was said, "Records kept for two years at the Bronx Municiple Hospital Centre by two New York psychiatrists showed that fewer persons sought psychiatric care during full moon periods than at other times of the month. The study also showed that the psychiatric case-load varied only slightly according to moon-phases. From this finding, they dispute 'the old wive's tale' that insanity increases during the full-moon phase. [But the effect, if any, would apply only to mediumistic people and would tend to be hidden by other, e.g., psychological, cases.] At Duke University, however, experiments are being carried out which seem to contradict this view. Dr. Radvitz, working with electrobiological techniques, has established beyond doubt that electrical currents flowing [in the vehicle of vitality] from one part of a plant to another, or from one part of an animal to another, experienced a cyclical variation of fourteen days, corresponding to phases of the moon. He also found similar variations in human beings: the voltage jumped when the moon was full and lowered when it was new. Most observed patients were depressed by high readings, and showed pent-up hostility and apathy at such times. Low readings almost universally were accompanied by amiability and feelings of well-being."

Paul Brunton[48] advised the special practice of meditation on two days of the month—when the sun and moon come into conjunction and opposition, i.e., the new and full moon nights (or at dawn on the following day). Buddhist monks of high class are among those who use such periods for meditation.

Case No. 779—Mrs. Margetts

Mrs. H. Margetts, of 91 Rhode Lane, Bridgwater, Som., sent me an account of an experience of her father's (not here cited and later (October 10, 1972) wrote:

"Since I last wrote, I have again felt myself falling and then seem to be partly outside myself: then the experience ends." This was, a partial projection: a falling sensation is felt when consciousness is largely in the physical body, a rising sensation when it is largely in the "double" that is in course of release from it. In a few cases, which we call "dual consciousness", the person experiences *both* sensations. Such descriptions strongly suggest that the "double" is not imagined (subjective) but "semi-physical" (objective, though not physical).

"Can you interpret the experience that a working-colleague related to me last week? Dorreen told me that she saw her 'husband' one night standing at the bottom of the bed. He did not say anything, but she was startled when she saw her husband was still in bed. As she shook his sleeping form, the figure [part of released vehicle of vitality] vanished [into his body]. Dorreen says her husband was apparently semi-conscious [since part of the vehicle of vitality was in, and part released from, his body]. This description corresponds to that published in 1923 by Dorothy Grenside and here cited first in our Introduction (p.2).

Mrs. Margetts then posed several questions which, of course, have been posed by many others. "Why isn't it possible to project at will?" (The answer is that people with tight vehicles of vitality project with some difficulty: that it is not necessarily a good thing to try to project at will—there is a time when the egg-shell breaks and the chicken emerges with safety, but it may be injurious to hasten the process. We do not recommend deliberate attempts at obtaining any psychic experiences.)

"When I fainted, I had no recollection of having projected [neither had Dorreen's husband]." This was answered in *More Astral Projections*, 1964, p.141: "Some readers may ask, 'If, as Mrs. Garrett declared from personal experience and Neville Randall discovered from correspondence, astral projections are common events that apply to quite "ordinary" folk, why have *we* failed to undergo one?' The answer is obvious—the failure is not in *the occurrence* but in *the memory of the occurrence*. The mistake is to suppose that it is easy to remember *an out-of-the-body experience* after one has *re-entered* the body. The physical brain must be involved in all that we remember in our 'normal' *in-the-body state*: but the physical brain was *not* involved in the astral projection; as Bergson said, 'The physical brain is the organ whereby we *forget* [out-of-the-body experiences, telepathic, clairvoyance and other psychic experiences].' This matter was mentioned by the present writer in 1961 (*The Study and Practice of Astral Projection*, University Books Inc., New York, U.S.A., pp. 32, 43, 55, 56). We have no means of assessing statistically the 'blinkering' effect of the physical brain on psychic experiences, involving either (i) the "semi-physical" vehicle of vitality only, with no consciousness, *no experience*, as in the case of Dorreen's husband or (ii) the "super-physical" Soul Body only, as in our First Group of *experiences*, i.e., St. Paul, Wm. Gerhardi, etc., or (iii) both the vehicle of vitality and the Soul Body, as in our Second Group of *experiences*, i.e., Prof. Harlow, Lattinger, etc. It is a mistake to suppose that people are simple and "alike" and all behave identically—they are actually highly complex (with the three ultra-physical bodies just mentioned) and their ultra-physical bodies, like their physical bodies, are not all equally-developed and organised as instruments of consciousness, including memory. Moreover, people are not static: on the contrary, just as the physical body can be rendered a more efficient instrument of consciousness by proper use (food, rest, exercise in fresh air), so the Soul Body can be rendered a more efficient instrument by proper use (the acceptance of moral responsibility) and the same is true of the Spiritual Body (which is organised by selfless love and the search for truth and beauty)."

Mrs. Margetts further said, "I do not understand why some people can get out of the body by first relaxing [this facilitates the release of the vehicle of vitality which normally circulates in and animates the physical body] when others get close to death and remember it as a harrowing experience [on the contrary, I have seen many cases in which this was a very happy experience and none whatever in which it was harrowing—see *Intimations of Immortality*, James Clarke, 1965, pp. 3, 4, 130]. Some people felt very giddy before projecting [they were feeling the vehicle of vitality loosening preparatory to projecting from the body]."

Case No. 780—J. S. Hindle

Mr. Hindle, a Roman Catholic, wrote: "One morning I woke at 7 a.m. My son, John, starts work at 7.30, leaving the house at 7.15.

"Not hearing him downstairs, I guessed he had overslept. I rose . . . and went along the passage to his room. His bedroom door was half-open. As I attempted to pass through it, I was surprised to find myself [released 'double'] in the room without the door moving. John was still in bed, his head covered with the bedclothes, his right arm hanging down the side of the bed . . .

"The next moment I had *an unpleasant sensation of falling from a great height, to find myself awake in my own bed.*

"It was still 7 a.m. I went to John's room to find him in exactly the same position as I had seen him in my 'dream'. He had overslept."

Case No. 781—Clifford Thomas

Mrs. H. Margetts sent me the experience recorded by her father, Mr. Thomas.

"He was recovering, in hospital, from an injury. He lay in

bed resting when *suddenly he [released 'double'] became suspended in mid-air.* He was astonished to see himself lying in bed and yet hovering in the air.

"A man in the bed next to his said my father was yelling, 'I can't get back!' The man questioned this and my father repeated it.

"*Then he was suddenly jerked back into his body.* He felt that he had been in two places at once [= 'bilocation'].

"My father is a very rational person and would not accept that this experience was a psychic one, but I believe that it was.

"As for myself, on two occasions, just as I have been waking [= returning to body] I have been aware of rising and descending—it is a delightful sensation: but I did not find myself looking at my physical body. On three other occasions, I have found myself cataleptic, completely paralysed [= with vehicle of vitality projected from body]. I have been psychic —flashes of ESP—since a girl, and have been trying to find an explanation for these rising-and-falling and cataleptic experiences."

Case No. 782—Mrs. E. Bullinger

"Three years ago I read a book on out-of-the-body experiences. I started to practice [*sic*] it. I did this five ore [*sic*] mornings in succession.

"On the last attempt I was lying for half an hour and thought to myself, 'This is all baloney. If anyone saw me they would think I was stupid!' Anyway, I had to get up to let the dog out. I sat in my chair when such *a melancholy feeling* came over me, strange music ore [*sic*] *a whirring noise* [= releasing part of vehicle of vitality]. My head flopped to one side. I tried to snap out of this funny feeling. Then I thought, 'No! Whatever it is!' So the next moment my eyelids closed and it was like sticks sticking them down—try as I would, I could not open them. Then I started to see all the room lit up in a lovely radiance. I saw everything a lot clearer but the funny thing about it was I ['double'] *was floating around the top of the sitting-room, yet I [body] was there in the chair.* My sight and faculties were a thousand times more clear.

"Then I was drawn to the mantelshelf were [*sic*] an ashtray was and in the ash-tray was a fairly [?large] amount. Right on the bottom was a needle which, earlier on, I was searching for and could not find.

"The next moment my attention was drawn to a big glass

cabinet at the bottom of the living-room and from this were *streams of power [=ectoplasm] coming* and this *strange noise*. In the centre of this power was a gap and in this a pair of sandalled feet appeared. *It was building-up in quick jerks.* Then a long white gown. I was scared. It built up to about the shoulders. I was terrified.

"*The next instance [sic] I was back with a bump [=the released ectoplasm returned to her body]. All had vanished. I was 'coming to'.*

"I argued with myself, 'It was all a dream!' But I knew different. I thought about the needle and when I looked it was there alright [*sic*] under a good coating of ash which no naked eye could see. I had to move the ash away to find the needle.

"Anyway, this stopped my attempts to experiment. But on the third day after I sat in the same chair when this feeling came over me again. So I rushed into the bathroom and dashed cold water into my face. This seemed to shake it of [*sic*].

"Three weeks later, it happened again. I was sat in the same chair. Once more cold water did the trick.

"I wish you would explain this. I can't find an answer. Have I lost something that could have been a gift through being scared?"

Case No. 783—Jane Roberts

Jane Roberts exercises that type of astral projection which is called "travelling clairvoyance"—largely out of the body, she reports to those present through her largely-vacated body. The details of a number of her excursions (like those of P. E. Cornillier's artists' model Reine) were corroborated.

On the first occasion, Mrs. Roberts saw locations in different towns and states. On the second she said, "I was definitely 'out', yet Seth ['control'] described what I saw". She began by finding herself ('double') "descending through the air" and standing near a motel. There was a man in a business suit and carrying a brief-case. This was Mr. Gallagher. Her descriptions of the latter and of the motel were accurate.

Case No. 784—Cornillier's model

P. E. Cornillier[50] produced "travelling clairvoyance" in a young artists' model, Reine, by hypnosis (or, rather, by mesmerism, i.e., with the use of "passes").

Cornillier "sent" Reine's projected "double" to see "D", a sculptor-friend (concerning whose studies she is quite ignorant). "She appears to be really there and sees him working." He then "sent" her to an apartment on the fifth floor. "She describes the bathroom very exactly. She appears really to see it herself and not in any way to be accepting my thought-images or suggestions. For example, in spite of my insistence, I cannot make her mention the window, but she discovers the curtain which, as was proved later, had been drawn over the window."

Several similar examples of "travelling clairvoyance" were given.

Case No. 785—Dr. Nandor Fodor's cases

Fodor[51] cited several cases of "travelling clairvoyance" when he mentioned Sir William Barrett (*Psychical Research*) as considering that the evidence for this is even more widespread than that for telepathy. Fodor mentioned "a letter written to the Marquis de Puysegier in 1785 from Nantes: a girl followed the movements of her 'magnetiser' when he went into town and described everything that was taking place around him", Adolphe Didier's work and the projections, recorded by Alphonse Cahagnet with Adèle Maginot. He quoted F.W.H. Myers to the effect that "the clairvoyante will frequently miss her way and describe houses and scenes adjacent to those desired."

Case No. 786—Alex. Erskine

Erskine[52] gave several examples of "travelling clairvoyance".

One case concerned a youth, the son of Jack Mardell, a friend of Erskine's. Asked where his father was, the youth replied, "I don't know!"

"Will you let me put you to 'sleep'?" asked Erskine. He was soon "off" and I put the question again. He answered me at once, giving the minutest details. I wrote down what he said, noting the time on the margin of the paper.

"His father, it seemed, had gone out. For three hours I made the boy [released 'double'] follow his father through the streets of London, into various houses and out again. Without hesitation the boy told me all . . .

"I got into touch with the father and saw him privately and showed him what I had written. He was staggered. He admitted that his son's account of his movements, of the people to whom he had spoken, etc., was accurate.

"Two promises he asked, and these I readily gave; one, that I would never divulge what I had written, and the other, that I would not repeat the experiment with him."

Case No. 787—H. Willmott
Willmott (*in litt.*,) said, "When my first projection occurred, I knew nothing at all about it and wasn't at all interested in the subject.

"I was laying [*sic*] sideways on the sofa with our dog curled up by my feet. *Suddenly I found myself [released 'double'] floating face downwards with my arms outstretched at mantelpiece level. I could see my earthly body on the sofa with eyes closed and the dog still there.* I could see everything in the room, but I was looking at it from a separate [*sic*] body. I was in this state two or three minutes, then I was drawn down to my body. The remarkable thing is that *I wasn't surprised: it seemed a very natural thing.* This was eight years ago.

"The second and last time I was laying [*sic*] on my back on the sofa watching T.V. My wife was sitting in an armchair next to me. *I suddenly found myself ['double'] floating on my back, just below the ceiling. After about 30 seconds I was drawn down to my body.*"

Case No. 788—Miss Victoria Laird
Miss Laird wrote (*in litt.*): "Just before Christmas, 1970, I was taken to hospital for a 'check-up'. The trouble proved to be 'a tired heart' and angina (I am 75). But what might interest you, as it did when the hospital consultant called to examine me, was this: The night before he came, I had an out-of-the-body experience—not the first but the most beautiful and comforting one. *My sight seemed to be in the 'cord' that held me to my body on the bed,* for I could see both my spiritual self [here = Soul Body, not the True, Transcendent Spiritual Body] and my physical body, though all feeling was in the spiritual [here = Soul] Body. I was thinking how wonderful it was to be free and young again and happy. Yet, as I thought, *I could see myself [Soul Body] looking a lovely seventeen or eighteen: my hair, which used to be a reddish-gold, shone with all the brightness it did at that age.* [Compare the description of an Australian, Miss Zoila Stables, B.A., our Case No. 73, who said, 'I was in youth: in physical life I am middle-aged and my hair is grey—in the projection it was dark.' This highly significant phenomenon was discussed in detail in *The Jung-Jaffé View of Out-of-the-body Experiences,* World Fellowship Press, 1970, pp. 34, 45, 84, where it was shown to apply not only to 'astral projectors', such as Miss Laird and Miss Stables, but also to people who undergo pseudo-death and, according to

both clairvoyants and 'communicators', in Great Britain, America, Germany, South Africa, etc., to those who became permanently free from the body—the so-called 'dead'—the same thing applies. We concluded, 'The hypothesis that the Soul Body is the primary, and the physical body only a secondary and derived organ of consciousness, is supported by numerous facts in connexion with pseudo-death, astral projection, clairvoyance, etc. On the one hand, the "level" of consciousness of mortals is described as relatively low, while the release of the Soul Body from its physical condensation is often observed to be accompanied by an elevation and extension of consciousness.' We quoted Sir Oliver Lodge as considering that consciousness (which primarily uses the Soul Body) is not directly associated with physical matter (and therefore with our physical bodies) but via 'an "ether" body'—the 'semi-physical', ultra-gaseous electro magnetic portion of the total body—which we call the vehicle of vitality.]

"My figure, always a slight five feet two, looked as young as my face, and I was smiling happily. *I seemed to be in a cloud of golden light* [*=Paradise conditions, corresponding to the unenshrouded Soul Body*, the 'double' here being simple, whereas enshroudment, due to a significant amount of released vehicle of vitality, the released 'double' being composite, caused contact with the dim Hades conditions, corresponding to the vehicle of vitality—see below]. A sudden violent pain drew me back into my body: I awoke in bed.

"Other experiences have happened during sleep [which condition is due, on our hypothesis, to a slight disconnection of the 'bridge', the vehicle of vitality, from the body, necessarily also disconnecting the Soul Body]. I have always struggled not to return to my body. The light around me has never been golden [Soul Body only] before, but always *a dim half-light* [*due to the enshroudment of the Soul Body by the vehicle of vitality, i.e., a composite 'double'*. Miss Laird's vehicle of vitality is naturally slightly loose, so that the tendency, at least at first, is for the released 'double' to be composite].

"Other times I have been conscious of leaving my bed which is in a curtained alcove: sometimes it has seemed as though the curtain caught my hair as I floated through it, and I tossed my head to free it [because this 'double' was not Soul Body only but included much of the 'semi-physical' vehicle of vitality also]. I have walked in streets and there seemed to be other *grey shadowy forms* [=*Hades conditions, corresponding to the vehicle of vitality*] about.

"When I lived in a tenth-floor flat, I was outside the building and suddenly wondered if I had my key [= directed attention back to flat]. But no sooner the thought than I was in the flat and looking at the door I had passed through [in the released 'double].

"*I have often struggled to keep my legs from floating to the horizontal before being forced to enter my body again* [the typical position for *composite* 'doubles' that were *either leaving or re-entering* their bodies: the position was described both for leaving the body in *The Study and Practice of Astral Projection*[53] and re-entering the body[54] and in *More Astral Projections* for leaving the body[55] and for re-entering it[56]. The horizontal position is never described in cases in which the Soul Body only was projected]. My 'astral body' [here = composite 'double'] seemed quite firm to my touch, though it looked like a solid cloud and always my mind and feeling was in the 'astral' body [which was primary] and not in my material body [which was secondary and derived] on the bed.

"I think I have, since my childhood, had 'astral flights' during sleep, as I used to talk about my flying dreams. [Compare Case No. 822 and *Out-of-the-body experiences. A Fourth Analysis*, 1970, p.56 where S. A. Wildman, a lawyer, is cited as discussing the significance of 'dreams' of flying, etc.] I often tried to 'take off' from my bed after waking: it seemed the natural thing to be able to fly. But my attempts were never successful.

"I bought your book, *During Sleep*, T.P.H., 1964, and believe that, at times, I have crossed the 'border' [= Hades the 'borderland' corresponding to the vehicle of vitality, between earth and Paradise, corresponding to the Soul Body, the 'journey' consisting of shedding the vehicle of vitality from the composite 'double', i.e., of passing through the second 'death'] during sleep and helping on 'the other side' . . . *I seemed to pass through a dim tunnel* [=*consciousness was dim during the second 'death', the brief period when the vehicle of vitality was separating from and freeing the Soul Body from envielment—Compare Case No. 800*] *before coming to a golden brightness* [=*Paradise*]. That was how it was when I met my father recently. He had 'passed' in 1939. He had no belief in an after-life and, living, I had hated him as he had made my mother unhappy. But *I saw him younger*, waiting for me. I kissed him, saying, 'How lovely to see you, Dad!' He smiled in a shy, bashful way, as though asking if he had done well, and wanting my approval. I feel sure that he had been in 'dark' [Hades] places for a long while and was just emerging into 'light' [Paradise]. As I left him I thought how glad I was that we were now friends and, when I woke next morning, I had a warm feeling of love for him that I had never felt when he was 'living'. I wondered if I had helped him [I have little doubt that Miss Laird helped her 'deceased' father to emerge from a prolonged stay in the Hades state—he had been 'earth-bound' because body-bound, retaining the vehicle of vitality, which, with average decent folk who die in old age, lasts only about three days of our time. I have known very similar cases].

"Often I seem to be in a dim, shadowy place [Hades] looking through a glass partition [the enshrouding vehicle of vitality] into a brighter place [Paradise]. It was like that when I saw a brother, who had 'passed' previously at 69, meet with outstretched hands and smiles an elder brother. Though the dark form, that left my side to meet him, I could not recognise, I knew it was one of the family and a letter which reached me later confirmed that it was my eldest brother (who I did not know was ill). I am certain that my younger brother is a healer or helper on 'the other side': he wanted very much to be a doctor but lack of funds prevented that on earth.

"I used to write of various psychic experiences to the late T. C. Lethbridge: he said that my spiritual body [here = the 'semi-physical' vehicle of vitality and not the 'super-physical' Soul Body, much less the transcendent True Spiritual Body] was loosely knit with my physical body."

I wrote to Miss Laird and she replied (April 11, 1972) that she had not read about out-of-the-body experiences and the "silver cord"—extension prior to herself having had projections: "It was my interest in the use of the pendulum by Lethbridge that first made me write to him, as the pendulum works for me also". She said that it was a month after she had died, her mother appeared: "A glorious vision in a luminous cloud of light which lit the room". The account continues, "She smiled and wordlessly assured me she was well and happy and I was not to grieve. She looked radiant [? younger than when she had died] then was gone"—all very typical. "When I first had out-of-the-body experiences it seemed I was beside my bed, feeling wonderfully happy ... Then, after a time, I would float to the ceiling, looking down on the bed and my body on it. Once I saw myself high in the sky, under the deepest of blue skies. *As I looked over my shoulder [compare the numerous cases of people who 'turned round'] it seemed as though a narrow gleaming silver ribbon was stretching from me ['double'] as far as I could see.* Then I thought I must not go too far and immediately I was waking in bed. That time, instead of the *convulsive jolt,* I experienced something like *an explosion* in my head [*=repercussion caused by the re-entry into the body of a 'double' which was composite in nature, i.e., which included 'semi-physical' substance from the vehicle of vitality*].

"Once I wakened, I could not move a hand or foot [*catalepsy, due to the release of much of the vehicle of vitality, which constitutes a 'bridge' between the Soul Body and the physical body, from the latter*]. I could see a shadow [*the released vehicle of vitality*] over my body. As it and my body became one, I came to life with a jolt. Other times I have wakened cataleptic and, for a few seconds, was not able to move.

"It is only of late years that I have read about this subject."

Case No. 789—Brad Steiger's cases

Certain of Steiger's cases contain details that are of obvious significance. Mrs. Sara Norris awoke at 3 a.m., the time when she should feed her baby, and went over to the cot [= directed her attention to the baby]. Returning to her own bed, she [released 'double'] saw her own physical body. A seven-year-old girl who had "died" for fifteen minutes visited a beautiful place which she thought must be "heaven" where she saw her (deceased) father at the end of *a "footbridge" (compare "gate", "door", "bridge", "window", "mirror", etc.,* in other accounts). He sent her back. Carlotta Van Buren, when giving birth to her child, *felt "a whirling sensation" which went faster and faster until she was above her body lying on the bed* [= *the reverse of the "tingle" when quitting body*]. *Later she felt "a tugging or pulling"* [*from the "silver cord"-extension*] *and entered "a tunnel with a light* [*that of earth*] *at the end"*. Then she was back in her body. Mrs. M. Walker, out of her body after a surgical operation, seemed to stand in *"the doorway* to a grey hall [= Hades]." Each time she moved forward, however, *"something"* [= *the "silver cord"-extension*] held her back. She said, *"I wanted to stay there and not return. I know now that death is nothing to fear."* P. M. Vest almost drowned but found "himself" (released "double") a dozen feet above his struggling body. The significant statement then followed: he "watched the drowning body dispassionately—as you might watch an old coat being discarded". Since then he no longer thinks of his body as "I"—he regards it as a "garment". Mary "W", in pain after an operation, released her "double" (her "real self") and when the nurses tried to revive her, was reluctant to return. "T.P.H.", twelve years of age, had bronchitis and released his "double". Seeing the doctor reviving him, he thought, "I'll have to go back to *that clumsy, imperfect body*". (Disparagement of the body, as well as indifference, is common.) *Finally, he was "sucked back" into his body* (a description used by several others—see More Astral Projections, pp. xviii, Case Nos. 52, 105, 287, 291, 360, 368, 748). The phrase "sucked back" was also used by Reine (*op. cit.*, 1921, p.197) to describe her return from mesmeric trance.

Thereafter he did not fear death.

Case No. 790—Mrs. J. Alwood

Mrs. Alwood wrote: "I was praying one afternoon. I became quite relaxed, sitting in my chair, and felt myself ['double'] leaving my body. I moved at a great speed. *At first, all was dark around me* [=Hades, because the vehicle of vitality enshrouded the Soul Body].

"Suddenly [*evidently after the second 'death' though the process seems to have been un-noticed*] *I was moving at a still greater speed amongst flowers that were so beautiful that I could only marvel at them. There were flowers that I had never seen* [=Paradise conditions in the un-enshrouded Soul Body]. Then I saw the most beautiful babies in beds.

"Finally I saw a great light ahead of me—so great that it blinded me. I then re-entered my body."

Case No. 791—Mrs. E. Thirlway

"On December 8, 1968, I was in a car accident in California. My nephew was driving. I don't remember the impact. The next thing I did know, *I was about thirty feet in the air looking down*. I could see myself lying on the side of the road. No one was near me. They were all busy with the cars. I seemed to be up there for some time. There seemed no hurry. *The cord from my body was like a neon light.*

"I was not upset. I seemed to be interested in what they were doing down below.

"I don't remember going back into my body but since this experience I find great peace."

Case No. 792—Stanley G. Price

Mrs. J. R. Bierstein, of Harrisburg, Pa., U.S.A., a Fellow

of the Spiritual Frontiers Fellowship, U.S.A., passed on two experiences of Mr. Price to me. He lives in Alexandria, Va., U.S.A.

"In the first he was under an anaesthetic for nine hours but knew what was said in the operating-room and also observed a nurse in another part of the building, locked out of the floor she wished to enter, being forced to go out of the building and enter by another door. When, later, he recounted this to his surgeon, the latter was dumbfounded.

"In his second experience he awoke one morning, aware that he had been out of his body. He recalled having been in Egypt, in a hot desert. That morning when he went to work his secretary asked him where he had gotten such a sunburn? (On that day there had been snow.) He went to a mirror and saw he was sunburned. He opened his shirt and saw that the burn extended over his body. He subsequently peeled. He has witnesses to verify this."

A similar phenomenon, suffered by the "travelling clairvoyant" Adèle Maginot, according to Dr. Nandor Fodor[57], "the first French medium, whose phenomena were carefully recorded and well-attested". Fodor (*op. cit.*, p.47) said, "Actual harm was suffered by the medium. A M. Lucas was anxious about the fate of his brother-in-law. With the mother of the vanished man, he visited Adèle Maginot. To quote: 'That which astonished this good woman as well as M. Lucas —and the other persons present at the seance—was to see Adèle putting her hands before the left side of her face to shelter from the burning rays of sunshine of that climate . . . She had a violent sunstroke which made all the side of her face bluish-red . . . This deep colour only began to disappear 24 hours later. The heat was so violent at this time that you could not keep your hand on her." (In such cases the medium "reports back" to the sitters what she is observing via her released "double": the cord-extension between "double" and body probably has a considerable content of substance from the "semi-physical" vehicle of vitality, so that it transmits physical stimuli to the body. The phenomenon probably also occurred in connexion with some cases of witchcraft with stigmata.

Case No. 793—A. J. Martin

Mr. Martin wrote from California: "My psychic experiences have occurred during some degree of trance-state or deep slumber—the most extraordinary during the latter.

"One 'nightmare' I have had since childhood. This is an

example. Some years ago I was rooming temporarily in an old house and felt some sort of force-field—*intense humming and pulsing—and became partly numb and paralysed. There was also a sense of oppression and a need for light.* After a struggle I was able to leave the bed, walk over to the floor-lamp by the window. But I was unable to turn it on. Then I recalled that, in the hall outside my room, the light was on. So I walked to the door and opened it. But, instead of the dimly-lit hall, *I was in a large, very dark room in a strange house. And a Thing was waiting—as usual—a parasitic psychic entity of some sort that was trying to fasten itself to me.* [What Robert Monroe calls a '*sucker*', probably what the ancient Hindus called '*an astral shell*', i.e., a vehicle of vitality which had been discarded at the second '*death*'—see *The Mechanisms of Astral Projection*[58].] When I did manage to waken I realised that physically I had not left the bed.

"On a higher level of awareness, I have a feeling of spiritual elation, move freely and see everything in clear focus. Here is an example: I was on a long train-trip and *was nervously fatigued* and dropped off into a sort of trance-sleep. I felt elated with *a slight tingling, humming sensation* [*vehicle of vitality being loosened*]. *Then, in a velvety blackness, I saw an opening* [='*door*', '*gate*', *etc.—compare Case No. 789*], which, as a bodiless awareness ['double'] I moved towards . . . I was in a room in a friend's house: he was there, sat at his table. Then the train gave a lurch and snapped me awake. I noted the time—10.00 p.m. When I arrived at my destination I wrote my friend and asked him if he had been sitting at his table that night at 10.00 p.m. He had! In other experiences I have a 'body' but it lacks the density of the physical body: it doesn't seem such an encumbrance. *I have always returned from such experiences with reluctance and regret.*"

Case No. 794—Mrs. B. F. Leary

Mrs. Leary, who is seventy two years of age, wrote from British Columbia, Canada: "I was coming out of an anaesthetic. *Suddenly I found myself above my body,* looking down at it and saw doctors and nurses putting in sutures on the last skin layer. At this point the doctor (Leeder) was explaining to the nurses the uses of new types of suture . . .

"Then I knew no more until I came out of the anaesthetic. The strange thing was that I had felt nothing [no physical pain because the primary body for feeling, thinking, etc., had been disconnected from the physical when the vehicle of vitality was ejected by the anaesthetic] but my mind was keen and alert.

"Later, I discussed the incident with Dr. Leeder. He looked at me rather strangely and said, 'Oh! So you are one of *those* people, are you?' He did not appear to be at all surprised."

Case No. 795—Wanda Sue Parrott

Miss Parrott, who contributes regularly to the Los Angeles *Herald and Examiner,* wrote (*in litt.,*): "Projections started with me when I was quite young, with a feeling of travelling —I was going 'home'. I knew I would come back to my body.

"When I was 20 I saw my body below me. I went to a girl who was about to kill herself. I touched her. Energy flowed from me to her. The girl fell back, asleep. Next day she called on me and thanked me."

Case No. 796—Mrs. D. E. Munroe

Mrs. Munroe, of San Bernardine, California, wrote (*in litt.,*): "I am sixty seven, and had never heard of astral projection when I first had these experiences.

"When *about seven years old* I was very ill with measles and rose high above my body: I watched my writhing body on the bed. After floating there for some time, I heard my mother coming and all was back to normal.

"When I was a young married woman with one baby, a farm accident put me into hospital. My mother-in-law had taken the baby. I lay in hospital *worrying and wishing I could see my baby* [=*directed attention towards it*]. Then suddenly I was in my mother-in-law's bedroom, floating near the ceiling over my baby's cot. I have no recollection of returning to my body.

"Later, when my husband and I were doing a lot of quarrelling, I was in hospital for surgery next day. I was quite ill. A nurse gave me a sedative. She left the room and *I found myself wishing to see my husband* [=*directed attention towards him*]. Then I was floating near the ceiling in my own home—over the bed. Then someone called my name and I was back in my body.

"Many times, over the years, I have re-lived these and other episodes. I have never told anyone. I have never tried to project purposely."

Case No. 797—The Rev. N. A. G. Sieme

The Rev. Sieme, rector of the Parish Church of St. Mary, Springfield Centre, New York, wrote (*in litt.,*): "On the night of August 2, 1966, shortly after I had retired, *I felt an odd tingling sensation accompanied by a buzzing sound* [= the vehicle of vitality loosening from the body—compare Monroe and many others], *whereupon suddenly I seemed to be out of my body in a clearer and more peaceful* [Paradise] *world . . . I seemed to hover, several feet in the air,* above some roses I had planted near the Parish Church. When I looked across the road, which physically is a lovely landscape with a gentle rolling hill, the field, which at this time of the year is quite green, was covered with Easter lilies [= Paradise conditions]. Then I was back in my body.

"This does not seem to be an astral projection to a physical locality, for although the roses were real, the lilies were not [it was a projection with dual consciousness—awareness of both earth and Paradise: had Mr. Sieme 'gone further', the earth would have disappeared from his view]."

Case No. 798—Mrs. M. J. Holland

Mrs. Holland, of Chicago, Ill., U.S.A., said, "I am writing to you to tell you about two experiences in the last two years when I was in 'astral projections', except that I did not know that term.

"On April 1, 1969, I was in hospital in very great pain. They had given me a 'pain-killer'. I thought I was witnessing my mental crack-up. I was able to detach my functional body ['double'] and watch myself [physical body].

"Six months later I left my body in bed and went to Tucson, Arizona, where some dear friends, Helen and Abe, live [= direction of the attention]. When I saw them I was alarmed as Helen looked very drawn and leaned on Abe as she walked.

"The next morning I mentioned my 'dream' to my husband and, at his suggestion, wrote my friends and sent it by air mail. In a few days I got my answer—on that particular evening Helen had a very bad pain in her back and Abe helped her to get to the doctor's office."

Case No. 799—Mrs. B. Doty

Mrs. Doty, very ill, was taken to hospital and became physically unconscious, but she remembers seeing "a beautiful golden city in which everything was bright and dazzlingly beautiful" [= Paradise]. Then she was back in her body. After this she is convinced, *"Death is the doorway to a life beyond the earth—earth-life is a shadow of things to come"*.

Case No. 800—Margaret Livermore
Mrs. Livermore, of Pontac, Michigan, U.S.A., wrote: "In reading your book, *Out-of-the-body Experiences*, I am sure I have experienced astral projection but unlike any of the cases in that book—I didn't see my 'double'. I will set down the experiences just as they happened and let you be the judge. If you could throw light on these things, I would greatly appreciate it.

"My first experience was deliberate. *I directed my thoughts to God and His goodness and asked that He would help me. I was suddenly standing beside my body, looking down at it. Then I was suddenly in a blue-black tunnel.* I was a very long tunnel and I went fairly quickly [passing through second 'death'—compare Case No. 788], thinking, 'This is what I have been looking for!' There was a grand sense of peace. *At the end of the 'tunnel' there was a 'light' and a man in white robes beckoning to me* [=Paradise conditions]. *I thought, 'I never want to go back!'* Immediately I was back! This really happened. I felt very refreshed.

"My other experience: I dozed off and found myself ['double'] racing through space and as though something was pushing at the back of my head. I saw no 'double'. Finally, I was standing beside my bed, looking at my body and thinking, 'Now, if you can only get back!' I woke up, but *knew I had had difficulty in getting back 'in'. I can't tell you how I knew*, but I did and it was such a frightening experience that I shall never forget it.

"I have seen beautiful places in my 'dreams', so real that, when I wake up, I want to cry. I feel as though I don't belong here on earth. This feeling stays with me all day.

"Now, I'm not a 'nut', or in any way neurotic: it is just that these 'dreams' are so real that they leave this life empty and dream-like.

"Another thing that puzzles me: *often when I first start to doze off* [disconnecting the vehicle of vitality] *I am awakened by a loud 'explosion'* ['click', 'snap', etc.].

"Also I sometimes [in the early, hypnagogic state, when the released vehicle of vitality enshrouds the Soul Body, giving glimpses of Hades conditions] *see horrible, evil faces* [those of would-be 'hinderers'—Mrs. Livermore is evidently somewhat mediumistic, her released 'double' being composite at first and simple—Soul Body, with the glimpses of Paradise— only after *the second 'death'* has been passed, though, like Mrs. "I. Beach", Case No. 778, she does not describe that event]. Can you shed any light on this?"

Case No. 801—Jimmy E. Ward
"I read your article in *Fate* magazine. I was interested in your theory of multiple—[actually two—] stage projections [with mediumistically-constituted persons, first the projection of a 'double' that was composite, contacting Hades, which, secondly, became simple—Soul Body only—at the second 'death', and contacted Paradise]. I had something like this some years ago. But I found no one who entertained that idea. My first experience happened twenty five years ago and lasted, on and off, for three or four days.

"I was born somewhat psychic and was *very sickly [as with Muldoon, tending to project the vehicle of vitality] as a youngster.* At the age of sixteen I was an active member of the Civil Air Patrol Cadets and *working until midnight seven days a week [=causing the vehicle of vitality to project in search of cosmic vitality and so become re-charged]* and then found myself with nothing to do. I had a 'breakdown'.

"I awoke one morning and people had ceased to exist for me. I knew they were around but *couldn't see, hear or feel them [because much of the 'bridge' represented by the vehicle of vitality was projected]. I seemed to be half-asleep.* I got up, dressed and lay down on the couch in the living-room when *suddenly I found myself [now completely released, composite 'double']* standing in the doorway, looking at my body lying on the couch. I felt no fear, not even surprise. It seemed perfectly natural that I should leave my body when I knew it was worn out and needed time to re-build itself. I 'knew' my body would be safe as long as I returned to it every few hours. *I never felt so 'alive' in my life.*

"I loved to fly and the next thing I knew was I was doing just that—I was soaring above a large, beautiful cloud-bank, without a 'plane'. After a time I saw an air-liner and looked in at the people in it. They did not see me, except a girl of eight or nine: she looked at me and smiled.

"*I thought of [=directed the attention towards]* sightseeing and *suddenly I was flying low over villages, lakes and mountains.* Then I found myself standing in front of the Sphinx. Then the scene blurred and I was back in my body at home.

"From this point until the present time, when I leave my body, it has been a slow, gradual process and I have never seen my body after I left it. I will return to this in a moment.

"When I lay back down, I stared at the corner of the ceiling and saw 'clouds' forming. Sometimes I would never go beyond this dual scene and I seemed to be in two places at once and aware of 'me' in both [=*dual consciousness—cf.* No. 751].

"One morning I woke up feeling great and then assumed that all that had happened had been mere 'delusions' caused by my 'breakdown'. I forgot all about it until some years later.

"A friend and I had been conducting experiments in telepathy, off and on, for some years and got fairly good at it when she decided to visit a mutual friend in Sweden. Before she left, we agreed to try and contact each other by telepathy during her visit [=direction of the attention]. Instead of trying to send messages to her, I decided to try to 'see' her surroundings and what she was doing. Eventually she verified 80-90% of them in her letters.

"One night I felt particularly lonesome and wanted to be with her. I lay down on my couch and made a mental picture of Rosemary. This is the way I found easiest to establish contact with her over any distance. [It was mentioned by 'Julia', communicating to W. T. Stead, in 1896]. I failed to make contact for some time, then *suddenly I saw her sitting in front of a fireplace, wrapped in a quilt* . . . then saw Ella asleep: I kissed her cheek and was back in my body.

"I wrote letters telling them what I had seen. Letters crossed. Rosemary said, 'I woke up, thinking about you, and could not get back to sleep. I got up, wrapped a quilt around me and sat in front of the fireplace. I felt your presence but could not see you. Then Ella screamed. I ran into her room and she was sitting up in bed with her hand to her cheek crying, 'Jimmy was here and he kissed me!'."

Case No. 802—Jerome Paul

Mrs. Sylvia Paul, of Brooklyn, New York, in a covering letter, said that her son, who had this experience at the age of eighteen, "does not read much about psychic subjects and could not have been influenced by anything he had read.

"June 5, 1970: Jerome first had a very funny feeling: his body had chills, as if freezing [=releasing vehicle of vitality]. He lay in bed feeling very light ['double'], though *both arms felt numb* [*catalepsy*].

"When he looked up at the ceiling he saw himself lying in bed [=dual consciousness—compare Case Nos. 751, 801, etc.]. He saw his father at work (not in his room). Although the room was in complete darkness, it seemed to become very bright.

"April 22, 1967: my husband, Seymour Paul, had a 'dream': he felt as if being hypnotised by *a whirling buzz-sound* [compare Monroe, Case No. 793 and others—the vehicle of vitality was loosening away from the body]. Then [projected] he felt at peace. *He saw 'a white star'* [= an incipient materialisation—Compare Case Nos. 744, 745, 747, 768, 778] and woke up.

"April 10, 1968: Seymour saw his own body on the bed. He felt a spinning in his head, and heard *a humming noise*. When he returned to normal [= re-entered his body] the humming sound ceased. This time *he felt his body plopping back on the bed* [= repercussion]."

Case No. 803—Ida R. Fettelberg

Mrs. Fettelberg wrote from Lake Worth, Florida: "On October 5, 1966, my dearest friend died. (Only a few months earlier my father had 'passed away'). I began to feel 'funny' [vehicle of vitality loosening from body]—since then, after much reading, I believe it was a trance. I attended the funeral and the feeling became 'funnier'. When I drove home it was still with me and most pronounced when I had to work alone. I enjoyed the feeling and seemed to go through motions like a robot—as if I were doing them without personal control [approaching catalepsy]. I watched my hands typing as if they were not part of me. It fascinated me.

"Two weeks later, *I suddenly felt something like a cord, or rope, snap. I never saw the cord or rope and I had never even heard of astral projection or O.O.B.'s, let alone knew or read anything about it. Therefore, I still can't understand how I knew it was a cord or thin rope.* [Many people who did not see their 'cords' nevertheless felt that they were there, and they pulled them back because they were elastic, etc.—see Cases Nos. 67, 73, 75, 172, 174, 177, 289, 762, 767 and 789.] *I remember being astonished that I could have possessed such an appendage, and not known about it until now.* [But she did not 'possess' it until it formed when her 'double' separated from her body] . . . *I wondered why it wasn't common knowledge that human beings have such things and to what mine had been a link* [to the body] *I was convinced it was now severed. Mine seemed to have been attached near the lower ribs, on the right side, because that was where I felt the snap. Immediately after, the 'funny' feeling lifted and my hands were normal again.* [This is one of the answers to Sir Cyril Burt who suggested that all descriptions of 'cords' were not actual observations but were merely copied from *Ecclesiastes* xii, 6. See also our Case Nos. 18, 71, etc., in which the feature was clearly mentioned but not as a cord—'I did not know what it was', 'Is it a cord? To me, it's just a stream of light', etc.]

"Was this astral projection? Was what I thought to be the breaking or snapping of the cord or rope, as if something had been *broken off* from my physical body, actually the snap of the 'astral' body *returning* to my physical body [i.e., was it a *'repercussion'*, i.e., a coming-back and not a going-out?—Yes, of course, the snapping (in the sense of breaking) of the cord when going out would cause physical death]. Did the snapping of the cord actually take place in *the front of my anatomy [solar plexus—Compare Case Nos.* 742, 744, 748, 768, 770], *rather than in the back or side, where I seemed to have felt it?* [Yes—doubtless—since this is the typical place for people who have loose vehicles of vitality—she had the 'funny' feeling, the 'vibrating' or 'tingle', which many felt as their vehicles of vitality were loosening from their bodies]. *How did I know of the rope's existence when I never saw it and had never heard or read of astral projection, 'doubles' or O.O.B.'s? Why didn't I see it as others do?* [Muldoon, the most accomplished projector of all, stated that there are many reasons why some people, out of the body, fail to see their cords. We ourselves have pointed out that if the 'double' has risen above the body (in the early stage of projection) the cord will not be seen unless and until the projector 'looks down' towards his body. And if the 'double' has erected and is moving away from the body (in the later stage of projection), it will not be seen unless and until the projector 'turns round and looks back' towards his body].

"If this was an O.O.B., what caused it to begin—the death of my friend is obvious [Yes]. I can easily go into the 'funny' state by fixing my gaze on an object or person [inducing hypnosis, which involves the projection of part of the vehicle of vitality—see *The Study and Practice of Astral Projection*, 1961, p.135]. Candle- or fire-light will catch and hold my gaze, causing the 'funny' feeling. Is the latter a kind of trance? [Yes.] Help me to understand!"

Case No. 804—Linda King
Mrs. King wrote from Burbank, California: "I have had spontaneous projections for years. I never know when it is going to happen—or consciously try to make it happen.

When first I started, *I had strange sensations, almost like an electric current [compare the 'tingle', Case Nos. 742, 750, 751, 765, 778, 793, etc].* It seemed to raise me to a high vibration [the vehicle of vitality is at a higher vibration than the body]. It frightened me and would wake myself up.

"After a time I decided to experiment with it and see what happened. *I found that after this strange 'buzzing' process is over [loosening the vehicle of vitality] the inner body [here a composite 'double'] is released and comes out.* With me it comes through the top of the head. On some occasions I seem to have a Guide who instructs me where to go—but I never see him.

"Mostly, when I feel that I am by myself, I do not go out of my apartment. *Once I was chased back to my body by two evil-looking characters ['hinderers'].* After that, if I felt I was leaving my body, I asked for protection. I had no more frightening experiences.

"Many times I have gone out of my body and went around doing things and went back to check for sure that this was really happening and to check-out my body sleeping on the bed. One time I took hold of my hand and found it quite cold.

"Last year I left my body by the vibrating process and was told [by 'helpers'] that I needed to go and help someone [='co-operation'—see *During Sleep*, 1964]. I went at a terrific speed to Utah, my home town. I travelled so fast I prayed for someone to slow me down when I got there: *I felt that, at that speed, I would not be able to stop [this is a common phenomenon in the projections called 'flying dreams', those due to rapid motion by cyclists, racing motorists, airmen, etc.: there is no physical resistance from the ground as in physical life].* However, when I came over the town I did slow down. They [the 'helpers'] directed me to a house in the town and told me that a boy, staying there, was in danger. They wanted me to go and frighten the woman, who I know has a bad temper and a past of mental illness. In the house I took a vase from one spot to another [telekinesis, possible only when the 'double' includes much of the 'semi-physical' vehicle of vitality]. The woman immediately got frightened and stopped cursing the boy as she had been doing when I entered. Although she couldn't see me, she said, 'I know someone is there! You can't fool me! You get out of my house!' Whoever was directing me [the 'helper'] told me the boy was no longer in danger and I could go now. I returned to my home in California.

"On my trips around my apartment I have learned how to walk in the lighter-feeling body and found it hard to keep balanced with its lightness. I haven't read any book on astral projection."

Case No. 805—Albert R. Johnston
Mr. Johnston wrote from Pasadena, California: "I am fifty four. For the past fifteen years I have been bothered by a disturbance that I do not at all understand. Although not always amply justified, I am described by my acquaintances as a cool, calm, collected individual and I lead a normal life —except when I am about to go to sleep! [=when the vehicle of vitality slightly disconnects from the physical body].

"And then it happens. *As I am about to drift off to sleep, suddenly it seems that a loud 'bang' or 'click' explodes in my head and I feel as if I were suspended in another world* [composite 'double' has been released] *and I cannot easily get back to this world which I love so much. I struggle (or so it seems) to get back and I feel as if I were suspended in some nether land* [=Hades, the 'borderland' between earth and Paradise] *above my body.* Often I find myself [released 'double'] trying to meet myself [vacated body] on some common ground. On one occasion I found myself ['double'] outside the house before my bodies came together.

"About fifteen years ago, when this first happened, I had talked to a medical man about a minor ailment. I timidly mentioned these occurrences and he just laughed and said it was 'nerves'. But I am not a nervous person.

"About a year after this I casually mentioned my problem to a friend. He suggested that I was beginning to travel astrally. At first I paid scant attention to the idea but later read all I could find about it. The sensations the authors described agreed with mine and one author [Muldoon, *op. cit.*, 1929, p.46] even suggested that those who had this experience should 'let go' and see what happened (instead of fighting it). But, truthfully, I am much afraid to do this as I sincerely believe that I would not get back [into the body].

"I am sometimes reluctant to go to sleep because of this sensation as I know it will come over me perhaps three or four times before I am actually, and thankfully, asleep, *when I literally jolted into wakefulness* [= the 'repercussion' as a composite 'double' re-enters the body]. When, eventually, I go into blissful sleep [with the 'double' completely released]

I am not bothered any more. Personally, it is difficult for me to believe that this is the beginning of astral projection, but some tell me that it is. They think I have achieved something special but, believe me, having the hell scared out of you is nothing special. I wonder if you would explain this to me. It frightens me and I must have some answers."

Case No. 806—Professor Charles T. Tart's marijuana cases
Professor Charles T. Tart, Professor at University of California, has published profound studies on out-of-the-body experiences and an article on marijuana intoxication. It is with the latter that we are here concerned. The effects of the drug were classified as (1) those that are common, (2) those that are infrequent but significant and (3) infrequent effects that seem to be very significant.

(1) These not only include visual, auditory, touch, taste, smell and space-time effects but also perceptions of the body: subjects said, "My body may feel very light or even *as if I float up into the air*"; "I have lost all consciousness of my body during fantasy trips"; *"I get feelings in my body—of energy of some sort flowing"*; "I become very aware of my breathing"; "pain is easy to tolerate if I keep [direct] my attention elsewhere"; *"I feel a vibration or tingling in some or all of my body . . ."*

There were telepathic contacts and psychological effects: "I feel what they feel"; "the group takes on a much greater sense of unity"; "I feel emotions much more strongly"; "I almost invariably feel good"; "my mood becomes greatly amplified"; "I feel very powerful, capable and intelligent"; "I feel . . . at one with the world".

(2) "Getting 'stoned' has a religious significance for me"; "I have spiritual experiences . . . which have had a powerful long-term religious effect on me"; "I feel in touch with a Higher Power or Divine Being"; "I feel in contact with the spiritual side of things"; *"I feel located outside the physical body"*; *"I lose control of my actions and do things that harm people"*; *"I have been 'taken over' [by a 'hinderer'] by an outside force or will which is hostile or evil in intent for a while"*; *"I can perform operations that affect objects or people [=telekinesis]"*.

Professor Tart observed, "Although the validity of the descriptions cannot be proved, there is at least a great deal of agreement among the respondents . . ." He is now writing a book on this subject.

Case No. 807—An electronic engineer
"I was meditating when I perceived that I was looking down on myself . . . The ground passed under me as if I was flying . . . the return was instantaneous".

Case No. 808—A motor cyclist
"I was riding my motor cycle with a girl passenger . . . I was watching my motor cycle, with the girl and me, from a distance of 6-8 feet above our physical existence . . . Physical sound did not register. I thought I was hearing wonderful . . . music. The experience was remarkably enjoyable".

Case No. 809—A man who had a fall
"I saw, from above, a crowd collect around my body . . . on pavement. Perception and cognition very sharp for three days afterwards".

Case No. 810—A teacher's projections
"I sometimes view my body, and the sequence of functions it follows in a particular environment, from some operator's or observer's vantage above and behind my body. The whole scene is then more obvious to me in that I have a sense of 360° perception rather than 180-200°: I am now conscious of what is actually behind me".

Case No. 811—An L.S.D. case
A young clerk described an "acid" trip in which he and a friend "changed places": he said, "I was inside his head looking at my body and hearing my voice when he talked: he was looking from my body into his face and when I spoke it was with his voice". [? mutual "possession".]

Case No. 812—Katherine Beaton-Troker
This case was kindly sent me by Phil. Phillips, of Iowa City, Iowa, U.S.A.
"A number of times during sleep, my astral body would leave on distant flight. During the winter of 1943, my astral body floated face downward, over the snow-covered North, passing over Air Force men's quarters in different sections of the country. Conversation could be heard distinctly.
"Since it was no concern of mine, I proceeded, leaving them immediately. Sometimes, an apprehensive fear would come over me—that of not knowing where to return to. Generally, however, there was much happiness on my flight."

Case No. 813—Peter Freuchen
This case also, from *Arctic Adventures,* came from Mr. Phillips:
"We hunted narwhales in the fjord. White whales (Belugas) appeared too. It was at this time that I experienced the trance, or 'kayak disease'. I sat in my kayak day after day waiting for seals. The hunter must not move, for the slightest shift of his body will disturb the small craft and frighten the seals away.

"*It is then that the mind begins to wander crazily. I dreamt without sleeping, resurrected forgotten episodes from my childhood* [= *the review of the past life as the vehicle of vitality loosens—Compare Case No.* 760]. *Suddenly great mysteries became for the moment plain to me* [the 'double' was released]. I realised I was in an abnormal, or supernormal, state and revelled in it. I cannot explain the feeling exactly, but it seemed that *my soul, or spirit, or what you will, was released from my body, and it soared impersonally, viewing everything as a whole. I was at home in Denmark and saw all my people once more.* I have often wondered if this was a touch of brain fever, or 'kayak disease'—or merely a state which everyone experiences at one time or another. I have never known, and no one seems willing to talk about it. But I do know that on sunny days, sitting in a kayak on the surface of a still sea, I approached a comprehension of mysteries otherwise denied me.

"In Greenland, when the hunters row out in their kayaks on still water they are often becalmed with *the sun's bright glare reflected in their eyes as from a mirror* [hypnotic effect]. *Suddenly they are gripped with a cataleptic paralysis which prevents their moving a muscle. They sit as if petrified.* Then, if a slight wind curls the surface of the sea, they are freed of the spell and come out of it. Or if a companion happens to see them and paddles close, rests his hand on their kayak or touches it with his oar they are enabled to move again."

Case No. 814—Dr. Aniela Jaffé's case of re-entry
"I went into my room, and as it was still a bit early for dinner, lay down on the couch. I must have dozed for some minutes, and on awaking suddenly had the curious sensation of being empty inside. *I wanted to get up, but was unable to do so. I was unable to move* [catalepsy]. My head was quite clear and told me that I must have died, since I could no longer feel my body. Strangely enough I did not feel sad.

I was only worrying about how my spirit and my mind, which was still clear, would detach themselves from the dead body. As I lay like this and thought things over, something most singular happened. To my right a dark shadow came floating slowly towards me. This shadow lay horizontally in the air [the common position on release—Case Nos. 729, 739, 743, 750, etc], hovering quite freely, and its outline and size were exactly the same as those of my body. (The room was light, and I could see everything up to the last detail.) *This shadow now moved till it was at the same level as I and we were lying there side by side like twins; then it gradually went through me.* This gliding in of my second self took about five to ten seconds. I felt all of this physically more or less in the same way as one would normally feel rubbing one's hands together. At the same time I began to feel warm again from right to left, being able to move my right hand first, while the left was still lying there completely stiff."

Case No. 815—Dr. Jaffé's case of a released vehicle of vitality
"I had a daughter who was a pianist. One afternoon she was sitting at the piano practising. To my great surprise I saw another figure of my daughter sitting to her left, dressed in just the same way, but transparent."

Case No. 816—Dr. Jaffé's case of pain-avoidance
"The following letter, written by a man, describes a duplication process after a severe renal colic. I was in such terrible pain that I said to myself: 'You should somehow be able to get out of yourself, then the pain would stop'. *Suddenly I saw a 'man' in front of me who was walking towards the garden gate.* I watched him as though stupefied, till I realised: 'That's me!'—I jumped up with the sole thought of catching up with him. He had already gone round the corner of a side road and disappeared. Then I was seized with the most dreadful fear. I ran even faster and when at last I caught up to him and seemed to catch hold of him, the whole apparition dissolved into nothing, how, I cannot say. The pain, which I had not felt at all, returned once more. I was exhausted by the unaccustomed exertion and sat down again on the bench outside the front door. Soon afterwards my wife came out into the garden and said: 'Mrs. S. and Mr. K. have both just 'phoned and asked me what on earth was the matter with you. They said you were running along the street like a madman!'—These people had indeed seen me running, but had not seen my second self,

the one I was chasing, and for this reason I must have looked extraordinary from their point of view."

Case No. 817—Hannen Swaffer's medium
A medium told Swaffer how discarnate helpers trained her to leave her body.

"My guide began to withdraw my astral body from the human form. He withdrew it gradually, a little more each time, and then at last he announced that I was ready to go into trance. He promised that at the next sitting he would take the astral body away completely.

"Gradually I went deeper into trance and was often taken for a tour round the spheres, although sometimes I could remember nothing and it seemed that I had just been asleep. *The thing that has impressed me most about the spirit world [here = Paradise] is the vegetation. The flowers and the trees seem to be made of coloured lights, and are transparent and radiant.* The atmosphere suggests bright sunlight all the time, although there is no sun visible. I have only once met another spirit on my astral travels, and that was when I found myself by the side of my sister. I never see my guide, because when I go he takes charge of my body. *I remember once seeing my body in the chair as I left it. It was apparently sleeping, and I thought it looked rather stupid. Strange as it sounds, leaving the body seems perfectly natural at the time."* (Cf. No. 819.)

Case No. 818—James H. Neal
"*I seemed to be standing near one of the walls of my room looking disinterestedly at my own body reclining on the bed* [Compare Case Nos. 748, 767, 789]. *Then I passed right out through the bedroom wall.* Beyond was a vast, deep-blue space, and it struck me that I was travelling an enormous distance at extreme speed. I arrived finally in another illuminated area, only to see that a still more brightly lit passage led away from it. Then by some mysterious means I received a message to the effect that I could not yet enter this passage as my time had not yet come. I had to go back.

"Once more there was the speeding through the blue vastness, the re-entering of the bedroom through the wall, and again the sight of my own body lying there on the bed.

"As I went back inside my body—and it was an uncanny feeling of surrounding dampness—I became instantly aware of pain again."

Case No. 819—C. H. D'Alessio
Mr. D'Alessio wrote (28 March, 1972): "I strive my utmost to be accurate and truthful: you can rely completely on this.

"My earliest remembered astral projections were when I was between five and six years old: my present age is fifty eight. Between these two ages, some really extraordinary things have occurred. I seldom mention them because even those who love me are apt to look askance and change the subject. Your books have helped me. [cf. No. 817.] Sometimes I have moved as if floating face-downwards—quite natural! In a few days I will send you reportage. I have no doubt at all that we have more than one body in which we can be conscious." His next letter follows.

"On 11 March, 1972, I awoke at 4.30 a.m., and lay awake for half an hour when I drifted off to sleep again.

"About 5.30 a.m. I became conscious: I [released 'double'] was in the passage outside the closed door of my room; my physical body was still asleep in bed. *I knew, beyond any doubt whatsoever, that I was in my 'astral' body: it was shadowy and insubstantial, but as real and natural as anything ever is. I could see, the light was grey with patches of denser but non-solid areas where I recognised the walls and familiar objects [=Hades conditions, indicating that the 'double' included part of the vehicle of vitality, i.e., was composite].* I looked further, not more than a few yards, and moved forward—not by walking but just moving.

"Then I saw a sort of concentration of energy, of mass, and I felt apprehensive [? a 'hinderer']. Instantly I retreated *through* the closed door into my room. My consciousness had dimmed, but it now revived [compare Cases Nos. 32, 43, 64, etc., when consciousness also 'waxed and waned', doubtless because the Soul Body sometimes gained and sometimes lost —back to the physical body—part of the enshrouding vehicle of vitality]. I found myself just inside the door, facing the top of my bed. At this point my consciousness reached its maximum. My fear had vanished. I still saw the grey light. I knew exactly where I was. I said to myself, 'This is it! It has happened as I longed for to do it! It is a fact! I am awake in my 'astral' body! Now I will levitate!' I attempted to do so, but the upward effort somehow produced a painful sensation in the crown of one or both of my heads. Almost immediately I was wide awake in my body.

"I had a headache, but I was elated—overjoyed. My delight and enthusiasm are markedly with me today, nearly a month later. Most valuable of all, I have gained some priceless insights to do with the nature of existence and time. These are no dreams, and neither was that out-of-the-body experience."

Case No. 820—Léonie
This example of "travelling clairvoyance" was given in *Parapsychology Review*[59].

Pierre Janet, the epoch-making French physician and psychologist, made some very interesting experiments with "travelling clairvoyance". He had a good hypnotic subject, called Léonie. One day Janet set her "travelling". In her hynotic state she "went" to Paris to see Professor Charles Richet and a Mr. Gilbert who had left for Paris. Suddenly she said, "It is burning". But she soon woke again, saying, "But Monsieur Janet, I assure you that it is burning!" In fact Richet's laboratory in the Rue Vauquelin had caught fire and was burnt out that very day.

On April 21, 1969, Jarl Dahler carried out an experiment with pictures with Mrs. Z. After this I tried an experiment with "travelling clairvoyance". When she was in deep hypnosis I asked her to go to one of my friends whom she had met once. She had never been at the home of this man but described a scene in their living-room correctly, reported about a quarrel between the man and his wife, described the wife although she had never met her, then saying that the wife got very angry and hit her husband's face. She also said that the wife was wearing a bright green pullover and was "nasty and without humour". All the time Mrs. Z. had the feeling that she herself was present at the place of the "excursion" and when back again, she had a very distinct feeling of coming back into her body at the place of our experiments (a distance of about 12 kilometres).

This "travelling clairvoyance" experiment with Mrs. Z. was a spontaneous experiment without previous arrangements. The next day (April 22) I phoned my friend and asked him, just for a joke, if yesterday evening he got his ration of beating from his wife. I was very surprised, indeed, when he told me that he really was beaten by his wife and asked me why I happened to be joking about such an unpleasant thing. I did not want to upset him, but at the same time wanted to know if his wife really had a green pullover and if she, perhaps, was wearing it last night. I got a good opportunity when he asked me for lunch, saying that he had something he wanted to talk about. At lunch-time I did not need to ask what I wanted to know. He told me that there had been some rather deep-seated problems between him and his wife (about this I knew nothing before) and that his wife even slapped him in the face last night. When I asked how it came to such an unpleasant situation he told me that this probably had been going on for some time under the surface and that the quarrel yesterday evening began with a new pullover. The colour was bright green and he did not like it. (The matter of "clothes" on apparitions is very important. A number of psychologists, etc. have argued: "The 'clothes' of an apparition must be imaginary: hence the 'body' that seems to 'wear' them must also be imaginary, subjective and not objective. But the matter is not so simple. —See the writer's *The Next World—and the Next*, T.P.H., 1966).

Case No. 821—Shukracharya

The "story" of Shukracharya is here mentioned to illustrate how age-old accounts of out-of-the-body experiences are: Dr. B. K. Kanthamani described the *Yogavasistha*, written in Sanskrit, as "ancient". Other pre-historic accounts, of course, come from Tibet (Dr. W. Y. Evans-Wentz, *The Tibetan Book of the Dead*, O.U.P., 1927), and still others from China (Richard Wilhelm, *The Secret of the Golden Flower*, Routledge, 1931).

Ancient Chinese prints show, quite clearly, the "silver cord"-extension which unites the released "double" to the vacated body below: the ancient Chinese could not have read *Ecclesiastes* in the Revised Version (1881) and obtained that phrase from that source.

Case No. 822—Mr. and Mrs. Sage

Mrs. Sage wrote: "My husband *watched from a corner of the room* while his tooth was taken out under 'gas'. He was frightened.

"My seven-year-old girl says she '*dreams*' of flying in the garden and of gliding downstairs.

"I had my first experience when seven years old: *I returned too quickly and felt I had been hit in the middle* [*solar plexus*—compare Case Nos. 742, 744, 748, 768, 770, 803, etc.]. I have noticed that, when 'out' and fully conscious, *I see better, colours are brighter, no sound is heard and time seems endless.*

"Going out during sleep is easy, but *coming back is sometimes difficult, so it wakes me*: *my body feels too small and occasionally it is lying awkwardly. You can laugh at this—on three occasions I tried to fit myself in upside down* . . .!"

Case No. 823—Miss Carole Thraum
Miss Thraum, of St. Louis, M., U.S.A., wrote:

"During the past two years I have experienced a total of 18 projections. My experiences seem to be somewhat unusual in that *they are nearly always accompanied by certain peculiar sensations in the thyroid gland.* I have been wondering if other people experience these sensations as *I have not read of anything like this*—although I was interested in your account of Professor Whiteman's descriptions of 'stresses near the solar plexus' and 'a feeling of dying' in this connection, for *I frequently have a feeling of dying when I begin to project* and sometimes I become very frightened and quickly fasten myself back into my body. In addition to the complete projections I have had numerous partial projections of this sort. About ten years ago, when I was in my early twenties, I had a period of severe insomnia during which I didn't sleep for weeks at a time. During this time *I frequently would fall into a sort of trance in which I was fully conscious but disconnected from my body and completely unable to move* [cataleptic]. Associated with this were the stressful sensations in the throat chakram. This happened probably several hundred times.

"About two years ago I began experiencing full projections. The first time I was not aware that I was projecting. *I awoke feeling cold* and determined to get up and turn my gas heater up higher but was too tired and cold to get up. Finally I forced myself out of bed but when I attempted to touch the heater *my hand went right through it!* I then felt a strange drawing sensation in my throat and was drawn back into my body. I repeated the same procedure again and the same thing happened! After this I started paying close attention to the borderline state and finally discovered that when my chakrams were vivified in this way I could deliberately lift myself out. The sensation starts in my thyroid gland. Then I sort of gather myself up into my throat while the sensation spreads through my head and face and when my pineal gland 'opens' or becomes vivified I lift out through the centre. Although I usually feel the sensations in my chakrams first and then lift myself out, there have been several occasions, as the one I first mentioned, in which I wake up in my astral body and *proceed to get up, thinking I'm in my physical body*. It is only when I feel the drawing sensation in my head and throat that I realise I'm projecting.

"The scenery I contact varies: sometimes I find myself in

the same room where my body is, sometimes I am in completely unfamiliar surroundings. On several occasions I apparently contacted the realm of reflections [=Hades]. I was in my home but everything was on the opposite side of the room. Also some colours were reversed; for instance, a bluish-green washcloth appeared red. Once I found myself in my childhood home, and as everything appeared just like it was twenty years ago, I thought I had gone back in time and went through the house looking for a calendar or newspaper. I found a newspaper but somehow couldn't seem to determine the date. On one occasion I drifted up under the ceiling and noticed a brownish stain in a peculiar floral pattern. I decided to check it when I got back into my body and noted the exact design. Later, when I checked it physically, I had to climb a ladder to examine it closely and it appeared just as I had seen it during my projection, although it was small and I had never noticed it physically before. *On two occasions I saw my body* and this had a peculiar frightening effect on me. I suppose this is why I don't see my body more often. On those occasions I felt powerful drawing sensations and *had to fight hard against the pull of my body. The slightest attention or thought of my body seems to draw me back.* I can feel very vividly the points of connection at my thyroid and pineal glands. This sensation is very real and physical. This is how I know definitely that these experiences are not imaginary.

"*I don't think I am mediumistic* but *I do seem to be somewhat loosely 'connected' at my throat chakram,* as I occasionally 'slip loose' at this centre even when my attention is fully focused on the physical plane. At about the age of ten I had several experiences which apparently were partial projections of this sort, and, oddly it always happened at Church during evening services [when relaxed and passive]. I was fully conscious but somehow 'disconnected' at my throat and unable to move. This lasted for maybe five or ten minutes.

"At present, when I have these sensations, although I want very much to project, *I sometimes become frightened when the separation begins. This seems to depend on the degree to which my consciousness is focused on the astral or physical. If I am still fully oriented on the physical the disconnection feels like death, and in spite of my intentions I quickly bolt back into my body.* If my consciousness is more 'astrally' oriented [=towards Paradise] I feel no fear and know there is no death, and then I eagerly lift myself out through my pineal chakram. *It is probable that I project a part of my etheric 'double' as well as my 'Astral'* [='Soul'] *Body, although on a few occasions I apparently projected only the 'Astral'. On these occasions I did not feel physical sensations. At times I* [with little or no vehicle of vitality in the 'double'] *can go through physical obstacles and at times* [with much in] *they present a barrier.* Frequently I float around under the ceiling and sometimes bump my head. *Once I tried to go through a window* and seemed to be going through all right until I started thinking about the physical properties of glass. Then I got 'stuck' and felt 'glass' sticking in my heart and suddenly I found myself back in my body with stabbing pains near my heart. Frequently I try to notice things that I can check later physically. Sometimes this works and I am able to make some definite observation, but at times the deceptive, fluid quality of 'astral' matter makes this difficult. Once I noticed a small flaw in the fabric of my couch and was able to check this later physically, although I had never noticed it before.

"Most often the conditions I contact seem to be a sort of fog-filled counterpart of the physical plane [=Hades] and I am somewhat hampered in my observations, but *on a few occasions I found myself in the most beautiful surroundings imaginable* [=Paradise]. When 'astral' matter is beautiful it is more vividly beautiful than anything in the physical world. It has a brilliance and aliveness completely unlike a corresponding physical scene. On one occasion I thoroughly enjoyed drifting around in the most beautiful 'astral' palace. I went from room to room and was extremely thrilled by the vividness of the colours. On another occasion I was gliding along a beautiful country road with trees and vegetation that were breathtakingly beautiful.

"The manner of locomotion is not always the same. Sometimes I walk and sometimes sort of glide or float. I am presently trying to train myself to make more scientific observations of the various sub-planes which I contact."

Case No. 824—L. A. Woodworth
Mr. Woodworth wrote (*in litt.*) from 14 Hillside Road, Cowies Hill, Natal, South Africa, 10 October 1972: "I was manager of a new factory, making steel pipes. Due to faulty mechanism, about a ton of steel pipe fell into a deep trough of molten bitumen . . . Some of the men on shift received burns, but I was generously plastered down by right side,

head to foot, and a hat saved my life. The agony was unbearable, though I retained consciousness.

"I was aware of a *terrific grinding wrench* [as the vehicle of vitality—and therefore also the Soul Body—suddenly left the physical body] and hoped I was dying. I found myself [released 'double', composite, consisting of most of the vehicle of vitality plus the Soul Body] . . . high up. I could 'see' the five operators on the shift, and others coming from a different part of the factory . . . and appeared compassionate and yet *dispassionate and un-moved* . . . In particular I was sorry for the small smoking figure that was staggering on its feet alongside, about the middle of the trough of bitumen.

"My place of observation was the most inconvenient (normally) as I [in released 'double'] had to perceive through a brick wall and two partitions of corrugated iron. *As my attention focussed on* [= was directed towards] *'me'* [= physical body], I 'came back'.

"And now a miracle. I . . . gave clear instructions, first of all, First Aid and especially for the man whom I had perceived burned, then the running of the rest of the shift, especially from the safety angle. Then I told one of the men to 'phone for an ambulance and my family doctor.

"As confirmed later by Dr. Fehrensen, I was in an extraordinary state of *acute perception, lucidity, and peculiar elation* [because almost entirely free from the physical body]. . . . My right hand was saved, though badly scarred."

Mr. Woodworth stated that his experience had been published in *The Star newspaper* in 1954 and added, "As far as your interest lies, were there other developments? Some time later in life, and all in the same house, *that indescribable grinding uprooting sensation* [releasing vehicle of vitality]. Once I became conscious up, or through, the ceiling and once in the kitchen. I do not know how I 'saw' so clearly as it was very dark in each case. *Each time I was horrified and appeared to be bundled up and hurled through space* [? = shed the vehicle of vitality from the originally composite 'double', i.e., passed through the second 'death', so that the Soul Body was un-enshrouded]. This was followed by peculiar and most lucid 'dreams' [= experiences of Paradise conditions]. I woke several times in *the 'up-rooting'-stage* and found that I [physical body] was in a state of complete immobilisation [= catalepsy]. Once I became conscious and 'saw me' [physical body] lying on my back in bed, a most unlovely sight [= disparaged vacated physical body]: I 'saw' my wife in a twin-bed six feet away."

Mr. Woodworth's ability, while free from his body, to contact and instruct others is by no means unique: we cited a similar experience by Cromwell Varley, F.R.S. (our Case No. 121) whose released 'double' also included much of the vehicle of vitality, since it was projected when he inhaled chloroform on a sponge: he said, "Mr. Varley was in the room above. *I . . . was powerless to move . . . I willed an impression on my wife's brain that I was in danger. Thus aroused, she came down and removed the sponge. I then used my body to speak to her. I said,* 'I shall forget all about this and how it came to pass, unless you remind me in the morning. Be sure to tell me what made you come down and then I shall be able to recall the circumstances.' "

Case No. 825—Mrs. G. Tuke
This represents an experience under an anaesthetic. The deponent had been told by "Eileen", a niece who had been "dead" for some years, and with whom she held frequent communication, that she would be taken and shown something of "the next world". The account was written immediately after returning to physical consciousness.

"Dr. J. gave me the anaesthetic and I could see K. [physically-embodied sister]. After a few minutes, *a luminous patch* [= *ectoplasm released from K's vehicle of vitality*] *grew at her side and I saw a hand in it: the patch grew bigger and I saw* [*the 'dead'*] *Eileen. She was radiant, full of vitality.* 'Dr. George' (who frequently spoke at 'sittings') was with her. 'Dr. B.' was with him . . . All three [who had discarded their physical bodies] appeared far more real than [the physically-embodied] K. and Dr. J., who now seemed misty and dim.

"Someone said, 'Now come!' I felt weight and heaviness [the physical body] slip away from me and I was standing by Eileen. I could see my body lying there, but did not feel I had lost any part of myself—it [released 'double'] was *me*, complete and alive . . .

"I saw them take my body to the theatre and went too . . . I could see the [physically-embodied] surgeon, the nurses and the doctor, but they were indistinct and dark. *I did not feel any sort of sympathy or regret for the body lying there: it did not matter, because I felt far more alive and conscious without it* [= *indifference to the vacated body*].

"Then Eileen said we would go . . . and we were standing on cliffs which I have often visited in 'dream' or 'trance' states [= Paradise conditions] . . . There was no sun [cf. Rev.

xxi, 23; xxii, 5]. The quality of the light was soft. I felt sustained by, but not dependent upon, the light. I learned that light was a very fundamental thing on that plane. The flowers were . . . consciously alive. I wondered if plant-life on earth was like that and we were too dull to appreciate it? They were not conscious in the same degree as I was. We went through lovely gardens to Eileen's 'house' . . . Eileen was dressed in white [cf. Case Nos. 778, 782, 800] . . . I seemed to have a yellow dress . . .

"I asked her how far away they were on earth, and *she told me to think of [=direct my attention towards] them* [cf. Case Nos. 823, 824, etc.]. The light grew dark, the atmosphere thick and heavy, and I could see my bed with 'me' on it and the nurses and Dr. J. Then Eileen told me to come back and all the darkness went and I was in the beautiful room again. She told me she was being allowed to take me to a Service but that I would probably be able to appreciate only a small part of it . . . *I was not free from the earth-body but still tied to it [by the 'silver cord'-extension]* . . . Someone spoke to us and I understood things which, now I am back, I do not understand any more, but I know that my Spirit knows.

"Eileen told me that, though I felt so well, it was nothing to what they felt, as I was still linked [by the 'cord'] to earth-conditions . . . Everything was far more vivid, the whole range of sound and colour was far greater. *I was in no strange place but in familiar [Paradise] conditions. When Eileen told me I must go back I was most unwilling* (cf. Case Nos. 788, 789, 793) . . ."

Case No. 826—Josephine Lambert

Mrs. Lambert, of 381 London Road, Stoneygate, Leicester, wrote of her "one and only" experience: "It happened many years ago when I was 13 or 14 years of age. The subject was completely unknown to me at that time and . . . it was not until some years later that I realised the possible significance.

"I had been taken to a farm to visit some friends unknown to me. The young son of the household, who was about my age, was escorting me around the farm and we were walking across a field when suddenly I became aware of the fact that I was watching both of us from about twenty feet away. The boy and I had our backs to this 'other consciousness' and I could see us talking but could not hear properly. The consciousness that contained the 'I' I knew it thought, 'I cannot hear nor do I know what we are talking about, so I had

better get back!' Instananeously [sic] I was back in my body
..." This case should be compared with that cited by Prof. Ian Stevenson in J.A.S.P.R., 1970, p.108, one of schizophrenia.

Case No. 827—Mrs. A. Johnson

Mrs. Johnson wrote from R. D. Five Waters, Chelps, N.Y. 14532: "I was sitting, in 1967, on my mother's couch, doing nothing in particular. In a matter of seconds I was away out above and beyond earth, looking down at it . . . I was terrified and seemed to 'yop' right back into my body. I had not heard of astral projection at that time. I told my mother and she said I was just emotionally upset . . . But it did happen to me and I want to know why.

"Another time, my husband said he had awakened in the middle of the night and seen my body lying beside him and another 'me' sitting up as though I was out of my body from the waist up [cf. Case No. 775 and Dorothy Grenside's Case]. *My projection led me to believe in a life-after-death."*

Case No. 828—A legal Correspondent

This correspondent wrote (August 27, 1972): "I have had two specific types of projections of the type where the eyelids are closed but images are clearly visible to me. The difficulty with this projection in the two instances I refer to is that I see handwritten documents, in block (not script) roman-style lettering, but find I cannot read them. In other words, the problem appears to be that the 'astral' body contains only sensory perception but lacks intellectual ability. This phenomenon has occurred to me twice . . . I am at a loss to explain why I cannot read it when it occurs, in spite of my ardent attempts . . . It is like an illiterate person looking at written matter and clearly seeing it there but being unable to comprehend it in any way. I am extremely curious as to whether any person has ever had any projections of this or any type wherein intellectual ability came into need, and the result of the attempt to use the intellect in these situations.

"My other projections have been standard types—*moving through walls in horizontal positions* (cf. Case Nos. 729, 768, 776, 788), slight movements out of the physical body; instantaneous projections to places unknown to me; *tunnels* (cf. Case Nos. 751, 761, 767, 768), but I have yet to enjoy the wonder of looking at my own physical body, since my projection to the unselected site is always immediately followed by my conceiving that I have left my body. I also am totally unable to select my 'destination' in such 'astral' travel."

I replied: "My suggestion is that the two experiences in which you saw letters that you could not decipher indicate incomplete projections, that the partially-separated vehicle of vitality gave partial perception without sufficient activity in the (also partially-separated) Soul Body. Some memory-images, probably distorted, might be seen, since the vehicle of vitality keeps a record of all that we have seen, heard, etc. (as a drowning or a dying person may find)."

Case No. 829—E. C. Colley

Mr. Colley wrote from 2330 Napoleon Avenue, New Orleans, Louisiana, 70115, on July 6, 1972: "My friend (Warren) had a motor-cycle. We were going at about 80 m.p.h. and came to a bridge over a canal. For some reason, the front of the bike went down. Warren stayed with the bike and came out unscathed. I too tried to hang on but was thrown into the railing of the bridge. I tried to cushion myself against the rail but was catapulted over it and was hospitalised.

"The strange part of this story—and I may add that no one believes it—is that *I saw the chain of events just described: I saw everything as a by-stander. I saw myself being flipped from the bike and trying to grasp the rail.* I was shocked back into reality when I hit the water. My view was as if I were standing on a platform about 30 feet behind the scene. When I saw your article, I was glad that someone else had had this type of experience."

Case No. 830—Alma R. Clarke

Miss Clarke, Secretary-Treasurer of the California Parapsychology Foundation, wrote (*in litt.*) from their Headquarters at 3580 Adams Avenue, San Diego, California, U.S.A.: "I was first aware of being out of my body and standing at the head of a flight of stairs. It was an old mansion . . . A blond woman was coming out about 3.00 a.m. She looked up, saw me, and stepped back, startled. Then *all turned black* [= a momentary 'blackout' or lapse in consciousness as the released 'double' re-entered the vacated body—cf. Case Nos. 745, 748, 751, 761, 717, 768, 828] and I found myself back in my body. I felt myself return to the body through the top of the head . . . On another occasion I was seen by a close friend, Tom, in his house, late at night. He was startled. He said he was just about to enquire what I was doing there when I disappeared. He telephoned the next day. I myself had no recollection of this experience, though I did confess to him that a problem had arisen on the previous day and I had thought of inviting his assistance [=directed attention towards him].

"During the time my father was staying with me, I had two more experiences. Both times I felt myself separate from my physical body, which was lying in bed, and aware of my 'astral' body standing up: I was thinking, 'Away we go!' I then found myself heading through the front door head-first, as though I were flying. As I came to the front door, I closed my eyes, but instead of going through the door, I found myself back in my body.

"The second experience I would not close my eyes and went out of the front door head-first. I decided I would go to my mother's house: I could see myself going by buildings. I never got to my mother's but went back into my body instead.

"When my son, Mark, was six years old I woke up one night to find him standing next to my bed . . . He slowly disappeared and I went to his bedroom and found him peacefully asleep."

Case No. 831—H. Brennan

On July 30, 1967, in announcing the items to be covered, a B.B.C. radio announcer said that they would deal with "the dangers of astral projection". It transpired that Mr. Brennan had written a book entitled *Experimental Magic* and that it included a projection: having retired to bed for the night, and, having fallen into a deep sleep, he wanted to pass water. He went to the lavatory for this purpose but, to his surprise, found that it was his released 'double' that had made the journey and not his physical body. He had left the latter in bed, fast asleep. The experience was repeated several times before he could rouse his body: no danger was mentioned.

However, Isaiah (xxix, 8) pointed out that a hungry man, during deep sleep, dreams that he eats food and a thirsty man dreams that he drinks water, satisfying the mind if not the body. We can only suppose that Mr. Brennan escaped one, at least, of "the dangers of astral projection" by failing to dream!

No human activity is entirely free from dangers and even complete inactivity has its dangers. In all my books on projection I advise against deliberate attempts to project. The chief reasons are two—those who are not morally prepared may have definitely unpleasant experiences, and it is one thing to open a "door" at will and another thing to close it at will. Drugs of any kind should not be taken for this purpose. The study of testimonies is a very different matter: this can be most profitable and illuminating, practically as well as theoretically.

Half a century before Mr. Brennan had had his projection, S. J. Muldoon, an American youth who had read nothing about these matters, in *The Projection of the Astral Body* (Rider, 1929) told how he ensured projections in his sleep by previously swallowing an eighth of a teaspoonful of salt. Once asleep, he felt a strong need to drink water: his physical body would not move but his (somewhat "loose") vehicle of vitality left it and went to the tap.

Both of these men, Brenner involuntarily and Muldoon voluntarily, used the principle of the direction of the attention to release the "double"—in each case the attention was strongly directed away from the physical body with which it is normally associated, to some distant place: the body was inert, the "double" left it temporarily.

Case No. 832—Jean Tunniscliffe

The deponent, of 78 Pohutukawa Avenue, Chope, Bay of Plenty, New Zealand, wrote: "My first experience took place when I was seventeen: I found myself leaning against the wall of a dance-hall, watching 'myself' [released 'double'] dancing. I was interested but not alarmed. Later I had many similar experiences. I knew nothing of astral projection. Then I read Carrington and Muldoon's book and realised what had been happening. Experiences, when they happened, then took on a different meaning. I found myself in other countries.

"My last experience, eight years ago, was in full colour [involving the Soul Body] as opposed to the black-and-white of the earlier ones [when the Soul Body was enshrouded by part of the vehicle of vitality]: after I visited a healing sanctuary I ended up in a very depressed area [in Hades, i.e. the Soul Body had become enshrouded]. Here I met a man in an orange robe who told me I was not strong enough to continue. I returned home."

Case No. 833—Kelvin J. Drab

Mr. Drab wrote from 94 Wilsmere Drive, Northolt, Middx.: "The experience occurred in a dentist's office. There was a state of awareness and alertness, unlike the usual anaesthetic state. I did not see any connexion between my experience and that of others until many years later. I was first aware of looking down from a height of seven or eight feet. I was aware of my body in the dentist's chair and of my past life [=review of past life], I felt detached, as if I were merely an observing intelligence ... I could see my whole life-involvement of both my earthly self and everybody else ... as well of being aware of my body in the chair. I thought how senseless it was to continue to strive after the 'shadows' of earthly life ... There was no fear, but a vague longing to remain in that state [=reluctance to return]."

Case No. 834—Mrs. M. Blanton

Mrs. Blanton wrote from Box 51162, Tulsa, Okla., U.S.A.: "My youngest boy, then aged fourteen, bought a cycle. He followed his sister who was driving a car. She stopped suddenly and the boy applied his brakes but hit a hole in the road. His body was thrown from the cycle—but he stated that 'he' [released 'double'] was standing on the curb watching it all from some six feet away. Then he became conscious in his body.

"Later he went to stay with his grandmother and became very dissatisfied: he had a second experience. As he approached a tree, suddenly it was the tree in front of our house and he [released 'double'] could look around and see the corner of our house. In this case he was conscious all the while."

Case No. 835—W. H. Hudson

Hudson told how he was very seriously ill for some six weeks (i.e., with his vehicle of vitality released from his body to a considerable extent—necessarily disconnecting the Soul Body also). To his amazement—for he never felt "properly alive" when out of touch with Nature—he "never felt confinement less", and "had a marvellous experience". He had "a wonderfully clear and continuous vision" of his past. The remembering, he observed, was not, as is usual, awakened by some sight, sound or smell—he had gone back to his childhood and remembered it in great detail, e.g., his relationships with other children and people. This review of his past life continued throughout his illness, i.e., so long as his vehicle of vitality was, to a large extent, released from his physical body. He wrote many details down.

Hudson had experienced the first (and non-emotional) review of the past life, sometimes described by those who leave the body temporarily (e.g., Case Nos. 32, 34, 211, 304, 343, 345, 379, 380) and often described by those who have left it permanently and subsequently communicated via mediums (see *The Supreme Adventure*, 1961, pp. 12, 86, 98).

Although his body lay on the sick bed, he described himself (Soul) as many miles away, "rejoicing in that long-lost, and now-recovered, happiness".

Case No. 836—Kathy Roberto

Miss Roberto's account, directed by the A.S.P.R., was sent from RD I BX 472 B, High Falls, N.Y. 12440, U.S.A., in October, 1972. She stated:

"I have had three astral journeys, two the result of fainting. I felt fantastic, floating and looking down at the ground. I wasn't frightened—only pleasantly surprised. Both times I looked back down at my body, to see people slapping it and applying salts. *I reluctantly returned,* just to protect myself (cf. Case Nos. 788, 789, 792, 825, 833, 835).

"The first experience happened when I was 16 and the second about 6 months ago: I am now twenty seven.

"I was in a darkened room the third time, lying down on the bed, staring at the light-fixture on the ceiling [an autohypnotic proceeding, tending to release part of the vehicle of vitality]. As I stared at it, *I rose out of my body in the exact [horizontal] position my body was in* [cf. Case Nos. 729, 768, 776, 768]. I looked down through my 'body' at my body on the bed. I noticed that the light-fixture was of porcelain with tiny pink rosebuds and gilt edging—all of which was impossible to see from the floor. I turned my face aside quickly and, with that motion, *returned to my body in the same (horizontal) position* [cf. Case Nos. 750, 768, 814]. I emphasise this because the first two times [the fainting-spells] I seemed much freer—I moved and flew. This time I drifted stiffly, I don't know why. Also the feeling of exhilaration was missing. If you have an explanation, please give it. [The 'double' released on the third occasion—with some hypnotic stimulus—contained more of the vehicle of vitality than that on the first two occasions: hence this 'double' was 'body-bound', occupying the same position as the physical and being less free to move; the greater enshroudment of the Soul Body gives less exhilaration.] I wasn't feeling quite well that day [another factor that tends to release part of the vehicle of vitality—it tends to reach out, away from the physical body, to avail itself of cosmic vitality, as it normally does in sleep for the same purpose, when one is tired towards the end of the day]. I was visiting friends in their new apartment when I felt the need to lie down. After my experience I turned on the light but could not see the fixture clearly at all.

"I have tried consciously to duplicate these experiences, but with no result. I contacted the A.S.P.R. and they told me of you." [We do not recommend deliberate attempts at projecting: we are convinced that a study of these experiences yield invaluable insights into the nature of human beings—and that it is supremely wise to *act* in accordance with those insights: "If you know this, happy are you if you *act upon it*"—John xiii, 17; on the other hand, to "hide your 'talent' in the ground" inevitably brings regret and misery.]

Miss Roberto sent a further experience which clearly involved precognition and asked, "How could I have travelled into the future? Does that happen?" The answer is, of course, the "super-physical" Soul Body is not subject to physical space or time. (There are many references to this in *The Interpretation of Cosmic and Mystical Experiences*, James Clarke, 1969, p.174). In this latter experience she made references to what the present writer sums up under the general heading of "the direction of the attention". She said, "When I thought about something deeply, I would 'zoom in' on it".

Case No. 837—A.S.P.R. investigations

In 1951 (*The Phenomena of Astral Projection,* Rider), Dr. Hereward Carrington pointed out that neither the British nor the American S.P.R. had reviewed his *The Projection of the Astral Body,* Rider, 1929, written in conjunction with S. J. Muldoon. In 1972, A.S.P.R. Newsletter (No. 12), Dr. Karlis Osis, Director of Research of the A.S.P.R., made the following welcome announcement: "The A.S.P.R. is starting a new research-project on out-of-body experiences". He said that a person may feel himself floating near the ceiling while seeing his body lying on the bed, that he may be able to reach a friend's house, report back what is going on there and have his report verified, that he may be seen by others at the place he has "visited", etc. Dr. Osis observed, "Such extreme cases suggest that some part of the personality is actually projected outside the body and is capable of perceiving and being perceived". Readers were to send reports of their experiences to Miss Jane Mitchell, his Chief Assistant, at the A.S.P.R. Headquarters, New York.

In Newsletter No. 14, 1972, Dr. Osis spoke of "an ectosomatic aspect" of human beings equating it to Myers'

"phantasmogenetic centre" and also calling it "man's 'spiritual self'," terms that include both (a) the bodily aspect, i.e., our "vehicle of vitality" and/or Soul Body (or an admixture of the two) and (b) the cognitive aspect (the Soul, the Thinker and Feeler who uses the Spiritual, Soul and physical bodies). Over 100 individuals have already come forward. Of these, the major subject is Ingo Swann who "sits quietly in a semi-dark room, attached to a polygraph (in an adjoining room) which records data concerning his physiological state (brain waves—EEG—heart-rate, respiration, etc.). The targets are on a shelf suspended 2 feet from the ceiling: this shelf is divided by a partition, on each side of which is a tray containing an arrangement of target-objects placed so as to look distinctly different as seen, say, from the south or from the north. We used objects having strong form and colour (e.g., an umbrella, a black leather scissors-case, an apple).
"We asked Mr. Swann to tell us the position from which he saw the objects. He gave us verbal descriptions of the targets, as well as sketches. We developed psychological scales for rating the quality and clarity of his OOB vision . . . *Perception*—Mr. Swann's OOB perception was organised in much the same way as if he were indeed looking at the stimulus shelf from the point where he felt he had projected his spiritual self. So OOB-vision seems in one respect at least to be more like normal vision than does ESP . . . Does OOB-vision follow *the laws of optics*? On the shelf we arranged stimulus material (e.g., a small 'd') inside a closed box with a small opening and a two-mirror system. We wanted to see whether, in the OOB-state, Mr. Swann could see the target through the opening, as he would normally see it from that point (as reflected via the mirror), or whether he would see it directly by clairvoyance, without using the mirrored image . . . We are now developing optical systems for testing the ectosomatic hypothesis of OOBE: physicists (Messrs. L. F. Barcus, T. Etter, R. J. Kleehammer and J. Merewether) psychologists (Miss B. Preskari and Dr. C. K. Silfen) and engineers (Messrs. J. Cohen, M. Ruderfer and G. M. Smith) are co-operating. *Physiology*—The autonomic nervous system responses seem quite within normal range, indicating that there is no danger to the organism during OOB states . . . Voltage-changes appear to be important." Dr. Osis asked for further help from readers. This experimental approach is, of course, supplementary to ours. The latter was mentioned in the Preface to our *Out-of-the-body Experiences,* University Books, N.Y., U.S.A., 1970, as follows:

"When, as has often fallen to the lot of the present writer, one undertakes the microscopic investigation of a petrified stem, it is necessary to take transparent slices ('sections') from it at various angles. The first series of sections is made across the stem, the second series goes down its middle, and the third is tangential: this procedure leaves no tissue unrevealed. The investigation of out-of-the-body experiences demands an analogous psychological procedure: that is, one analyses the testimonies of those who claim to have had them from various angles." For this purpose, the present writer divided the testimonies into (a) natural and (b) enforced and the deponents into (a) mediumistic and (b) non-mediumistic types (see classification, p.12). This procedure leaves no reasonable doubt as to the reality of such experiences.

Case No. 838—Drs. R. L. MacMillan and K. W. G. Brown's patient

These medical men published an account in C.M.A. Journal, May 22, 1971, vol. 104: it concerned a 68-year-old man. "The patient remembered in details the events surrounding his cardiac arrest, and the following account is his own. 'I had been admitted to the Intensive Care Ward . . . I was lying flat on my back because of the intravenous tubes. My head flopped over and I thought, "Why did my head flop over—I did not move it? I must be going to sleep!" This was my last conscious thought.

" 'Then I am looking at my own body from the waist up, face to face (as though through a mirror). Almost immediately *I saw myself leave my body, coming out through my head and shoulders. The "body" leaving me was not exactly in vapour form,* yet it seemed to expand very slightly once it was clear to me. It was somewhat transparent, for I could see my other body through it. Watching this, I thought, *"So this is what happens when you die!"* (although no thought of being dead presented itself to me).

" 'Suddenly I am sitting on a very small object travelling at great speed, out and up into a dull blue-grey sky . . . Down below I saw a cloud-like substance and thought, "What will happen to me when it engulfs me?" and "You do not have to worry—it has all happened before and everything will be taken care of!" . . .

" 'My next sensation was of floating in a bright, pale-yellow light—*a very delightful feeling . . . I have never experienced such a delightful sensation and have no words for it. Then there were sledge-hammer blows to my left side*

[? = re-entering body] . . . and opened my eyes. Immediately I was in control of all my faculties: I asked the nurse, "What has happened?" and she replied that I had "a bad turn" . . . I have read about heart-transplants in which it is claimed the brain dies before the heart stops. In my case, *my brain must have been working after my heart stopped beating for me to experience these sensations.* If death comes to a heart-patient in this manner, no one has cause to worry about it—I felt no pain and, while it was a peculiar experience, it was not unpleasant. The floating was strangely beautiful and I said to a doctor later that night, *"If I go out again, don't bring me back! It's so beautiful out there!"—and at the time I meant it* [= *reluctance to return*: cf. Case Nos. 788, 789, 793, 825, 833].'"

The medical men commented: "It is unusual for patients to *remember* the events surrounding cardiac arrest . . . This description is extremely interesting. *The patient saw himself leaving his body and he observed it 'face to face'. This could be the concept of the Soul leaving the body which is found in many religions. The delightful feeling, etc., and not wanting to be brought back may provide comfort to patients suffering from coronary artery disease, as well as to their relatives."*

THE RELEASE AND RETURN OF COMPOSITE DOUBLES (VEHICLE OF VITALITY PLUS SOUL BODY)

Simple doubles are extremely rare: they consist of either (a) the "semi-physical" and "semi-mental", "fluidic" (electromagnetic) *vehicle of vitality only* (representing "ghosts" of living persons), the first group of cases in our Introduction, or (b) the "super-physical" *Soul Body only,* our first group of out-of-the-body experiences, or (c) the True, Transcendent *Spiritual Body only,* our third group of out-of-the-body experiences.

The vehicle of vitality is not an instrument of consciousness; the Psychic or Soul Body provides psychic experiences, i.e., awareness of other Souls, whether in-carnate or discarnate, and the Spiritual Body permits mystical, or Spiritual experiences, i.e., awareness of God. The extremely few people who tend to project the vehicle of vitality do so only because that portion of the total physical body is in loose association with the chemical body; the event tends especially to occur during illness or abstraction (especially that which involves the direction of the attention towards some distant place or person). People who tend to project the Soul Bodies only chemical body) possess Soul Bodies that have been rendered efficient by their moral and spiritual activities in daily life: Soul Bodies that are so organised, with the "sense" organs, the "chakras" of the Hindus not dormant but active, can be used as instruments of consciousness *independently of the physical body* and these people therefore have psychic, or Soul, experiences (telepathy, etc.). The relatively few people who project the Spiritual Body from both the physical and the Soul Body have it organised by Spiritual activities, chiefly love, so it can be used separately from those two denser bodies. They have occasional awareness of God—Spiritual experiences.

In addition to the three above-mentioned types of double (*simple* doubles), we recognise composite doubles, our second group, consisting of (a) *part of the "semi-physical" vehicle of vitality plus the "super-physical" Soul Body*: hitherto no medical man, psychiatrist or psychologist has envisaged this, the most frequent type of double.

When, towards the end of an active day, the physical body is more or less exhausted of "nervous" or "vital" forces and needs "re-charging", *there is a tendency for everyone's vehicle of vitality to disconnect slightly from the body* and the event has several results. First, since the vehicle of vitality is intermediate in nature (in "vibration"-rate, etc.) between the chemical body and the "super-physical" Soul Body (man's primary Body for thinking, feeling and willing), it operates as a "bridge", "link" or "ladder" between the two. On the one hand, our emotions and ideals affect our actions and, on the other hand, our actions affect our Souls. "That which a man 'sows', that shall he also 'reap' ". We (Souls) only "live" in the physical body ("on earth") via our vehicles of vitality.

Secondly, the *disconnection* of the vehicle of vitality from the physical body necessarily also affects the latter—it "*sleeps*": but the Soul (in its Soul Body) is not then (at least not always) asleep—sometimes it is more awake than in daily life (when working through both the Soul Body and the physical body). It often has telepathic, clairvoyant and precognitive experiences, few of which we become aware since, in order that we become aware of them in "waking" life, they must pass through the physical brain (which organ was not concerned in those experiences).

Joel (ii, 28—see also Acts ii, 17) said, "Your old men

[whose vehicles of vitality have begun partially to loosen from the body, preparatory to completely loosening at death] shall dream 'dreams' and your young men [whose vehicles of vitality are not yet fully immersed in the body] shall see visions."

Most people doubtless have numerous psychic experiences during normal sleep, but rarely, if ever, "remember" them: "The night-time of the body is the day-time of the Soul".

With people who have definitely loose vehicles of vitality, the latter may not merely *disconnect* from the body but may largely, occasionally almost entirely, *project,* in which case *the body gets little vital force and is in trance, death-like, immobile, cataleptic*—and the psychic experiences may be much greater (though they are usually known only to others who are present). Sleep may pass into trance and vice versa —it merely depends on how much of the vehicle of vitality —which, unlike the physical body, is "fluidic"—leaves the body.

It is not strange that medical men and psychologists have failed signally to explain so "well-known" a phenomemon as sleep (and that of trance), since they have paid little attention to psychic matters and therefore not envisaged the existence of the vehicle of vitality, a bodily feature for which there is coercive evidence in "physical" phenomena. Dr. Hereward Carrington (*The Story of Psychic Science,* Rider, 1930) pointed out that none of the orthodox hypotheses that have been advanced to explain the phenomena (and experiences) of sleep—a condition common to all who live, who have ever lived, or ever will live!—entirely fulfils that purpose: they include the chemical hypothesis, the circulation of blood in the brain hypothesis, the glandular hypothesis, the muscular relaxation hypothesis and the deprivation of physical stimuli hypothesis. We can go further and claim that all these hypotheses together also fail to account for these universal phenomena. Carrington said, "We shall never arrive at a satisfactory theory of sleep, doubtless, until we admit the presence of a vital force [circulating in the 'semi-physical', electro-magnetic portion of the total body, the 'vehicle of vitality'] and the existence of an individual human 'spirit' [better called the 'super-physical' Soul, with its own Body] which withdraws more or less completely from the body during deep sleep [which withdrawal, on our hypothesis, is due to the disconnection of the 'semi-physical' vehicle of vitality, the 'bridge' between the physical and the Soul bodies], deriving 'spiritual' invigoration and nourishment during its sojourn in the 'spiritual' world [here meaning the Paradise World, corresponding to the Soul Body, not the true Spiritual World, the true Heavens, which correspond to the true Spiritual Body]."

Dr. Nandor Fodor[60] noted that psychic experiences occurred in (or as) "dreams" during sleep and also in trance, hypnotic and other, and that F. W. H. Myers found indications that "the self of sleep is a 'spirit' [Soul] freed from ordinary limitations [= with the Soul Body no longer enveiled or enshrouded by the physical body and its vehicle of vitality] and this conclusion conforms to the hypothesis that we live in two worlds—the waking personality is adapted to the needs of earth-life, the personality-of-sleep [the Soul] maintains the fundamental connection between the 'spiritual' world [Paradise] and the body so as to provide the latter with energy while developing itself by the exercise of its 'spiritual' powers."

The true nature of mediumistic trance, Fodor (*op cit.*, p.388), pointed out, is unknown and he also (p.179) admitted that this also applied to hypnotic trance.

The American Psychiatric Association (February, 1961) stated, "So little is known of the nature of the hypnotic state that definitions usually reduce themselves to mere descriptions of the various manifested phenomena". In Professor Charles T. Tart's collection of essays entitled *Altered States of Consciousness*, (John Wiley, 1969), there is no attempt to explain the nature of, as distinct from the phenomena that accompany, sleep or trance, either mediumistic or hypnotic. These phenomena are of two distinct kinds, the first "physical" and the second "mental".

On our hypothesis, "physical" phenomena are due to the release from the body, of a considerable portion of, the electro-magnetic vehicle of vitality and the forces that circulate therein, explaining why they very rarely occur in connection with natural sleep (where, with non-mediums, the vehicle of vitality is merely *slightly disconnected* from the body) typically occur in mediumistic trance (where *much is projected*): raps, direct voice phenomena, telekinesis and materialisations occur in connection with those who have a particularly loose vehicle of vitality ("physical" mediums) commonly when they are in trance, sometimes when they are asleep. Illness and old age naturally increase the tendency.

"Mental" phenomena (telepathy, clairvoyance, precognition, etc.) occur either in trance or in natural sleep (since the

Soul Body is released from the physical body in both conditions). But, as already said, the "remembrance" of such phenomena is restricted by the physical brain. Professor Ian Stevenson[61] cited thirty-five cases in which telepathic impressions were received: among them, ten were "received" (*and remembered*) as the recipient awoke from sleep. Dr. Montagu Ullman experimented in his dream laboratory: subjects were asked to sleep in a sound-proof room. Before each subject retired to sleep he was told by the agent, "At various times during the night, *I* will concentrate on a 'target picture': *I* will try, by this means, to convey my impression of the picture to you in the hope that it will appear in *your* dreams". The subject was monitored by an electro-encephalograph ("EEG") which indicated to the agent that a dream was in progress. Rapid eye-movements ("REM") also indicated that a dream was in progress. As soon as it stopped, the dreamer was awakened over an "inter-comm." and asked to describe his dream. This took place on each occasion that the indications showed that a dream was in progress. In the morning, the subject was interviewed to obtain further information concerning his dreams.

The results showed 97 "hits" and only 37 "misses". In one experiment the agent randomly selected a picture showing children walking up a staircase which faced a large window: the subject said, "Somebody was going down a corridor . . . wandering down this corridor . . . the window looks like the windows in our house". In another test, the target picture showed two monkeys in a comical pose with a large white bird in the foreground: the subject described her dream as follows: "It was about a small bird . . . like a pigeon . . . an animal skin on the floor. In a third test the target picture showed a female walking up a road towards a church: the subject dreamed of "a lady, a typical old lady" who "came to this building . . . could have been a church . . . a great big dome . . ."

Dr. Gardner Murphy[62] commenting on such researchers, said, "There is pretty solid evidence that man . . . in the sleeping condition, is more easily able to make these long, remote kinds of contact than in the waking state . . . *It is only in the deep relaxation, and even to the point of sleep, that the 'windows'* [*of the Soul*] *get wide enough open* [*or, on our hypothesis, that the Soul Body gets sufficiently un-enshrouded, or un-enveiled, by the physical body and its vehicle of vitality*] *to make possible this kind of contact.*"

The above refers to telepathy received by mortals from

other mortals and the phenomena strongly supports the claims, in "communications", that telepathy is the normal mode of communication between those discarnate Souls who have reached Paradise conditions—and that they often try to impress their loved ones on earth (usually of course, with little or no success, since the Soul Bodies of mortals are enshrouded by their physical bodies). A number of our most eminent psychical researchers have concluded that telepathy is going on all the time between mortals (though they are, of course, very seldom aware of it): they include C. D. Broad, Gilbert Murray, G. N. M. Tyrrell, Whately Carington and H. H. Price in Great Britain, Henri Bergson in France and Hereward Carrington and Gardner Murphy in U.S.A.

Sir Lawrence Jones[63] referred to the mediumship of Kate Wingfield and said, "On four occasions my youngest daughter, aged nine, purported to communicate *during her sleep*, speaking with great animation and very characteristically. In the first, she was some fifteen miles from where Kate was staying. A correct version of certain happenings was given, through the body of the *sleeping* Miss Wingfield by this child." We submit that all the above facts are readily explained on our hypothesis concerning the vehicle of vitality and the Soul Body and their operation in sleep—and on no other hypothesis.

Out-of-the-body experiences also occur (even more commonly) in those cases in which *the Soul Body only* is released, i.e., our First Group of Experiences (as might be expected) and (again as might be expected) in those cases in which the released double is at first composite but—after passing through the second "death"—consists of *the Soul Body only*, i.e., our Second Group of Experiences. As already said, doubles that, when first released, are composite (and they are released by people with loose vehicles of vitality) are by far the most frequent—and the most significant. The various events and experiences that are described by the deponents can readily be explained on the hypothesis that these doubles are objective—"semi-" and "super"-physical bodies (vehicles of vitality and Soul Bodies respectively)—and not subjective (either mental images or "archetypes" in the "collective unconscious").

While the above was in course of printing, E. W. Russell and H. S. Burr produced two books which clinch the case for the existence of the electro-magnetic vehicle of vitality, the former *Design for Destiny* (1971), the latter *Blueprint for Immortality* (1972), both published by Neville Spearman. These I reviewed in *The Psychic Researcher and Spiritualist Gazette*, 12, 1973. The invention of the D. C. Vacuum Voltmeter enabled Dr. Burr to demonstrate the existence of the electro-magnetic "life-field" (our vehicle of vitality) in plants, animals and men: it acts as a "bridge" between man's Soul and his physical body, and is primary to the latter, the mould upon which it is formed; its partial breaking makes one dreamy, sleepy, in suspended animation, etc., and complete severance means bodily death. Russell gave the name "Thought-field" to what we call the Soul Body, regarding it as primary to both the vehicle of vitality and the chemical body.

THE SUCCESSION OF *EVENTS* AND *EXPERIENCES* IN THE *TEMPORARY RELEASE* OF COMPOSITE "DOUBLES", WITH CORROBORATIVE DATA
A-*EVENTS* IN THE FIRST STAGE OF *RELEASE* (THE FIRST—PHYSICAL—DEATH = THE FIRST UN-VEILING OF THE SOUL BODY)

(1) *"Mist", "fog", "vapour", "cloud", "smoke", even "water", "a shadowy form", "a shadowy replica" of the body, "a waxen image", "something like chiffon", "like white intestines"*, etc. (also felt as *"electricity", "tingles", "vibrations", "pins-and-needles"*, etc.) *left the physical body: they represent part of the electro-magnetic vehicle of vitality, via which the body is normally vitalised.* "Fog", etc. (sometimes "condensed" to "water") were mentioned in our Case No. 778 and in earlier cases Nos. 13, 17, 59, 90, 244, 258, 307, 368, etc. Monroe (No. 749) saw "something like grey chiffon", Mrs. Spaulding[64] "a gauze curtain", Frank Hives (No. 49) "a shadowy form" and "a wraith", Mrs. Eileen J. Garrett, "a shadowy form of myself" and Edgar Cayce "a waxen image"[32]

"Mist", "fog", etc., often more or less luminous, again obviously representing the "semi-physical" vehicles of vitality, are described in *situations other than out-of-the-body experiences* (such as the above).

(a) People who had no claim to be clairvoyant claimed to have seen the phenomena with the physical eyes, in connexion with death (see E).

(b) *Permanently-released vehicles of vitality*, i.e., the "bodies" of Souls who had recently survived physical death, have often been described as resembling "luminous mist", "shining smoke", etc. Frau Hauffe[65], the German seeress, in 1829, said, "A ghost appears to me like a thin cloud", and added a significant observation: "I do not see it when my eyes are closed or when I turn my head away": The physical eyes were used.

(c) *"Ghosts"* of the objective type (including the vehicle of vitality) have often been seen and also *photographed (indicating objectivity)*: they are "mist-" "smoke-" or "cloud"-like—see, e.g., the photographs published by Dr. H. Baraduc (*Mes Morts, Leurs Manifestations,* Paris, 1908, of persons who were dying and those of "ghosts" by Mme. d'Espérance[66]).

(d) *"Communictors"*, i.e., the "dead", in this connexion as in all others of moment, give descriptions that are obviously comparable to those of astral projectors, clairvoyants and non-clairvoyant observers of the process of dying: "luminous magnetic mist" and "pearly vapour" are among the terms used.[67]

It will be seen that five groups quite independently provide accounts that accord with the statements of (mediumistically-constituted) people that, at an early stage of their projections, an objective fog-like substance began to leave their bodies. This process—the projection of the electromagnetic vehicle of vitality—had important effects. ("Mist", "chiffon", etc., are also described at appropriate stages later—in projections.)

(2) *"Cold winds" and depletion, and therefore apprehension, were sometimes felt, doubtless due to the loss of part of the animating vehicle of vitality from the body*). It should be noted that such phenomena occur (a) in out-of-the-body experiences of people who show signs of having loose vehicles of vitality (mediumistically-constituted people) and (b) those of trance mediums.

Among the projections here given we note Case No. 749. It was also mentioned by Marjorie T. Johnson (Case No. 53) who said, "These travels were characterised by the rushing 'spirit-of-the-wind' sensations, followed by a heightening of the faculties and exaltation". Professor Whiteman (No. 244) said, "A vivid sense of cold flowed upon me". See also Acts ii, 2. It is not purely subjective, since in some cases it affects thermometers. It is not surprising that (a) when produced by a medium in trance, it is usually followed by "physical" phenomena (raps, "lights", direct voice, telekinesis, materialisation) and (b) when produced by a mediumistically-constituted person he sees a "ghost" (since he provided the electro-magnetic "bridge" by means of which the "earthbound"—because "body-bound"—Soul manifested his presence). Lord Adare, at a seance with D. D. Home, felt "strong rushing winds". Sir Wm. Crookes[68] found that "physical" phenomena in general were usually preceded by "cold air" and sometimes by "a decided wind": he added, "A thermometer lowered several degrees" (showing that the phenomenon was objective and not merely imagined). Prof. E. Bozzano described "icy air" at seances, the temperature falling 20 degrees. Dr. Alan Gauld (*Proc.* S.P.R., 55, 1971) reported "cold winds". The famous healer W. J. Macmillan[69] found that when he healed by "passes" his patients felt "intensely cold". The same phenomemon was described in France by Dr. H. Durville who used "passes" to release the doubles (including the vehicle of vitality) of subjects. The astral projector *Fox (Case No. 31) correlated "winds" with "water" (=condensed "mist", "fog", "cloud", "steam", etc.)* when he referred to hearing "sounds like the surging of an angry sea and rushing winds". *A "communicator"*[70] *correlated "mists" with "a river"* (compare the description of death as "crossing the River Jordan", etc.): after passing through the second "death", and entering Paradise conditions in the unshrouded Soul Body, he said he had been trained to eliminate fear, etc. so that he could re-enter the "mists" which hang over the great "river" [=Hades] that separates the physical world from Paradise [just as man's vehicle of vitality separates his physical body from his Soul Body]. He said that, "All Souls must pass through these 'mists' on leaving their physical bodies for the last time." He was thus able to help "Spirits in prison", i.e., the "earthbound" who were delayed in Hades conditions. Nevertheless, some of the unpleasant inhabitants of Hades affected him on three occasions. Mme. d'Espérance[71], who produced materialisations, when entering trance (due to releasing much of her vehicle of vitality), felt "cool breezes" and then felt as if she were covered with "spider webs" (both =ectoplasm being released from the vehicle of vitality) after this, she saw before her luminous "white vapour" or "steam" and this became a definite "materialised" form. On other occasions, faintly-luminous "threads" left the pores of Mme. d'Espérance's skin, evidently corresponding to the "luminous threads", i.e., "silver cord"-extensions of the vehicle of vitality, reported by many other "physical" mediums. Turvey (our Case No. 21), an "astral projector" who clearly had a loose vehicle of vitality since he exercised PK, said, " 'I' (double) seem to make use of the medium's psychic [=ectoplasmic] force which 'I' appear to draw from her wrists or knees as a sort of red sticky matter". i.e., the medium's power "boosted" his own and rendered PK possible. This description by an English "astral projector" resembles that of a young French girl-medium, Reine[72], when her (composite) double was released from her body by mesmeric "passes": she described the permanently-released (composite) doubles of "earthbound" Souls as "reddish" in colour: moreover, when they touched her, they felt "like snails". A French lady, Mme. Bouissou[73], investigated the mediumship of "Eva", also described the released vehicle of vitality as feeling like snails. The "earthbound" communicator of J. S. M. Ward (*Gone West*, pp. 236, 240, 245) described his own "aura" (vehicle of vitality) as "dull red", "lurid red" and "full of red rays".

Dr. Fodor[74] made several references to these matters: with Margery Crandon, in Canada, the temperature dropped from 68 to 42 degrees after the "cold breezes" had blown for a time, while she also felt as if there were "cobwebs" on her face. In Poland, Dr. J. Ochorowitz, experimenting with the "physical" medium Tomczyk, himself felt "a thread" that resembled "a spider's web": its objectivity was beyond doubt, since it supported a pair of scissors above the table. As already said, in France, Dr. H. Durville [75] released the vehicles of vitality of several persons by means of mesmeric "passes": anyone who approached these projected doubles felt cold (since ectoplasm was withdrawn from their own vehicles of vitality): Durville himself touched a released double and it felt "humid".

The above-cited observations of "ectoplasm", released from a person's vehicle of vitality, as "sticky", "snail-like", "cobweb-like", "spider's-web-like" or "humid", it is surely significant, were made by the natives of Polynesia, who could neither read nor write and very many years before psychical research began. Max Freedom Long[76] reported that they described "the aka body", obviously meaning the electro-magnetic vehicle of vitality, and said "the aka body sticks to anything we contact—it is like touching fly-paper with the finger". Long added, "The idea of an 'aka-thread' or 'cord' is closely related to the idea of a flow of 'mana', i.e., vitality, —the root 'ka' means 'a cord'." Again there is a suggestion of correspondence with the "silver cord"-extension between a released vehicle of vitality and the body it left.

The anthropologist, Dr. Ronald Rose[77] was similarly told by Australian aborigines, who could neither read nor write, how a kind of "cord" left the body of "a clever man" (medium) at the mouth and navel (solar plexus): this "cord" was "like black cobwebs".

These "threads" can be used as "feelers". Two clairvoyants, Phoebe Payne and Eileen J. Garrett[78], advised one who wishes to develop psychic abilities—psychometry by handling "links" or rapport-objects that have been much worn by people, the type of healing that involves the laying-on of hands, telepathy, etc.—to *project "feelers", i.e. ectoplasmic "threads", "cords", "rods", "pseudo-pods", etc. from his electro-magnetic vehicle of vitality*, which "semi-physical" extensions interpenetrate the physical rapport-object or the physical body of the subject and merge with its "semi-physical" double, for every stone and every plant, as well as every human being possesses a double. We mentioned this matter in *The Interpretation of Cosmic and Mystical Experiences* (Table, facing p. 130—see also *The Supreme Adventure*, pp 69-72) in explaining certain healings and psychometric "readings": "The vehicle of vitality merges with that of another being "and" this *bodily at-onement* renders possible a *mental at-onement*—one temporarily shares the life of another creature or being".

Alice Gilbert, Douglas Fawcett and Richard Jefferies are among the many who advised us to *touch trees,* etc., while the "communicator" of *The Thinning of the Veil*[79], Dr. J. W. Achorn[80] and the great naturalist W. H. Hudson[81] all advised us to *touch the soil*. Hudson's mother's feelings for flowers, chiefly wild flowers, amounted to "little short of adoration": she regarded them as "Divine symbols of a place beyond our power to imagine [=Paradise]". Hudson himself was more affected by trees than by flowers. He made a further observation which is of interest in view of the fact that the [*"fluidic"*] *vehicle of vitality is said to be affected by the moon* [hence our word *"lunatic"*]—"*the trees always affected me most on moonlight nights . . . I* used to steal out of the house alone when the moon was at its full to stand silent and motionless near some trees . . . The sense of mystery would grow until it was no longer to be born and I would escape to recover the sense of reality indoors where there was light and company . . . The large locust or white acacia trees (*Acacia blanca*) seemed more intensely alive than others, more conscious of my presence and watchful of me."

Hudson compared the sensations which he thus experiences among his trees with the "thrill" of one who was in the presence of "a silent, unseen super-natural [—physical] being" who regarded him intently. He also mentioned **a man** who sat among trees in his garden and, before returning to the house at night, visited each tree in turn *"resting his hand on the bark of each tree"*, being "convinced that the trees knew of, and encouraged, his devotion".

So far from claiming that he was exceptional, Hudson maintained that many people receive this kind of impression from flowers, trees, the soil, etc. They can certainly be encouraged and developed with great advantage, and we give a few suggestions. With regard to conditions: (1) The physical sensations of sight are best excluded in order that the more delicate impressions that come via the ectoplasmic "feelers" may be noticed; if it is not dark, the eyes should be closed; (2) Similarly, physical sounds should be excluded —one is best alone and in quiet surroundings; (3) one's physical touch should be as light and gentle as possible, since a rough touch or grip would yield a physical sensation of roughness or solidity that tended to mask the more delicate impressions sought. With regard to oneself: (1) One should begin with relaxing the whole body; any tenseness prevents the releave of ectoplasmic "feelers" from the vehicle of vitality, imprisoning the latter in the body (note the conditions required for successful seances); (2) Since the vehicle of vitality is "semi-mental" (as well as "semi-physical"), its substance is "biddable", "commandable", under control (though of the "sub-conscious" mind rather than the conscious will—it will do what you expect, what you "have faith" in); the putting-out of "feelers" and their interpenetrating an object is therefore aided by imagining that process taking place. (3) Discordant emotions of fear, distrust, vanity, etc., affect the delicate ectoplasmic "threads", distorting any impressions that might be transmitted by them; peace, tranquility and trust are a sine qua non to clear impressions. (4) The direction of the attention is clearly important: the attention should be withdrawn from one's own thoughts, feelings and judgments and it should be aroused, alert, directed to receive impressions coming from the rapport object or person concerned; (5) Rhythmic breathing (taking, say seven, breaths slightly deeper than usual, pausing slightly on each intake and on each release) steadies both the emotions (No. 3) and the ectoplasmic "bridge" represented by the "feelers", minimising the distortion of the impressions received. This, according to clairvoyants, astral projectors and "communicators", is a merciful provision: while in physical embodiment, our main duty is to live the normal everyday life (expressing, of course, by appropriate words and deeds, the moral and Spiritual laws, bringing "the Kingdom of God" to earth)—glimpses of the Soul World (Paradise) and the True Spiritual World (Heaven) may well come and provide stimulus and comfort. A typical statement was made in France by Reine, an uneducated artists' model (*op. cit.*, 1921, pp. 44, 142): if she remembered much of her out-of-the-body experiences she would think herself "extraordinary" and her "normal life would be disturbed". Nevertheless, she did receive ideas from which she *"unconsciously* benefited". All make these statements. Mrs. Rhys Davids[82] held—we believe rightly— "It is in the shifting from one body [the physical] to the other [the "super-physical" Soul Body via which the impressions are cognised] that we may find some clues to the provoking oddities in dreams"—i.e., it is in the intermediate "semi-physical" vehicle of vitality that genuine impression can be distorted and appear to us as mere meaningless fantasies. The "communicator" of Kate Wingfield[83] similarly stated that most "dreams" are not, as they appear to be, mere fantasies, but are distorted genuine impressions and observations. "H.J.L.", communicating to J. S. M. Ward (*Gone West, Rider*, 1917, pp. 156-7), gave the same reason for the distortion of out-of-the-body experiences. He said, "Experiences on the 'astral' [=Hades] plane, being akin to earth, become distorted as the 'astral' [vehicle of vitality] re-unites with the physical body: it is as though the physical brain [with three dimensions] attempted to explain 'astral' [with four dimensions] phenomena by physical laws . . ." Later (p. 165) "H.J.L." said, "Many people occasionally remember, in a distorted manner, fragments of their [Hades or Paradise] experiences."

Dr. Alice Gilbert[84], engaged in telepathic experiments with her son, Philip. He died and then explained, "The telepathic image, passing with difficulty through the crowded images of the sub-conscious memory [in the vehicle of vitality—hence the first, non-emotional review which often occurs when that bodily feature quits the physical body, either temporarily or permanently] may be halted, becoming, in sleep, a 'dream', blurred and distorted." On the other hand, when his mother 'dreamed' of green meadows, etc. [i.e., of Paradise conditions, "Paradise" being an old Persian word for "a park"], he assured her, "These 'dreams', vague as they are, are not ordinary dreams [=not purely fantastic], but the beginning of true [un-distorted] sleep-life memory".

We can go back hundreds of years to find the above idea

in the Vedanta (Upanishads) of India, interpreted by Sankara-Acharya in the 9th century A.D. "Moonlight" (from the "moon body" = the vehicle of vitality) was described as conveying truth but as necessarily distorting it (see G. A. Gaskell, *Dictionary of the Sacred Language of all Scriptures*, Geo. Allen, 1923, pp. 511, 806). The great Sanskrit authority, Max Muller, observed, "Unless we learn to understand the metaphorical or hieroglyphic language of the ancient world, we shall look upon the Upanishads, and on most of the Sacred Books of the East, as mere childish twaddle".

The "communicator" who provided "The Palm Sunday Case" (*Proc.* S.P.R., 52, 1960, p. 181), probably the most evidential of all survival cases in the whole of psychic literature, gave an essentially identical statement and went further: he made the claim that "glimpses of 'the real world' [= Paradise, in which he lived] do not wholly pass away", even if they are not specifically remembered on re-entering the body and awakening to physical life, (1) "The knowledge has been registered" (in the Soul Body) and (2) it will, at some future time and on some appropriate occasion be "utilised". Nothing of any value is ever lost.

It will be observed that the explanation given by the clairvoyant Mrs. Davids of the distortion of observations and impressions (made via the Soul Body) when they enter "normal", i.e., physical-brain, consciousness was the same as that given by at least three independent "communicators", namely, those of Miss Wingfield, Ward and Alice Gilbert: it is difficult for "super-physical" impressions to pass undistorted through the "semi-physical" "bridge" represented by the vehicle of vitality without undergoing distortion. The clairaudient Edith Ellis (Wilfred Brandon, *Open the Door!*, Alfred A. Knopf, 1935, p. 67) gave the same reason. She pointed out that, "The Soul is most active during natural sleep [when free from the physical body]. It is then functioning on its own—without using the brain . . . Usually it is concerned with the welfare of an absent friend: space is nothing; the image of the friend in the consciousness [= the direction of the attention] will bring them together—many words of cheer are exchanged in this way." According to her, what we call "complexes", etc. are "manifestations of the Soul . . . seeking to co-ordinate its desires with physical life" [= "super-physical" impressions, received in sleep], have very little relation to everyday [physical] life. (Edith Ellis, the clairaudient, also described the ("semi-physical") aura of an angry person was "dull red"—precisely as did the hypnotised Reine[85], the astral projector Vincent Turvey and the "communicator" of J. S. M. Ward.)

The practices suggested above provide a means by which enquirers can test, by personal experiment, the important claim of (a) clairvoyants, (b) astral projectors and (c) "communicators" that the "semi-physical" vehicle of vitality acts as a "bridge" between the "super-physical" Soul Body and the physical body. (This is, indeed to be expected—the Soul Body itself, in turn, must act as a "bridge" between the personality and the "Spirit" or Over-soul, for their could be no interaction within the total human being without complete continuity.)

Professor Ian Stevenson[86] reviewed the "physical" phenomena which occurred in connexion with three *"poltergeist"* cases ("Are poltergeists living or are they dead?"): the three cases included such phenomena as telekinesis, apports, raps and winds and concerned a living and an ostensibly dead woman. He drew attention to the importance of examining any such phenomena that takes place in the presence of *trance mediums,* saying, "With trance mediums the presence of discarnate spirits is usually a reasonable working hypothesis, at least initially". We have recorded the occurrence of *telekinesis, raps and winds* in a number of *out-of-the-body experiences ("astral projections")* of people who showed signs of possessing a loose vehicle of vitality, releasing "mist", etc. in the early stage. The fact is that the possession of a loose and extensible vehicle of vitality is the cause of such phenomena in all these apparently different conditions—by poltergeists, trance mediums, (certain) astral projectors (certain sleepers)—and *certain of the dead*—those who, having retained the vehicle of vitality for an unduly long period and, at the same time have their attention directed earthwards, are "body-bound" and therefore "earth-bound".

In *The Jung-Jaffé View of Out-of-the-Body Experiences,* World Fellowship Press, 1970, p. 92, I cited a number of experiences and phenomena that occurred in connexion with sleep (=when the double was more or less released from the body): "Dr. Jung began to see the apparition while he was *asleep*: A. V. Burton, "Kenwood", Sherman, Reine, etc., like Jung, all began to see an apparition during their sleep. In addition, (1) The released double of *a sleeper* has been recorded on a photographic plate; (2) materialised apparitions have formed during the *sleep* of certain mediums; (3) a *sleeping* medium has "boosted" the psychic powers of another medium; (4) "communications" from living persons have been received while the latter have been *asleep*; (5) super-normal raps occurred during the *sleep* of Hetty Wesley, E. H. Green's child and Dr. Henry Slade; (6) super-normal stone-throwing occurred during the *sleep* of a native servant of W. G. Grottendietch; (7) telekinesis (plus raps) occurred when Charles H. Foster *slept;* (8) transfiguration was observed by Dr. J. Maxwell during the *sleep* of a sick man; (9) transportation occurred during the *sleep* of the Marquis Centurione Scotto. It will be seen that most of the phenomena which occurred during the sleep of a subject were of the "physical" type.

Dr. Nandor Fodor[87] mentioned other phenomena that occurred in connexion with sleep: they included astral projection (the well-known method of determining, prior to sleep, to appear to a friend, the fact that the Rev. Father "H's" released double was seen while he himself was asleep, the fact that Frau Hauffe (who was normally more than half-released from her body), asleep, cried out, "Ach Gott" when her father was, in fact, in the course of dying, and the fact that E. A. Brackett saw the materialised doubles of mediums while they themselves were asleep.

The normal function of the electro-magnetic vehicle of vitality is to act as a "bridge" between a mortal's Soul Body and his physical body. It can also act as a temporary "bridge" between a discarnate person's Soul Body and the physical body of a medium (the "dead" man using it to speak, write, etc.). It can further make certain physical substances (especially wood which seems readily to absorb electro-magnetic forces and emotions that accompany them) so that they act, in part, like a "dead" person. The Revd. Canon L. W. Grensted, Nolloth Professor of the Christian Religion at Oxford, at once a trained psychologist, eminent theologian and "a rather sceptical person", did not find "cross-correspondences" (e.g. "The Ear of Dionysius") as convincing as a table—which, he said, "came and caressed my knee!" Dr. Joseph Maxwell[88] found that wooden pegs were better than metal nails in tables that were used in connexion with psychical phenomena—metals seemed to conduct the electro-magnetic forces away and so prevent their accumulation. Dr. Fodor[89] said, "The motion of a table may express humour, emotion, personality: it may climb up into the sitter's lap as a mark of affection, it may chase others all over the room in a hostile manner". The first sign that a table is thus impregnated with electro-magnetic forces which are transmitting emotions and personal characteristics is "a quivering motion" [="vibrations"] under the sitters' hands and the table eventually pulsates. Fodor said, "The wooden surface appears to act as a reservoir of externalised nervous force. Carrington said of his seances with Eusapia Paladino that the table appeared to be somehow alive . . . After the vibratory stage, the table may jerk, jilt, stumble about, and may eventually become entirely levitated. Apparently there is an intelligence behind these movements. If the letters of the alphabet are called over the dark, the table, by tilting, knocking on the floor, or tapping the sitter, indicates certain letters which connectedly spell out a message, often purporting to come from someone deceased. The intelligence which thus manifests has personal charactertics. In repeated sittings it is soon noticed that the skill with which the table is manipulated, or the eccentricities of its behaviour, is indicatory of the presence of the sane entity. The strange, solid or clumsy behaviour of the table immediately denotes that a new visitant is tampering with the contact." George F. Long[90] found that one person who "communicated" in this fashion was still in the flesh. People who are obsessed by the either/or argument suppose that cases of the latter type negative the possibility of communicating from the "dead": actually, of course, each case should be decided on its merits. In our present connection, these are various examples of the electro-magnetic ("semi-physical") forces from a vehicle of vitality acting as *a "bridge"* between a "super-physical" Soul Body, exhibiting will, emotion and thought, and physical matter: the "bridge" transmits emotion, etc.

Judge Edmonds, in U.S.A., observed that, with some entranced mediums, "cold winds" were accompanied by *"strong scents"*. These are pleasant (e.g., of violets) with mediums of high moral and spiritual type, e.g., Mrs. Piper, but with those who contacted haunts they resemble the stenches of decaying corpses, which matter is mentioned below—under "hinderers". Dr. Alan Gauld (*Proc. S.P.R.,* 55, 1971) reported scents.

It is significant, indicating objectivity and not subjectivity, that "cold winds" were also encountered when the vehicle of vitality left the composite double in the second "death" and when it returned to the body.

In *The Interpretation of Cosmic and Mystical Experiences* (James Clarke, 1969, pp. 105-114), I drew attention to the large number of investigators who had concluded that the *"mental" phenomena of psychical research, chiefly telepathy and clairvoyance,* were not the special prerogatives of a few (and therefore "strange") people, but were normal to all mankind: the investigators included Neville Randall, Frances Banks, H. H. Price, Calder Marshall, Walter F. Prince, Henry H. Hillers, the Rev. Canon Wm. Rauscher, J. B. Rhine, W. H. Clarke, Dr. A. Jaffé, G. N. M. Tyrrell, Herbert Bland, Henri Bergson, Gilbert Murray, R. Warcollier, Hereward Carrington, Gertrude Tubby, Joseph Maxwell, Audry Butt, A. P. Elkin, etc. Numerous "communicators", in England, U.S.A., Germany, South Africa, etc., had stated that telepathy, clairvoyance, etc. were normal faculties of all mankind years before these investigators had arrived at that conclusion (*ibid.*, pp. 114-116). The conclusion is supported by the fact that clairvoyants and people who had out-of-the-body experiences (again as well as "communicators") all independently declare that everyone has a "superphysical" Soul (or Emotional) *Body,* the organ which is used in telepathy and clairvoyance.

In *Journ.* S.P.R., 1966, K. J. Batcheldor, a psychologist, observed that cases of instances *of "physical" phenomena of psychical research, chiefly PK, table-tilting and levitation, super-normal noises (raps, footsteps), strong winds and cold winds, touches, lights and, occasionally, apports,* were not the special prerogative of a few ("strange") people but were normal to all mankind: if several "ordinary", i.e., not obviously mediumistic, persons would form a group and meet regularly under well-known conditions they would obtain such "physical" phenomena. This also had previously been said, independently, by "communicators", e.g., by that of Fr. J. Greber, a Roman Catholic Priest in Germany fifty years ago, and by that of Mrs. Cora L. V. Tappan in U.S.A. a century ago. This conclusion also is supported by the fact that clairvoyants and people who had out-of-the-body experiences all independently declare that everyone has a "semi-physical" and "semi-mental" vehicle of vitality (or vital *'body'*), the organ by means of which the "physical" phenomena are produced. Both Batcheldor (*loc. cit*) and Dr. Alan Gauld (*Proc.* S.P.R., 55, 1971) reported table-tilting, strong winds, cold winds, lights (incipient materialisations) and scents.

(3)*Sensations of "stress" and "vibrations" were often felt in the solar plexus region of the body.* We include the "vibrations" in general under experiences (A 1). The observations not only tie up with each other but also with the fact that those mediumistically-constituted who claim to have seen the "silver cord"-extension between their released doubles (composite, i.e., including the vehicle of vitality as well as the Soul Body), e.g., P. T. Sullivan and Evan Powell, J.P., described their "cords" as attached to the solar plexus (whereas (a) those who release the Soul Body only, and (b) those mediumistic people who have passed through the second "death" typically describe the "cord" as attached to the head): the vehicle of vitality chiefly leaves via the solar plexus region so that the "cord"-extension is attached at the solar plexus while the Soul Body chiefly leaves via the head so that the "cord"-extension is attached at the head. This condition is noted herein in Cases No. 742, 744, 748, 768, 770, 803, and also in earlier Cases No. 419, 425, etc.

We note that, among "astral projectors", Muldoon and Monroe in U.S.A., Whiteman in South Africa and Rosamond Lehmann in England (all showing signs of a loose vehicle of vitality) all felt stresses and cramps in the solar plexus region. Among "physical" mediums (who are characterised by extremely loose vehicles of vitality), that of Dr. J. Maxwell[91] in France and the Rev. Wm. Stainton Moses (whose phenomena convinced F. W. H. Myers), in England, also felt these sensations. Among people whose vehicle of vitality was largely forced out of the body, a French engraver[92], almost suffocated by fumes from a lamp, saw "light", i.e. luminous, "cords", etc. coming from his "epigastrium", i.e., "solar plexus", the chief exit of the vehicle of vitality.

Almost a century ago, Adolphe d'Assier[93], an agnostic, made observations on (composite) doubles that were released from their physical counterparts by "magnetic passes": he considered that the phenomena provided a complete answer to the hypothesis of the survival of the Soul (in the "superphysical" Soul Body)—that it was the "larva", i.e., the "semi-physical", "semi-mental" electro-magnetic vehicle of vitality only that survived bodily death. Our present point is that he called the latter bodily feature (part of the total physical body) "the epigastric personage".

The solar plexus is used by those mediums who readily release part of the vehicle of vitality. George Valiantine was a "physical" medium: his solar plexus region was *bruised* (indicating objectivity) when released ectoplasm returned suddenly to his body, i.e., it caused a "repercussion" (cf. the "jolt", "jerk", etc. experienced by astral projectors who have loose vehicles of vitality which return suddenly to their bodies—see Summary of Events and Experiences, A 3, C 6 and L 7).

As early as 1829 the unlettered German seeress, Frau Hauffe[94], who was "more than half dead" for some years prior to actually dying (i.e., with more than half of her vehicle of vitality released from her body—hence her clairvoyant abilities which were almost entirely with "earthbound" Souls) claimed to be sometimes helped by her discarnate grandmother: Frau Hauffe, significantly, said that she saw her grandmother "direct 'passes' to the epigastric region" of her body.

The released Soul Body sometimes uses the solar plexus to "feel" or "see", though not very distinctly. In France, in his studies of the transposition of the senses, Tardy de Montravel, as early as 1785, found that some subjects under hypnosis, i.e., with part of the vehicle of vitality released, could "see" via "the pit of the stomach". In Germany, Dr. J. Kerner recorded the same phenomena with Frau Hauffe without the use of "passes"—as already said, her vehicle of vitality was already considerably released. In U.S.A., Mrs. Garrett, once a trance medium and eventually one of the truly great women of all time, described how the solar plexus can be so used. In Switzerland, Dr. C. G. Jung, the great psychiatrist, produced raps supernormally (i.e., via the vehicle of vitality): before the phenomena appeared he felt as if his "diaphragm" was "made of iron" and was "red hot". Some hypnotisers see "rays" from the solar plexus of the hypnotised. T. Lyon, a miner, produced "raps": in his case, *photographs* showed an extension of the vehicle of vitality which came from the solar plexus and caused the phenomenon. James H. Neal[95] was attacked at the solar plexus by "hinderers".

(4) *The released (composite) double was almost always above the vacated body.* This applied to Cases herein Nos. 729, 739, 743, 750, 760, 762, 767, 769, 770, 777, 778 and also 369, 411, 415, 416, 424, 433, 441, 463, 781, 782, 783, 787, 791, 794, 796, 797, 800, 803, 806, 807, 808, 813, 822, etc. Typical phrases used by these *astral projectors* are "floated down", "hovered above" (body) and "looked down on" (body). Identical phrases were used by people who had suffered *pseudo-death*. This condition is, as it were, half-way between normal out-of-the-body experiences and *death*. "Communicators" who describe their own "passing" use similar terms.

(5)*The released (composite) double was at first commonly in a horizontal position above the body.* This remarkable initial position is indeed to be expected since the vehicle of vitality represents the electro-magnetic portion of the total body—this (composite) double is "body-bound" (and those discarnates who retain the vehicle of vitality for an abnormally long period after death are, therefore, "earth-bound", unable to leave Hades—the electro-magnetic portion of the total earth—and so enter Paradise). This position accords with the *objective nature of the vehicle of vitality*.

The horizontal position was herein described in Cases Nos. 729, 768, 776 and 788 and in earlier Cases Nos. 20, 32, 38, 49, 60, 68, 72, 73, 74, 78, 85, 90, 95, 100, 102, 177, 185, 192, 202, 212, 226, 243, 250, 268, 280, 294, 336, 395 and 364. Terms used by these *astral projectors*, besides the common "horizontal", include "level", "a lying position", "supine", "prone" and "parallel to the body". Observers of *the dying* (e.g., W. T. Pole, Alice Mortley and T. E. Morgan) also used the word "horizontal". It is significant that the composite double was also horizontal just before it re-entered the body.

(6) *A temporary extension (the "silver cord") united the released double to the vacated body.* This was described herein as seen by deponents in Cases Nos. 740, 744, 748, 770, 778, 791 and as felt though not seen in Cases Nos. 762, 767, 789 and 803. It is described in many of our earlier cases— Nos. 388, 390, 392, 393, 394, 396, 400, 401, 406, 415, 416, 417, 419, 420, 442, 443, 444, 446, 453, 455, 463, 475, 486, 493, 497, 516, 524, 525, 526, 527, 528, 529 and 530.

Terms and phrases that were used by "astral projectors" to describe their "silver cord"-extensions include the following:—

"a cord", a "silver cord", "a silvery cord";
"a chain" or "ribbon";
"a strand" or "string";
"a tape" or "band";
"a thread" or "arm", or "pipeline".

"Silver cords" were also often observed by people who saw the double leaving a body permanently: J. C. Street observed "a slender cord", Mr. "G" "a cord", Dr. R. B. Hout "a silver-like substance" which streamed from the head of the dying person. He said, "as I watched, the thought, 'the silver cord', kept running through my head. I knew, for the first time, the meaning of it: this 'silver cord' was the connecting-link between the physical and the 'spirit' [Soul] bodies, even as the umbilical cord unites the child to its mother." P. M. Urquhart saw "a wisp of connection" that united, "for some little time" his newly-dead father to his corpse. The Revd. Dr. R. J. Staver used the same term.

E. W. Oaten saw "an umbilical cord" unite the newly-dead Daisy to her vacated body. Rose Harley reported "a silver thread" which "snapped" and the person died. V. D. Rishi described "a 'cord' similar to the umbilical cord of earthly birth". H. A. Curtiss mentioned "an 'astral' cord, something like an umbilical cord". Florence Marryat saw "cords of light, like electricity", Leslie Curnow quoted Mrs. Watts' description—"A delicate gleaming line or cord of light". Geoffrey Hodson observed, "a stream of flowing forces which shone with a delicate silver light", Mrs. J. Taylor "a very fine silver cord", Charles Moore "a psychic umbilical cord", Dr. A. J. Davis "a bright stream or current, of vital electricity . . . the life thread".

Professor M. Eliade reviewed the prehistoric accounts of projections but did not realise the importance of the "cord". We mentioned this in *Out-of-the-body Experiences*[96].

Illiterate natives used terms such as: —
"a cord" (Australia);
"a ribbon" or a "rainbow" (Hawaiian Islands, Japan, etc.);
"a rope" (Tibet, Manchuria, etc.);
"a thread", a "bridge as narrow as a hair" (Africa, etc.);
"a stick" or "post" (Hungary, Asia);
"a ladder" (Tibet, Borneo, etc.);
"a vine" (New Zealand).

The "silver cord" was not imagined, nor were all the descriptions copied from Ecclesiastes. It was an objective extension between temporarily-separated objective bodies.

The fact that some astral projectors reported a "silver cord" which was attached to the solar plexus while others reported one that was attached to the head caused some to doubt their testimonies, but five different groups of people have observed both conditions in a single person (in whom, of course, *two* bodily separations were taking place—the vehicle of vitality from the physical body and the vehicle of vitality from the Soul Body). These were indicated in *Events on the Threshold of the After-Life*, 1967. (a) The Theosophists (e.g. A. E. Powell) have always described two cords. (b) An astral projector[97] informed T. C. Lethbridge that it applied to him (p. 98). Another astral projector, Mrs. Gladys Osborn Leonard (Case No. 44), noted that many projectors saw their "cord" attached at the head but added, "I believe there is also a connexion . . . with the solar plexus"; An Indian *clairvoyant*[98] and two Americans[99] [100] claimed to have seen both cords; (c) French sensitives who were in *mesmeric trance* told their mesmeriser, Dr. H. Durville[101] that they saw "a wave-motion that comes from two centres, i.e., the solar plexus and the head and (d) Major W. T. Pole[102] observed both cords when a relative was *dying*. Here is another refutation of the psychologist who claimed that all who have described the "silver cord" merely borrowed it from Ecclesiastes—the latter mentioned one "cord" but not two!

Another point is this: many deponents whose doubles had risen above their bodies did not state that they saw their "cords" until they said that they had "looked down", and others whose doubles had begun to move away laterally from their bodies (and were no longer over them) did not state that they saw their "cords" until they said that they "turned round" (see, e.g. Case No. 778)—as would be expected if they were reporting actual observations and not merely repeating a Biblical text the meaning of which is obscure to theologians.

Oliver Fox[103] provides a further strand in the evidence that many who claimed to have seen their "cords" when temporarily free from their bodies were giving actual observations. Fox *felt* the presence of his "cord" on several occasions: he said, "My body was tugging hard . . . At last I could withstand the call no longer. It was as though a mighty cord of stretched elastic . . . overpowered me. I shot *backwards.*" Again, "One is drawn *backward* to the body". Still again, "The *backward* motion . . . very often occurs . . ." It is not surprising that he failed to *see* his "cord" (though the fact did not occur to Fox since he did not realise that *the "cord" is a temporary extension between two temporarily separated bodies*). He neither "looked down" nor "turned round".

(7) *Dim Hades conditions were contacted.*

(8) *The physical body was often cataleptic.* This is to be expected since it had temporarily lost much of the vehicle of vitality (via which it is normally vitalised). The condition is described herein in Cases Nos. 403, 414, 419, 425, 429, 739, 742, 763, 765, 768 and 778. In addition it is mentioned in Cases Nos. 223, 781, 788, 792, 801, 802 and 803.

Typical phrases used include: "powerless to move", "utterly powerless to move", "cataleptic", "absolutely paralysed" and "numb". Miguel Serrano, the Chilean diplomat, united his experience of "vibrations" with catalepsy—"vibrations" continued until his body "became immobile".

It is significant that when Dr. C. G. Jung saw a "ghost" his body became almost cataleptic [the "ghost" could not "materialise" and therefore appear to him unless and until a significant portion of his vehicle of vitality had been withdrawn from his body for the purpose].

It only remains to point out that the death-like condition which is so often described by *those who had out-of-the-body experiences* (many of whom, indeed, thought that they had died) and even more by those who had suffered *pseudo-death,* is comparable to *actual death.* Among the former, Hives (Case No. 59) said, "Anyone seeing my body would think I was dead". Mrs. Veitch (Case No. 311) "knew" she was dying —but she eventually re-entered her body and was "all right".

B—*EVENTS* IN THE SECOND STAGE OF *RELEASE* (THE SECOND—VEHICLE OF VITALITY—"DEATH" = THE SECOND UN-VEILING OF THE SOUL BODY)

(1) *"Mist", "fog", "clouds", "delicate drapery", "a gauze curtain", "a veil", "a black robe", "a silk robe", "a child's dress"* were seen to leave the composite double (= the vehicle of vitality was shed from it).

Cases herein include Nos. 774, 778 and 800. Cayce described *"mist",* J. H. Brown, Mrs. Joy and Mrs. Springer *"water".* On some occasions, Mrs. Piper, in Hades conditions, *"passed through* delicate blue drapery", on others "a veil", on others "a dark robe" and then glimpsed the bright Paradise conditions that correspond to the Soul Body. Lind's friend *"threw off"* a child's dress to get further away from the physical world, i.e., nearer to Paradise. Mrs. Spaulding saw what looked like *"a gauze curtain".*

(The identical phenomenon is described, not by the person concerned but *by observers of death,* of the *permanent* release of the vehicle of vitality: Mme. Isnard's body was seen by the two men present to release a figure which seemed to wear *"a grey veil".* Dennis Bardens recorded a case in which the observer saw *"what looked like a piece of diaphanous material".*

It is also described in "communications" by survivors of death: a "communicator" told Lord Dowding that, when he died, he had moved through *"water"* towards what looked "like a sunrise" [= Paradise]. Rosamond Lehmann's "communicator" similarly "slipped out of *the physico-psychic* [= *vehicle of vitality*] *shell":* his originally composite double had shed the vehicle of vitality: his Soul Body was un-enshrouded.

It is significant that the descriptions ("mist", "water", "a gauze curtain", etc., used to describe the vehicle of vitality when seen at the second "death", are identical to those used to describe the feature at the first death—see I A 1 above—and those used in the return of the double, the reverse of the second "death" C 1, E 1 below.)

(2) *"Cold winds" were sometimes felt* (ditto): these were reported in Case No. 59.

(3) *With this second "death"—the shedding of the vehicle of vitality from the composite double (unveiling the Soul Body)—the Hades sphere, with its "hinderers", was no longer contacted; the bright Paradise sphere, with its helpers, was glimpsed.*

C—*EVENTS* IN THE FIRST STAGE OF *RETURN* (THE REVERSE OF THE SECOND "DEATH" = THE FIRST EN-VEILING OF THE SOUL BODY)

(1) *"Mist", "a silk robe", "a shadow form", etc. (the released vehicle of vitality) re-enveiled the Soul Body.*

Hives (No. 59), Cripps (No. 90) etc., saw "mists". Mrs. Piper, in the Soul Body (a) felt as if something was being "poured over" her [Soul Body] and (b) saw "a silk robe" swirling over her [ditto]. Another saw "a shadowy form".

(2) *"Rushing winds" were sometimes felt* (e.g., by Hives).

(3) *With this re-constitution of a double that was composite (a re-enveiled Soul Body), Paradise conditions were no longer contacted: Hades conditions were re-entered.*

(4) *The double was above the body.*

(5) *The now-composite double re-assumed the (original) horizontal position, preliminary to re-entering the body.*

This was reported herein in Cases Nos. 750, 768 and 814. It was also given in Cases Nos. 44, 70, 74, 85, 99, 244, 301.

(6) *The "cord"-extension (at the solar plexus) was felt to tug the double*—as by Whiteman (No. 244) and Oliver Fox (No. 3), a phenomenon also reported when the double left the body—I A 6.

D—*EVENTS* IN THE SECOND STAGE OF *RETURN* (THE REVERSE OF THE FIRST—PHYSICAL—DEATH = THE SECOND EN-VEILING OF THE SOUL BODY)

The re-constituted composite double re-entered the body and the person concerned "awoke" to physical life.
N.B. *The essential events described as occurring when the body was vacated, i.e., the "mist", the "cold winds" and the horizontal position, were repeated not only in the second "death" (B 1 and 2) but also when the double re-entered the body. These remarkable facts have hitherto been overlooked by all who studied these phenomena: they are readily understood on the hypothesis of a "semi-physical" vehicle of vitality and a "super-physical" Soul Body, i.e., of objective bodies, but not on the hypothesis that the doubles were subjective (either mental images or "archetypes" in the "unconscious").*

THE SUCCESSION OF *EXPERIENCES* IN THE *TEMPORARY RELEASE* OF COMPOSITE DOUBLES
I-*EXPERIENCES* IN THE FIRST STAGE OF *RELEASE* (THE FIRST—PHYSICAL—DEATH = THE FIRST UN-VEILING OF THE SOUL BODY)

(1) *"Tingles", "vibrations", "pins-and-needles", "dizziness" and "giddiness" were felt.* These phenomena were herein described in Cases Nos. 742, 750, 751, 765, 779, 782, 793, 797, 800, 802 and 804, and in numerous earlier Cases (20, 64, 72, 392, 424, etc.). We interpret them as indicating *the loosening, preparatory to projecting, a significant portion of the electro-magnetic vehicle of vitality,* often seen as "mist", "chiffon", etc. and felt as "cold winds". In these cases, i.e., with people who showed signs of having a loose vehicle of vitality, the process continued until a *trance-like* bodily condition was reached (a condition beyond the *natural sleep of non-mediums,* since the vehicle of vitality of the latter merely *disconnects,* and does not definitely project from it. There are, of course, intermediate gradations between natural sleep and trance). The testimony of Mrs. M. Napier, given by A. J. Hill, correlates the "tingle" with the eventual catalepsy of the body (I A 9): her projections began with "a prickly sensation", "like a slight electric current" and the body became cataleptic.

Muldoon[104] observed, "Dizziness is a condition of looseness of the astral body [=vehicle of vitality]" and pointed out that it can be caused by a blow on the head, the abnormal functioning of a vital organ, etc. Other possible causes include anything that upsets the normal harmony of the vehicle of vitality with the body which it animates, a broken habit, the strong direction of the attention away from he body, a shock or jolt, great fatigue, whether mental or physical, illness, intense, unfulfilled desire, etc. He continued, "Regardless of cause, dizziness indicates that the astral body [vehicle of vitality] is not bound tightly to the physical body. When dizzy, we stagger because the astral body is loose and half-inclined to withdraw from the physical." Further, "Whirling will cause dizziness since it loosens the astral body—fakirs resort to whirling to accomplish astral projection."

A patient of Dr. Paul Gibier's, feeling tired, lay down. He said, "I felt dizzy and things seemed to whirl around me: suddenly I found myself [released double] in the middle of the room." G. Buck, cited by Muldoon and Carrington[105] felt "a whirling sensation" and then was "elevated in the air" above his body.

Dizziness often precedes the release of substance from the vehicle of vitality which culminates in *trance*. D. D. Home told the Dialectical Committee, "I feel for two or three minutes in a dreamy state, then I become *quite dizzy* and then I lose all consciousness [of the physical body and things —because the "bridge" between the Soul Body and the physical body has been broken]." With most astral projections (where the double released includes a significant part of the vehicle of vitality) with all cases of trance (where a large part is extruded) and at death (where the whole of the vehicle of vitality is expelled), there is often dizziness, etc., culminating in unconsciousness of the physical body and therefore of the physical world. Typical descriptive phrases include the following: —

"A strong vibration, like electricity";
"Like a continuous electric shock";
"A tingling sensation";
"Terrific vibrations";
"Like a dynamo";
"Like pins-and-needles";
"An odd tingle";
"Vibrations at a great rate of speed";
"Shuddered as from a strong shock";
"Currents like magnetic and electrical currents";
"A tingling sensation";

"An electric sensation";
"Delicate electric shocks";
"Terrific vibrations in stomach [solar plexus]."

Electric-like "tingles" are not only mentioned by those *astral projectors* who show various signs of having a loose vehicle of vitality, i.e., of being of the mediumistic bodily constitution. They are described by (a) mediums who developed the ability to perform *"automatic writing"*. Thus, Miss Howitt[106] described how her father, William Howitt, developed that ability after his wife had attended a seance (an example of "boosting" of psychic power): "Something *resembling an electric shock* ran through his arm and hand, whereupon the pencil began to move . . ." Mme. d'Espérance[66] similarly described *"a tingling, pricking, aching sensation"* in her arm before "automatic writing" began.

(b) The beginning of *trance*, as might be expected, was also heralded by electricity-like sensations. This applied to Mme. d'Espérance. Lord Adare reported that D. D. Home felt *"a tingling sensation"*, as though he were receiving *"an electric shock"*.

(c) *Super-normal raps* were produced by Mrs. de Morgan[107] with each "rap" there was *"a feeling like a light blow or shock of electricity"*.

(d) Allan Kardec described *transfigurations* which were produced by Mme. Krooke, the lady developing a thick beard and a marked resemblance to Kardec's deceased father: the medium felt, throughout her body, *"a prickling, like that of a galvanic battery"*.

(e) *Stigmata* (red pricks, some of which bled) were observed by Malcolm Bird[108] to form on the hand of the "physical" medium Frau Vollhardt: "the medium felt as though *an electric current* had entered at the skin and passed through the body". These marks were not imagined—they were photographed repeatedly by Dr. Schwab.

(f) Another feature which exemplifies the analogy which exists between psychic power and electricity is the "boosting" which often occurs: two or three mediums are better than one, producing stronger "physical" phenomena; contact with a medium (especially at seances) has often caused an apparently non-mediumistic person to become mediumistic—this applied even to Dr. Richard Hodgson the redoubtable S.P.R. investigator.

(g) *Metals are inimical* to both "physical" and electrical phenomena, since they seem to conduct the "current" away and prevent its accumulation. (Those who have undergone

Initiation may remember that they were divested of all metals and metallic substances prior to that event). Vincent Turvey[109] observed, "Silk, hair, and metals are not conducive to, but rather retard, clairvoyant as well as 'physical' phenomena". Rogers[110] described "electric girls" who were famous in 1838 and were investigated by scientists, etc.: when gilt paper was placed between them *"a crackling, like that of electric fluid"* was heard—but the phenomenon ceased whenever a piece of iron was placed on the table. Monroe[111] advised would-be astral projectors "Remove any jewellery or metal objects close to, or touching, your skin".

(h) Dr. Joseph Maxwell (like many others) observed that thundery weather and *electric storms* are inimical to mediumistic trance. He further found that the best conditions for "physical" phenomena (telekinesis, raps, etc.) were those which favoured the production of sparks under the wheels of electric trams, i.e., dry, quiet atmospheric conditions.

(i) P. E. Cornillier's "communicator", Vettelini[112], told him, in France, that when discarnate Souls who are in Paradise conditions "telepath" to mortals, they use the Paradise equivalent of our electric or magnetic currents. Dr. J. Kerner[113], in Germany, found that the strongly-mediumistic (because half-dead) Frau Hauffe was "much affected by electricity in all its forms". He also observed that if, when she was in trance, i.e., with almost all the vehicle of vitality exteriorized, she touched any persons they became clairvoyant (i.e., it caused a release of part of their vehicles of vitality). The above are only a few of the analogies between psychic "power" and electric power.

Many suppose that the study of psychic matters has no Spiritual implications. But the matter of psychic "boosting" appears to have its Spiritual equivalent. The Master[114] said, "If *two of you* agree on earth about any request you have to make that request will be granted by my Heavenly Father. For where *two or three have met together* in my Name I am there among them." (Compare Luke xvii, 21: "The Kingdom of God is *among* you".) St. Paul[115] advised, "See how we may best arouse others to love . . . *not staying away from our meetings* . . ."

(2) *Occasionally the "vibrations" were felt particularly in the solar plexus* (e.g. Case No. 70).

(3) *Noises were heard in the head*: the double, having been loosened, was actually leaving the body. They were recorded in our recent Cases Nos. 782, 797, 802, etc., also

Case No. 177, etc. Fox (No. 31) heard "crackling sounds suggesting electric phenomena", also "crackling and snapping noises": on one occasion (see No. 8) he heard a *"click"* in his head and found that his double was free. He had moved "as though struggling against *the pull of an elastic cord*" and he felt a pain in his *head*. Phrases used include:
"Hissing in the head";
"A buzzing sound";
"A whirring, buzzing sound";
"A whirring noise".

(4) *The release of the vehicle of vitality was sometimes accompanied by a panoramic review of the past life.* The experience was reported herein in our Cases Nos. 760 and 813 and in earlier Cases Nos. 32, 34, 210, 305, 343, 345, 379, 380, 438, 458 and 466. The vehicle of vitality is said to bear a record of all that happens to one throughout life and its stripping from the body exposes that record.

(5) *A "blackout" occurred in consciousness (or the feeling of passing through a dark tunnel—the former representing a rapid and the latter a slow release of the vehicle of vitality*). This was noted herein in Cases Nos. 745, 748, 751, 761, 767, 768, 793 and in earlier Cases Nos. 9, 13, 15, 65, 78, 87, 116, 123, 170, 254, 277, 321, 346, 361, 422, 427A, 451, etc. Phrases used are as follows:
"A period of unconsciousness";
"A blackout"; "A momentary blackout";
"A blackness"; "A moment's blackness";
"A dark tunnel" (into a new world);
"A dark passageway—a light at the end";
"A narrow corridor";
"A momentary clouding of consciousness";
"A lapse of consciousness";
"A second of blank unconsciousness";
"A state of utter blankness";
"A loss of consciousness";
"Fell asleep";
"All became dark"; "Everything was dark";
"Everything went void".

(6) *General dual consciousness (awareness of both the released double and the Hades environment and the vacated physical body and the physical environment) sometimes occurred,* as in our Case No. 751 (and earlier Cases Nos. 13, 19, 31, 39, 44, 56, 58, 61, 64, 78, 104, 105, etc.). Fox (No. 31) said, "Dual consciousness was pronounced—I felt myself

[double] among the stars and [body] on the sofa at the same time."

(7) *The sensation of falling (if consciousness is still in the physical body) or of rising (if consciousness is in the ascending double) was sometimes felt*: i.e., dual consciousness. These sensations were reported in our Case No. 754, also in Cases Nos. 5, 6, 26, 43, 48, 53, 57, 59, 60, 65, 68, 304, 315, etc.

(8) *A "click", or "snap" was heard in the head, as the double finally separated from the body.* This was described in Cases Nos. 20, 31, 49, 81, 180, 192 and 241.

The English actress Miss Nancy Price (Case No. 81) heard "a crackling sensation" in the body, after which there was "a sound like tearing silk" (cf. Mme. Bousissou in France who reported "a sort of silky rustle").

In *The Mechanisms of Astral Projection*[116] we cited P. D. Ouspensky as having observed, "A shock was felt . . . as though a spring clicked". It was also mentioned by Mrs. Keeler's "communicator" and cited in my *The Techniques of Astral Projection*[117], as well as by Mrs. Elizabeth Gaythorpe (*Light*, 1970).

Mrs. Piper, the famous medium, heard "snaps" both when she left her body in *mediumistic trance* and when she re-entered it, i.e., when her vehicle of vitality separated from, and when it re-associated with, the body. Those astral projectors who, having a loose vehicle of vitality, release a composite double could doubtless become strong ("physical") mediums.

(9) *The Soul Body left the physical chiefly via the head* (whereas the vehicle of vitality left chiefly via the solar plexus): this was described in Case No. 770 (also in earlier Cases Nos. 1-4, 23, 31, 47, 55, 60, 67, 69, 83, 90, 91, 97, 118, 213, 215, 220, 223, 224, 230, 245, 246, 254, 271, 287, 293, 360, etc.). Many of those who claimed that their Soul Bodies left via the head also observed that the "cord"-connection was at the physical head.

(10) *An easy release of the double was likened to leaving a glove, a coat, a sack, a garment, a bathing-suit, or like drawing the key out of a Yale lock.* Cases Nos. 770 and 774 are given herein and there are several early Cases (Nos. 15, 84, 95, 181, 277, 301 and 385).

(11) *The composite double (the projected vehicle of vitality plus the necessarily disconnected Soul Body) contacted a dim, "misty", "foggy", even "watery" environment, with "hinderers"* (=*Hades*). This was described herein in Cases Nos. 521, 748, 770, 774, 778, 800, 804, 806, etc., and in earlier

Nos. 17, 18, 25, 32, 43, 59, 73, 90, 97, 124, 126, 208, 244, 249, 258, 277, 296, 329 and 368. The description applies to *mesmeric trance*—see Anna Maria Roos cited in *The Study and Practice of Astral Projection*[118]. Oliver Fox (No. 31) described how he saw "a grinning face" and heard "mocking voices" just before he fell asleep (=when in the hypnagogic state).

"Hinderers" (and some helpers) occur in Hades, whereas the former are absent from Paradise. Attempts to contact the "dead" via the ouija board or "automatic" writing may attract "hinderers" who are delayed in Hades conditions—those who are "earthbound" because "body-bound"—retaining the vehicle of vitality: the direction of attention (the "call") attracts them; a loose vehicle of vitality, in mediumistic, passive people, offers them the "semi-physical" bridge. Two features, namely, *cold winds and tingles*, may indicate that contact has been made. In some few cases *a stench* shows the presence of particularly undesirable entities. It is clear that, although 99% of "obsessions" may be psychological, the 1% which are accompanied by these features are nothing of the sort: they are associations—highly undesirable associations—with discarnate Souls who are of low, even of dangerous type: some are definitely hostile. "Spirits" who are not "called" by particular mortals are unable to contact those mortals: those "spirits" who manage to contact certain mortals do so only because (a) "birds of a feather flock together"—there is a community of essential interest and (b) the mortals invited contact by deliberate passivity (at ouija board or writing table).

The idea that certain "ghosts" (earthbound Souls) may have a bad smell is an undoubted fact (and the reason for it is fairly obvious). In 1834 Dr. J. Kerner published an account of the mediumship of Elizabeth Eslinger in Germany: the "ghost" smelled like a decaying corpse. An account of a similar stench which accompanied a "haunt" near London was given in the *Daily Chronicle*, April 15, 1908: eventually when a decomposing body was found and destroyed, the nuisance ceased. Florence Marryat[119] describing "a charnel-house smell", one like that of "a putrid corpse" in connexion with the medium Miss Showers. Neal[96] was attacked by entities under the command of African "witch-doctors"—there was a stench as of a decaying corpse. "Communications" concerning these matters were given by P. E. Cornillier[120]. Fox (No. 31) felt "very melancholy" in the "dark, foggy" [Hades] realm. Like Muldoon (No. 20) he could perform telekinetic acts while his double included the electromagnetic vehicle of vitality.

Typical phrases in which "hinderers" are described include the following:

> Monroe described "dead" Souls who were "near insane";
> Whiteman felt "an undefinable menace";
> he found that "hinderers" formed "a barrier" to his progress;
> Reine and Yram also found they "formed a barrier";
> Cayce saw "shadowy figures" who "tried to side-track" him;
> Muldoon was attacked by an "earthbound" entity;
> Yram was attacked by "grey, unpleasant entities" who had "grinning faces";
> Stewart White reported "gate-crashers" and "intruders".

(12) *Many who released a composite double (and contacted Hades) found that, between the dim Hades (corresponding to the vehicle of vitatily) and the bright Paradise (corresponding to the Soul Body), there was a "gate", a "door", a "bridge", a "footbridge", a "window", etc., through which passage was difficult, if indeed possible* (for a mortal, i.e., one still attached to the physical body): some "fell", others were "told" to "go back" (to the physical body and therefore to earth-life).

This "gate", etc., to Paradise represents the Hades realm ("the half-way place") and was mentioned herein our Cases Nos. 728, 748, 754, 761, 762, 778 and 789. Mme. Bouissou (Case No. 277) observed, "In projection there is *a 'fringe'* which has to be crossed, the dangerous plane with these sinister fluids [= 'hinderers']."

(13) *There was a remarkable (to mortals an unnatural) (a) indifference to the vacated physical body and (b) even disparagement of it.*

These attitudes were herein mentioned in our Cases Nos. 415, 453, 474, 478, 767, 789 and 828 (and in many earlier Cases, e.g., 36, 331, 351, 354).

Phrases used include the following:

> (a) "I was conscious, in a detached sort of way, of my body";
> "I contemplated the body in a detached way";
> "I looked at it with complete indifference";
> "I did not care what happened to my body";
> "I regarded it with detached indifference";
> "I watched [the surgical operation] as though watching someone else being operated on";
> "That form meant less than nothing to me";

"I was not in the least concerned about my body";
"I looked at my body completely dispassionately";
"My body was no longer of any importance to me";
"My body did not interest me";
"I had a strange feeling of indifference";
"I didn't feel any pain—only indifference";
"My body seemed no longer important to me";
"I had a sort of amused pity for my body";
"I never thought of what I had left behind";
"I looked at myself [body] without emotion";
"I looked at my body with detached curiosity";
"I looked at it in an impersonal way";
"I looked down at it [body] in a wholly detached and impersonal way";
"I had a feeling of complete indifference and detachment";
"I looked down at my body with indifference";
"I felt quite indifferent to it";
"I couldn't bother with it";
"If my body didn't recover, it didn't matter";
"The Real 'I' could not care less";
"A poor, miserable thing";
"A mere physical shell";
"A prison"; "a cage"; "a garment".

The "dead" say the same sort of thing via mediums: thus "H.J.L." told J. S. M. Ward (*Gone West*, Rider, 1917, p.55) that his body, once discarded, meant no more to him than a piece of sculpture.

(14) *Many were reluctant to re-enter the physical body (and so to return to earth-life).* This almost incredible statement (which nevertheless ties up with Statement No. 13) was made in our Cases Nos. 788, 789 and 793 (and in earlier Cases Nos. 11, 13, 18, 19, 32, 40, 43, 44, 53, 57, 59, 61, 65, 66, 85, 90, 92, 113, 125, 127, 128, 130, 139, 164, 179, 208, 327, etc.).

Phases used include the following:
"Why did you bring me back?"
"Why have you brought me back?"
"Why did you not let me die?"
"I staged a rebellion at having to return";
"I felt acute regret";
"I had no wish to return";
"I scorned the idea of returning";
"I did not want to go back";
"To be back in the flesh was a sore trial";

"Returning was the hardest thing I ever did";
"I entered my body with reluctance";
"I was really cross";
"My heart quailed";
"I shall have to return—I shuddered";
"I hated to come back";
"I almost rebelled when I had to come back";
"I experienced a sense of reluctance";
"I wanted to remain there for ever";
"I returned regretfully";
"I had a strong desire to remain";
"It is with regret that one returns";
"I returned to my body with regret";
"I felt a peevish kind of resentment";
"I obeyed against my will";
"I was decidedly unwilling";
"I dreaded to go back";

J—*EXPERIENCES* IN THE SECOND STAGE OF *RELEASE* (THE SECOND—VEHICLE OF VITALITY—"DEATH" = THE SECOND UN-VEILING OF THE SOUL BODY)

(1) *A "blackout" (or tunnel-effect) as the vehicle of vitality was shed from the composite double.* This was described in our Cases Nos. 724, 731, 774, 788 and 800. Earlier Case Nos. in which the "blackout" or "tunnel"-effect are described when the vehicle of vitality left the (composite) double include Nos. 403. Fox (No. 31) walked through "a dark fog" [=Hades], then fell down "a dark tunnel or shaft", after which he saw the "bright colours" [of Paradise]. When in Paradise, a "helper" told him (mentally) not to be afraid.

Phrases used to describe this experience include the following:

"A sensation of being in deep 'water' ";
"A 'river' of darkness";
"A 'river' that has to be crossed";
"I saw a 'light' [that of Paradise] at the end of a tunnel";
"Suddenly I was freed from some blinding substance";
"I seemed to float in a long tunnel which gradually expanded into unlimited space" [Paradise];

"There appeared to be an opening like a tunnel, and, at the far end, a light";
"I fell down a dark tunnel or shaft";
"I went down a long dim tunnel"; "at the end was a speck of 'light' [that of Paradise] which grew as I approached it";
"I seemed to pass through a tunnel and emerge at the end into a scene of bright sunlight [ditto]";
"I passed through a tunnel with a light [ditto] at the far end";
"I was at the bottom of a chimney-like tunnel with a light [ditto] at the top";
"I floated in a tunnel and had a glimpse of a lovely countryside [ditto]".

It is surely significant that the experience of a "blackout" or "tunnel" was described as occurring at three different stages in the total projection: (a) when the vehicle of vitality left the body (= when the two were separating), (b) when the vehicle of vitality was separating from the initially-composite double at the second "death" and (c) when the re-constituted composite double re-entered the physical body: no mental images cause "blackouts" in consciousness.

It is also surely significant that the "blackout" was described by "communicators" as having occurred when they died, both in the first (physical) death and the second (vehicle of vitality) "death". "E.V." for example, told Jane Sherwood[121] that "communicators" compare the second "blackout", when the "etheric" body is shed, to "a deep sleep".

(2) *Hades conditions (corresponding to the vehicle of vitality) were now left and Paradise conditions (corresponding to the Soul Body) were glimpsed though not fully entered* (because the Soul Body was still attached—by the "silver cord"-extension—to the physical body, lowering somewhat its level of consciousness). The "light" mentioned in the phrases cited above (No. 1) was that of Paradise and, in addition to this, "unlimited space", "a scene of bright sunlight" and "a lovely countryside" are glimpsed: the vehicle of vitality of the earth [Hades] had been left and the Soul Body of the earth [Paradise] contacted, via the corresponding ultra-physical bodies of the deponents. This change in environment was mentioned herein in Cases Nos. 778, etc. The description of "a glorious park-like landscape" is of particular interest since the word "Paradise" is an old Persian

word for a park. Other significant descriptions include "blossoms and fruit" and "groups of children" (none of which are ever described as being in the Hades environment).

(3) *A second (emotional) review of the past life, the "Judgment", occasionally occurs.* Examples were given in *The Supreme Adventure*[122]. One lady saw "pictures" of her life on one occasion when she left her body and, on a later occasion, said she saw "the same pictures" but, in addition she had realised the motives behind the actions seen. Admiral Beaufort, almost drowned, saw the events of his past life "accompanied by a consciousness of right or wrong". Another man saw them and realised their "moral significance".

"Starr Daily", a criminal, in a coma, first saw "pictures" of the people he had injured—he said, "Every pang of suffering I had caused others was now felt by me": then he saw all his good deeds and men he had helped: then he awoke "with a sense of well-being, quite free from pain and fear".

The accounts of "communicators" as to their own "Judgment" experiences are given in *The Supreme Adventure*[123].

The few people who experienced the "Judgment" (like the many "communicators") had doubtless highly organised Soul Bodies: both had previously passed through the second "death".

K—*EXPERIENCES* IN THE FIRST STAGE OF RETURN (THE REVERSE OF THE SECOND—VEHICLE OF VITALITY—"DEATH"=THE FIRST EN-VEILING OF THE SOUL BODY)

The bright Paradise conditions (corresponding to the un-enshrouded Soul Body) were left and the dim but earth-like Hades conditions (corresponding to the vehicle of vitality) were re-entered. Before the second "death", when the double was composite, Dr. Kirkland (Case No. 327) found everything "grey" and Cole entered "a gloomy tunnel"; after this reverse of the second "death", when the double again became composite, Helen Brooks (Case No. 55) described "semi-darkness", Yram (No. 84) "greyness" and Miss Horngate (No. 184) "blackness", and so on.

L—*EXPERIENCES* IN THE SECOND STAGE OF RETURN (THE REVERSE OF THE FIRST—

PHYSICAL—DEATH = THE SECOND EN-VEILING OF THE SOUL BODY)

The re-constituted composite double re-entering the body and the person concerned "awoke" to physical life.

(1) *The re-entry of the composite double into the body sometimes caused "vibrations"* (as did its release). This occurred in Cases Nos. 724 and 798.

(2) *There was sometimes a "jolt" at the solar plexus.* This was experienced by Professor J. H. M. Whiteman (Case No. 244) who reported "a sharp jolt at the solar plexus". (This also repeats the experience of *release*.)

(3) *Noises were heard in the head.* Case No. 789 spoke of "whirring sensation", another of "a strange noise" and Mme. Bouissou (Case No. 277) experienced "the same gentle rustle" as when she left the body. (This again repeats the experience of *release*.)

(4) *There was often a sensation of falling* (consciousness was in returning double).

(5) *A "blackout" occurred in consciousness, or the feeling of passing through a dark tunnel, the former representing a rapid, and the latter a slow, return.* Cases herein include Nos. 398, 724, 747, 750. Among earlier Cases are Nos. 311, 327, 335 and 368. Typical phrases are as follows:
"I passed through a tunnel";
"There was a brief darkness";
"I passed through a passage or corridor";
"I lost consciousness for a few seconds";
"I had a sense of faintness and depression".

(Again we note that the experience in return repeats that of the release.)

(6) *Several described the (composite) double as "sucked back" by the body.* This applied to Cases Nos. 52, 105, 287, 291, 360, 368 and it is to be noted that the "communicator" of P. E. Cornillier[124] used the same word.

(7) *An easy return was likened to entering a glove, etc.* This was described in our Cases Nos. 458, 462, 482, 770 and 771 and in earlier Cases Nos. 53, 91 and 140. It was also given by Frances Banks[125]. (Still again we note that this experience of the return repeats that of the release.)

(8) *A very rapid re-entry of the composite double into the body caused a "jolt", "jerk", "click", "bang", "bump", "explosion", etc., i.e., a repercussion.*
Cases Nos. 398, 724, 731, 742, 747 and 750 herein and

earlier Cases Nos. 9, 20, 32, 68, 114, 238, 239, 243, 254, 258, 278, 293, 361, 378, etc., record this significant experience. Fox (No. 31), returning to his body, felt pain in the *head* (as on going out): he heard a *"click"* in the *head* and "was awake".

The following are typical phrases:

"I felt as if my whole self were being split in two";
"At the moment of coincidence, every muscle of the body jerked, and a penetrating pain, as if I had been split open from head to foot, shot through me";
"A jerk which shook me . . .";
"The body seems to jerk a little";
"I snapped back into my body";
"I felt a blow";
"I felt as if someone had hit me very hard";
"I felt as though I had received a blow, as if I had fallen from a height";
"Sometimes a slight, sometimes a sharp jolt";
"Like a flip on the bare brain with a wet towel";
"I received a jolt and woke up";
"With a sort of jolt I was back";
"A sudden shock back into the body";
"It seemed as if a gun went off and I was back";
"I was back with a gigantic bang";
"With what I can only describe as a 'thunderclap', I was back".

Here again, it will be seen, we have the claim—obviously un-noticed by the persons concerned and certainly un-noticed by any medical man, psychologist, parapsychologist or psychiatrist who has written on these matters—of a repetition of what was experienced when the body was vacated. Hives, indeed, made the observation—"*The journey back to my body is the reverse of what it was when coming through the 'mist', the 'rushing wind, followed by darkness' ['blackout'] and I came to my [physical] senses.*"

(9) *Re-entry of the double into the body caused a "blackout" or "tunnel"-effect.* This "blackout" was reported by Cases Nos. 2, 25, 42, 43, 47, 58, 59, 90, 95, 117, 126, 208, 226, 230, 243, 251, 296, 327 and 343. Phrases used include the following:

"A momentary darkness";
"A moment of darkness";

"Darkness and oblivion";
"My sight failed again for a moment and I became [physically] conscious"; [it had "failed for a moment" when the double had *left* the body]
"I fell 'asleep' again";
"I lost consciousness and found myself back in bed";
"There was a complete blackout";
"Everything was dark";
"A gloomy tunnel with shadows";
"A blank space";
"A momentary unconsciousness";
"I lost consciousness for a few seconds";
"An impression of blankness";
"A void until I entered my body";

Mrs. Dowell (No. 25) was among those who observed both this "blackout" and the first: "I 'blacked-out' at the same distance from my body when I approached it and regained my consciousness."

(10) *The person concerned no longer expressed indifference to his physical body (No. 13) or reluctance to re-enter physical life (No. 14): on the contrary, he was highly solicitous of his body and glad to resume physical existence.* Our detailed analyses of hundreds of independent cases confirm Hives' personal generalisation, cited above (No. 8): this repetition provides a remarkable, totally unexpected, and, until now, unrealised confirmation of their testimonies: they were not copied from each other (the deponents had never heard of each other, much less compared notes), they were not imagined (experiences that are imagined by numerous people do not conform to a highly logical pattern) and they are not "artifacts", i.e., deliberate inventions. *Verb. sap.* The repetitions apply to (1) the "tingle" or "vibration" felt (a) just before leaving and (b) just before re-entering the body; (2) certain sensations at the solar plexus (a) just before the double left the body and (b) just before it re-entered it; (3) the "blackout" or "tunnel"-effect at *three* stages, namely (a) when the composite double separated from the body, (b) when the vehicle of vitality separated from the composite double at the second "death" and (3) when the re-constituted composite double re-engaged with the body; (4) the "glove" (etc.) simile that was used to describe both (a) an easy release and (b) an easy return and (5) the noise, most often a "click" in the head, heard (a) when the composite double dissociated from the body and (b) when it re-associated with it.

SIMILAR SUCCESSION OF *EVENTS* AND
EXPERIENCES DESCRIBED BY "COMMUNICATORS"
VIA MEDIUMS REGARDING THEIR OWN
PERMANENT RELEASES FROM THE BODY, i.e.,
DEATHS (AND POSSIBLE *TEMPORARY* AND
PARTIAL RETURNS)

E—*EVENTS* IN THE FIRST STAGE OF *RELEASE*
(THE FIRST—PHYSICAL—DEATH = THE FIRST
UN-VEILING OF THE SOUL BODY)

(1) *"Mist", "a dark shadow" left the body.* This was described by a "communicator", cited in *The Supreme Adventure*, p.15[126], when describing his own death. In *The Techniques of Astral Projection*[127], a "communicator" stated that we human beings possess a "physical atmosphere" which is intermediate (a "bridge") between the physical body and the "Astral" (= Soul) Body, that, when released, "looks like a dark shadow" and that it corresponds to that "atmosphere" of the physical world which was called "the river of death", i.e., to the Hades realm of the Greeks (= the "Amenti" of the ancient Egyptians, the "Sheol" of the Jews, the "Kama Loca" of the Hindus, the "Bardo" of the scholastic theologians, etc.). "Communicators" often call it "the plane of illusion" (= of fantasy), the "greylands", etc., and many (e.g., those cited by F. H. Curtiss[128], *Realms of the Living Dead*, 1917, p.27) liken dying to crossing a river. Astral projectors provide all gradations between "mists" and "water"[129]. A person who received "communications" from "Browning", who was in Paradise, was told, "It is like trying to speak through water" (i.e., through the Hades belt of the earth). The title of a very important series of "communications" received by Geraldine Cummins—described by Prof. C. D. Broad as "strongly suggesting" survival—*Swan on a Black Sea* (Routledge, 1965), was taken from a question posed by one of its readers: "Is there an entity, the Soul, that rises, like a swan, from the black *sea* of death?" The reference was, of course, to the Soul the passing from the "misty", "watery" "semi-physical" Hades aura of the earth into the bright, clear light of the "super-physical" Paradise aura, i.e., to its passing through *the second "death"*. "Browning" had made a similar comparison when he passed through *the reverse of the second "death"* in order to communicate with a mortal: he had to borrow ectoplasm and thus passed from the bright, clear light of Paradise into the "misty", "watery" Hades

conditions. The total bodily condition of the person concerned—whether on earth or in Paradise—determines both the environment which he contacts and the level of consciousness that is available to him.

"Mist", "fog", "a shadowy form", etc., i.e., parts of the released vehicle of vitality, were also seen by many people, to leave *dying* bodies in many lands and at many periods of time. In the case of Mrs. Monk the phenomenon was observed by several people who were present at the death-bed. Dr. R. B. Hout saw "fog", Mrs. de Morgan "a white mist", Miss Tweedale "grey vapour" and T. E. Morgan "smoke". In U.S.A. Mrs. Dresser Mack and Louisa Alcott both reported "mist" as did Mr. Brittain and Mrs. Vivian in England. W. T. Pole saw "a shadowy form". In Australia Mrs. E. Herrick described the "mist" which left a dying person[130].

Because, when newly-released at death, the Soul Body is enshrouded by the whole of the vehicle of vitality, the immediate after-death environment [Hades] often seems to be "misty", "foggy", "dim", "dark", "grey", etc. A "communicator" of Mrs. Kelway Bamber who had been killed in war saw everything as "misty". Private Dowding similarly was in a "mist" which "blurred the vision".

This "fog", etc. (vehicle of vitality) has also been reported as seen leaving the bodies of dying animals, e.g., a cat.

(2) *The released substance was above the vacated physical body.* A number of "communicators" cited in *The Supreme Adventure*[131] described this elevated position.

(3) *The newly-released portion of the vehicle of vitality was often horizontal*[132]. (Death ensues when the whole of the vehicle of vitality is released from the body.) As already said (concerning the temporary release of a significant portion of the vehicle of vitality—A 5 above), this remarkable position emphasises the *objective* nature of the electro-magnetic vehicle of vitality, explaining why it typically remains near the body to which it belongs and to occupy the same horizontal position above it—this double is body-bound (and hence the Soul concerned, in its composite double, is "earth-bound"), contacting the "semi-physical" Hades aura of the earth and not the "super-physical" Paradise aura (which corresponds to the un-enshrouded Soul Body). These were personal observations of the "dead".

The same phenomenon was observed when *other persons* were dying (e.g., by Dr. R. B. Hout, *ibid.*, p.120, who saw the newly-released double of his aunt "suspended horizontally a few feet above the physical counterpart").

Wyatt Rawson[133] described William Blake's drawing of his brother's death—the newly-released double lay horizontally above the vacated body. A similar drawing was mentioned by Mrs. de Morgan[134]: a boy medium made this drawing. In *Intimations of Immortality*[135] we cited other cases of the elevated double (J. C. Street, G. M. Elliott, W. T. Pole, Florence Marryat and E. W. Oaten) and of the horizontal position (W. T. Pole and Mr. "G"). Mrs. G. Vivian, B.A.[136], saw her mother die: she saw, "From the top of her *head* came a *mist* and gradually took shape—like mother". The death of Elisha, about 850 B.C., as described in II Kings, ii, 12, is interesting: "There appeared *a 'chariot' of fire*" [=his luminous electro-magnetic vehicle of vitality] and he went *up* [=above body] by a *"whirlwind"*. The "horses" were doubtless imagined to draw the "chariot", to explain its (upward) movement.

(4) *A "silver cord"-extension was sometimes seen joining the released double to the vacated body.* (cf. A 4 and C 4.)

Phrases used by "communicators" include the following:
  "a cord" ("communicators" of Stead, Cummins, Robertson, etc.);
  "a cord of light" (Stainton Moses);
  "a cord of flame" (ditto);
  "a ray of light" (ditto);
  "a vital current" (ditto);
  "a magnetic cord" (Fitzsimons);
  "a fine, flimsy cord" (Heslop);
  "an 'etheric' cord" (Drayton Thomas);
  "a thin, luminous cord" (Keeler);
  "the cord of life" (Cummins);
  "the umbilical cord" (ditto);
  "a kind of umbilical cord" (Adler);
  "the spiritual life-cord, like the umbilical cord" (Evans);
  "a bond" (Stainton Moses);
  "a tie" (Dr. Vivian);
  "a fine line" (Keeler);
  "a life-line" (Thomas);
  "a 'light' thread" (ditto);
  "a thread of 'light' " (Pierpont and Morgan);
  "a fine electric hair-line" (Lees);
  "a channel of animation" (Livingston).

All the above-cited phrases are given by people who left their bodies only temporarily.

Similar cord-like connections between the released double

and the vacated body are recorded in a number of situations (described in *Events on the Threshold of the After-Life,* p.157): they include (1) hypnosis, (2) anaesthesia, (3) during the production of all "physical" phenomena, (a) telekinesis, (b) direct voice, (c) apports, (d) raps and (e) materialisations. Surely those who have suggested that all descriptions, by astral projectors, of "silver cords" were merely "borrowed" from Ecclesiastes, xii, were in error. Several projectors realised (what "communicators" say) that the snapping of the cord would mean physical death. Several observers of people who died claimed to see the "cord" and saw it snap.[137]

W. T. Pole, Mrs. Leonard and T. C. Lethbridge stated that there are *two* cords (one an extension of the vehicle of vitality and the other an extension of the Soul Body). "Myers", communicating, made the same statement.

(5) *The "silver cord" was often attached at the solar plexus.* This was described by T. Robertson's "communicator" in England while Mrs. Keeler's "communicator" in U.S.A. said, "The Astral [=Soul] Body starts to rise from . . . the solar plexus . . ."

(6) The physical body, vacated by the whole of the electro-magnetic vehicle of vitality, *actually died*: all connection between the vehicle of vitality and the body being completely severed, its re-entry (and therefore that of the Soul Body also, since it was the "bridge" between the two) was impossible.

F—*EVENTS* IN THE SECOND STAGE OF *RELEASE* (THE SECOND—VEHICLE OF VITALITY— "DEATH"=THE SECOND UN-VEILING OF THE SOUL BODY)

A "veil" or "skin" (=vehicle of vitality) left the (*composite*) double which became simple (Soul Body only).

The "communicator" of "A.L.E.H." said, "Hades is merely a condition of rest. For a short time after death the Soul [in its released Soul Body] remains in *a 'veil'* [=the vehicle of vitality which had also left the physical body, so that the immediate after-death double was composite]. This *'veil'* corresponds to the chrysalis[138]. The Soul [Body] eventually breaks through like a butterfly. Certain immature Souls remain in the 'veil' [=are body-bound and therefore "earth-bound"] and make no effort to go further [to pass through the second "death"—shed the vehicle of vitality—and so enter Paradise]. All their yearnings are for earth."

"Lancelot", who had died aged eight and managed to "communicate", gave an identical description of his second "death"—the shedding of his vehicle of vitality—calling it *"a skin"*: "I sort of cast *a skin* like a butterfly coming out of its chrysalis". He urged, "Tell Dad about my getting out of my *shell!* "

Mrs. Keeler's "communicator" (describing *temporary* and not *permanent* releases) said, "One has to go a certain distance from the physical 'atmosphere' [=vehicle of vitality] to get in touch with other [Paradise] planes". The vehicle of vitality "can be detached from the body just as the Astral [Soul] Body can. When it is so detached, a person going out . . . can take it with him [when his double could be composite] or leave it behind [when it would consist of the Soul Body only]".

G—*EVENTS* IN THE FIRST STAGE OF *RETURN* (THE REVERSE OF THE SECOND—VEHICLE OF VITALITY—"DEATH" *BY PROXY*=THE FIRST EN-VEILING OF THE SOUL BODY)

The composite double (either that of a newly-dead person —within a few days of physical death) or of a long-dead ("earth-bound") person, borrowed part of the loose vehicle of vitality of a mediumistically-constituted mortal and this formed a "bridge" between the two: this "bridge" could not be so effective as that which exists between the Soul Body and the physical body of every mortal, permitting the Soul to affect the physical body (and therefore world) and physical acts to affect the Soul. Moreover, it tended to affect the Soul Body of the medium, lowering the level of consciousness. Nevertheless, mental and emotional exchanges between the "dead" and the "living" were possible.

In *The Supreme Adventure*[139] we cited the descriptions of various "communicators" of the "semi-physical" substance which was borrowed: it was "a glow" (=luminous substance), "magnetism", "vibrations" that were "lower" than those of the Soul Body, "a lace-like substance" (cf. "chiffon", "dark shadow", "veil", "mist", "a gauze curtain", "a silk robe", etc., described in other contexts). The substance tended to enveil the Soul Body and so to lower the level of consciousness towards the sub-normal: the "communicators" complained that they tended to be "drowsy", "dazed", "dreamy", "half-alive", "suffocated", "obtuse", "befogged", "misty", etc., but they said that, via this "bridge" they could see, in a restricted fashion, into the physical world.

The "communicator" of "A.B."[140] described the substance as "cloud" or "mist" and that of Stainton Moses as "mist"[141]. That of the Rev. Drayton Thomas[142] described it as the medium's "psychic emanation" (= semi-physical aura). "Hatch", communicating to Elsa Barker[143] in U.S.A. spoke of it as the medium's "vitality", while "Heslop", in England[144] called it a "light", i.e., a luminous, though non-physical, substance.

In *During Sleep*[145] I cited other "communicators" who gave other descriptions of the substance they had borrowed from their mediums—"ether", "tenuous matter", "earthly vibrations", "something of earth", etc.

Kate Wingfield's "communicator"[146] gave highly significant descriptions: "There is a between-link (= vehicle of vitality) which binds the 'dead' to the 'living' . . . Were there no 'river' [Hades, corresponding to the vehicle of vitality] there would be no 'dead' [i.e., the two groups would intercommunicate without the need of the "bridge"] and were there no "bridge" there would be no communication . . . What most hinders the Soul is selfishness . . . selfishness makes it remain longer in the between world [= Hades]."

H—*EVENTS* IN THE SECOND STAGE OF *RETURN* (THE REVERSE OF THE FIRST—PHYSICAL—DEATH —*BY PROXY* = THE SECOND EN-VEILING OF THE SOUL BODY)

The discarded composite double united with the (largely-released) vehicle of vitality of a mediumistically-constituted person, passed from his vehicle of vitality ("aura") into his physical body (vacated for the purpose) and used it to speak, to write, etc.

M—*EXPERIENCES* IN THE FIRST STAGE OF RELEASE (THE FIRST—PHYSICAL—DEATH = THE UN-VEILING OF THE SOUL BODY)

(1) *"Dizziness", "giddiness"* (loosening of vehicle of vitality felt). These "vibrations" were described by Drayton Thomas and Mrs. Kelway Bamber: the latter's son, killed in battle, became "dizzy" and then had "the sensation of falling" (see No. 3 below).

(2) *"Blackout"* or *"tunnel"-effect.* Mrs. Keeler's "communicator" spoke of the "blackout" which occurred when astral projectors *left* their bodies only temporarily: "There is a moment of unconsciousness" and, he added, *"the same on returning"*. He also stated as a fact what the present writer had deduced: that it is *"at the moment of separation"* that this experience occurs: I pointed out that, just as changing gears in a car causes a brief loss of momentum, so changing bodies causes a brief lapse in consciousness.

An eminent lawyer's "communicator" said he had passed through "a tunnel"; "Nigel" told Geraldine Cummins he had "travelled down *a dark tunnel";* Lilian Walbrook's "communicator", hit by a bullet in war, said, "I felt only a nasty shock: I fell *asleep"* (= "blackout", as double left body). In France, Reine, in trance, described a "passing" in which "all became *obscure"* (ditto).

(3) A sensation of *rising or of falling* (according to whether consciousness was in the double or the body)—see No. 1 above.

The "communicator" of Drayton Thomas reported "a sinking feeling", that of Dennis Bradley "a feeling of sinking away", a third said, "I was falling down and through something, as one does in sleep" while a fourth "seemed to be lifted" above the bed on which he was dying.

(4) Soul Body left mainly via *head.* "Heslop", communicating, said, "The process of dying begins at the feet and emerges from the head".

Mrs. Keeler's "communicator", describing *temporary* release, stated that the Astral, or Soul, Body "finally passes out at the top of the head". "Heslop", describing death, said, "It emerges from the head".

(5) Easy release was like leaving *a glove.* The "communicator" of Sandhu Surdar Singh described release as "like drawing the hand out of a glove". "H.J.L.", having died, communicated to J. S. M. Ward (*Gone West, Rider,* 1917, p.28) and described his "passing" as follows: "I began to feel a heavy weight [= his physical body in course of separating from his double]: it was slipping away from me, or rather, I was sliding out of it, as if someone were drawing his hand out of a wet glove".

(6) *Dual consciousness,* i.e., awareness of both the (largely) released double and the (almost completely) vacated body

and the two environments that correspond to them was described as having obtained in the early stage of transition (before, with the breaking of the "silver cord", their separation had become complete). We mentioned this in *The Supreme Adventure*[147]. Pole's "communicator" saw "trees in a fair land" [=Paradise conditions] and was also aware of his dying body. We pointed out that it supports the idea that "the 'level' of consciousness is determined by the prevailing bodily constitution".

A few well attested cases exemplify this state (e.g., the "red scratch" case[148]) and that of Mr. Biberi[149]: it may have a bearing on too-early cremation.

Dual consciousness was also described by those who had *temporary* excursions from the body. Muldoon[150] described this and it is mentioned in our Cases Nos. 13, 19, 20, 31, 39, 44, 58, 61, 64, 78, 105, 142 and 177.

(7) *First (non-emotional) review of the past life* (due to the vehicle of vitality traces).

Many "communicators" describe the experience: they spoke of "scenes of the past life" passing before them:
"My entire life unreeled itself";
"Everything I did came before me";
"I saw the events of my past life in a long procession";
"I saw pictures of my life";
"My thoughts raced over the events of a whole lifetime"; but these particular experiences caused no emotion or sense of responsibility.

(8) *Dim Hades environment contacted* (with "sub-normal" consciousness, fantasies, etc.). We have already, under Events, noted the "misty", "foggy", even "watery" nature of Hades: it is often called "greylands". Earthbound Souls especially complain of "darkness", etc., while Souls who "descend" from Paradise to help the "earthbound" in Hades find the atmosphere "dense" and "suffocating" and say that they do this "at some cost" to themselves.

Mrs. Keeler's "communicator" stated that it was the "interspace" (between earth and Paradise) that gave rise to "the idea of a river of death".

(9) There was a *"cave"*, a *"door"*, a *"doorway"*, etc., the passing through of which meant permanent release. Two "communicators" saw a "door" through which they went in dying. Another entered "a cave", "the 'light' being much stronger outside".

N—*EXPERIENCES* IN THE SECOND STAGE OF RELEASE (THE SECOND—VEHICLE OF VITALITY—"DEATH" = THE SECOND UN-VEILING OF THE SOUL BODY)

(1) *"Blackout"*, *"tunnel"-effect or "sleep"*. Private Dowding "fell asleep for *the second time*", J.H.L. "slept *again*" (see *The Supreme Adventure*, p.17).

(2) Dim Hades conditions were left, bright *Paradise* conditions were entered. Various "communicators" now saw beautiful scenery—a bright and a glorified earth, with wonderful colours, no shadows, etc. Consciousness (in the now un-enshrouded Soul Body) "expanded", "broadened", "widened" and was "delightful". They realised that the Soul Body is the primary body: "the physical body is only the material shell of the 'spirit' Soul Body".

(3) Second (emotional) *review of past life* (due to Soul Body), i.e., the individual *"Judgment"*. This was considered in detail in *The Supreme Adventure*.[151]

"E.K.", communicating, said, "The events of one's past life come back into consciousness. Each incident brings with it the feelings not only of oneself but of all who were affected by those events"; A.L.E.H. was told, "I saw my life unfold before me in a procession of images. I was faced with the effects emotionally of all my actions"; Olive Pixley was informed: "All the pain he had given to people he experienced himself; all the pleasure he had given he received back again"; E.L.B.S. was told, "All my earth-life came through"; Harold Baily: "I watched myself as I had formerly watched and judged others"; Miss Gibbes's "communicator" saw "the emotional reactions" to all her earthly actions and became "a softer person".

Several "communicators" insist that this individual "Judgment" is a personal one: "It is a Judgment of God on us [personalities] through our Higher [Eternal] Selves"; "The Judgment-bar is the Innermost of yourself"; "There is an instinctive feeling that one must work out wrongs done. This way of recovery is in helping others who have exactly similar limitations, difficulties or vices".

(4) *Reluctance to re-enter the body*. "Etta", Drayton Thomas's[152] deceased sister, said, "I should not like to be back again in the body: this is such an interesting life".

O—EXPERIENCES IN THE FIRST STAGE OF "RETURN" (TO THE BODY OF A MEDIUM = THE FIRST EN-VEILING OF THE SOUL BODY)

(1) *"Blackout"* or *"tunnel"-effect.*
"Myers" described entering the body of a medium as like entering "a hollow log, cf. "tunnel".

(2) Bright Paradise conditions with super-normal consciousness were left, Hades with sub-normal consciousness was re-entered and finally the physical world again contacted.

Those "communicators" who are delayed in Hades (the "earthbound", retaining the vehicle of vitality) commonly (a) ask for the prayers of mortals ("Pray for me!"), (b) ask for the help of mortals or (c) try to obtain physical gratification from the contact or even (d) try to obsess. The last-mentioned can be recognised by "cold winds" (withdrawal of ectoplasm from the mediumistic person) and sometimes a stench. Like is drawn to like.

(3) Consciousness tended to be *"sub-normal"*.

Those "communicators" who are in Paradise conditions (in the Soul Body), in order to communicate must "bridge" the "vibrational" gap between their Soul Bodies and the physical bodies of the mediums concerned. They borrow part of the vehicle of vitality of the mediums, re-enveiling their Soul Bodies (and re-forming a double which was composite *but of two origins,*—the "communicator" (Soul Body) and the medium (vehicle of vitality). This obliges them, at first, to re-enter the dim Hades realm with the "sub-normal" level of consciousness that was theirs in the first stage of death (or, during earth-life, of astral projection). They use the following phrases:

"I was in a misty, half-alive state";
"It was like going into a trance or being drugged";
"I was in a sleepy, dreamy condition";
"I was semi-conscious";
"I found difficulty in remembering";
"It was like looking at a misty picture";

This temporary return to Hades, or near-Hades, conditions, with a temporary "sub-normal" (dream) level of consciousness accounts for many apparent errors in "communication".

P—*EXPERIENCES* IN THE SECOND STAGE OF "RETURN" (TO THE BODY OF A MEDIUM = THE SECOND EN-VEILING OF THE SOUL BODY)

The permanently-released Soul Body, having become composite by borrowing part of a medium's vehicle of vitality, may go further and temporarily "possess" his physical body, using it temporarily for speaking, writing, etc.[153]

We make the following observations concerning the above summaries and certain inter-related items.

(1) As regards *temporary* projections (the testimonies concerning which were given at first hand and were not communicated via mediums) and the "mist", etc. (interpreted as part of the substance of the electro-magnetic vehicle of vitality) reported: (a) "mist" was seen to leave the physical body, necessarily also disconnecting the Soul Body from it and forming a double that was composite in nature; (b) "mist" was described as later leaving the original (composite) double, thus un-veiling the Soul Body (a now simple double); (c) "mist" still later re-joined, and re-enveiled, the Soul Body, re-forming a composite double (which then re-entered the person's hitherto vacated physical body), completing the cycle of events—from "normal" (waking) consciousness, via (a) sub-normal consciousness and (b) super-normal consciousness, and back via sub-normal consciousness to "normal" (waking) consciousness. All these changes in the level of consciousness were determined by the bodily constitution at the time, i.e., physical body (a) vehicle of vitality plus Soul Body, (b) Soul Body only, (c) vehicle of vitality plus Soul Body and back to physical body.

(2) As regards *permanent* projections, involving the death of the physical body (the testimonies concerning which necessarily came to us via mediums) and the "mist", etc. (interpreted as the whole of the substance of the electro-magnetic vehicle of vitality) reported: (a) "mist" was seen to leave the dying physical body, necessarily also disconnecting the Soul Body from it and forming a double that was composite in nature and (b) "mist" was described as later leaving the original (composite) double, thus un-veiling the Soul Body (a now simple double): (c) although the (composite) double of the dead person could not re-enter his own body (because it had been completely emptied of the animating vehicle of vitality and any remaining cord-like extensions had been severed), it contrived, in a very few cases, to unite with the vehicle of vitality of a (mediumistic) person and, in still

fewer cases, pass thence into his (vacated) physical body, using it to speak, to write, etc.: this process involved the borrowing, by the discarnate Soul, of "mist" from the vehicle of vitality of the medium—the process was analogous to, though not identical with, that which occurred in temporary projections, a fact which has hitherto been overlooked. The (eventually composite) double of the discarnate Soul included sufficient "bridge"-material (vehicle of vitality, both his own and that borrowed from the medium) to control and use, in a restricted manner, an alien physical body, that of the medium.

Correlated with these bodily conditions and levels of consciousness were corresponding environments—the physical body with the physical world, the vehicle of vitality with the Hades aura of the earth and the Soul Body with the Soul Body of Paradise sphere of the earth.

A number of deponents gave descriptions which correlated two or more items as described by others (for the items are based on personal descriptions and are not entirely mutually exclusive): both certain astral projectors (Oliver Fox, J. H. Brown, Mrs. Joy and Mrs. Springer) and certain "communicators" (those of Lord Dowding) correlated *"mist"*, *"fog"*, etc. (= representing either the vehicle of vitality of man or the Hades aura of the earth) with *"water"* (hence the oft-mentioned "river" of death, "Jordan", etc.—see temporary projections A1, B1, C1, permanent projections E1).

Annie Brittain, the famous medium, correlated *"cold winds"* with "vibrations *at the solar plexus"* (see temporary projections A3, C6, I2, L2, permanent projections E3).

The numerous observations, made quite independently, by investigators of trance-mediums (Home, d'Espérance, Crandon, Tomczyk) and by illiterate natives of Polynesia and Australia (their "clever men", i.e., trance-mediums) provide a correlation between *"cold winds"*, *telekinesis* and *the "silver cord"-extension* which exists between the partly-released vehicle of vitality and the partly-vacated physical body, plus a correlation between *"vibrations"* at *the solar plexus* and *the frequent attachment of the "cord" at that point*. See temporary projections A2, A3, B2, C2, C6; permanent projections E5, I2, L2.

Oliver Fox[154] correlated the "fog" of the Hades aura of the earth with *a "tunnel"* (through which he underwent the second "death", passing from Hades into a Paradise—see temporary B1, C1; permanent F1). He also correlated *noises in the head* with *"electrical phenomena"*, (i.e. = *"tingles"*, *"vibrations"*, *"dizziness"*) (see temporary projections I_3, L_3; permanent projections F_1) and with the electro-magnetic vehicle of vitality. He further correlated *pain in the head*, felt when the Soul Body was released, with the point of attachment of the released Soul Body, i.e., with the "silver cord"-extension (see temporary projections I 8, 9) and this further with *a "click" in the head* on return (see temporary projections K_3).

The above takes into consideration only a few of the correlations between the several items described by different deponents, and not, of course, realised until they were analysed in detail. Critics are *invited* to take the testimonies which I cite in my books and/or any others that purport to describe either temporary or permanent projections, and to make a *coherent* summary which differs in *any* essential detail from those given above. Dr. F. C. S. Schiller said, "Single facts can never be 'proved' except by their *coherence in a system*. But, as all facts come singly, anyone who dismisses them one by one is destroying the conditions under which the conviction of new truth could arise in his mind". "What does 'proof' mean?" asked Sir Oliver Lodge. He replied, "A 'proof' means *destroying the isolation of an observed fact, the bringing it into its place in the system of knowledge*".

We have (above) cited Dean Inge that thousands desire a belief that does not rest on tradition, authority or evidence but *"on human experience"*. This we now have.

To conclude: physical death, so dreaded by so many, is a minor incident in a well ordered, and beneficent process; once it is understood it is accepted with gratitude.

SUMMARY OF *EVENTS* IN *TEMPORARY* RELEASES (A, B, C, D)
(v. of v. = vehicle of vitality; S.B. = Soul Body)

A. RELEASE: STAGE I, THE FIRST—PHYSICAL—DEATH: THE FIRST UN-VEILING OF S.B.
1. "Mist", "fog", "chiffon" (v. of v.) left body, disconnecting S.B. also. Released double therefore composite (v. of v. plus S.B.) cf. temporary B 1, C 1; permanent E 1, F, G.
2. "Winds" felt (= ectoplasmic phenomena from v. of v.). cf. temporary B 2, C 2.
3. "Vibrations" (v. of v. being released) felt at solar plexus. cf. temporary C 6; permanent E 5; temporary I 2, L 2.
4. Double above body. cf. temporary C 4; permanent E 2.
5. Released double often horizontal (it is electromagnetic part of a total body); cf. temporary C 5; permanent E 3.
6. "Silver cord"-extension between double and body. cf. permanent E 4.
7. Dim Hades conditions (corresponding to v. of v.) were contacted via composite double. cf. temporary B 3, C 3, E 6, G.
8. Vacated body was cataleptic, death-like, cf. permanent E 6.

B. RELEASE: STAGE II, THE SECOND — VEHICLE OF VITALITY — "DEATH": SECOND UN-VEILING OF SOUL BODY
1. "Mist", "fog", "a gauze curtain" left composite double, S.B. being no longer en-veiled by v. of v.; double now simple. cf. temporary A 1, D 1; permanent E 1, F. G.
2. "Winds" felt (v. of v.) cf. temporary A 2, C 2.
3. Bright Paradise conditions (corresponding to S.B.) glimpsed. cf. temporary A 7, C 3.
(Go to column on right)

(Compare events in permanent projections, E, F, G, H below).
The re-constituted composite double (v. of v. plus S.B.) re-entered the physical body: the projector "awoke" in his physical body and therefore to physical conditions. cf. temporary A 7; permanent H.

D. RETURN: STAGE II THE REVERSE OF THE FIRST—PHYSICAL—DEATH: SECOND EN-VEILING OF S.B.
6. "Silver cord" - extension at solar plexus. cf. temporary A 3, I 2, L 2; permanent E 5.
5. Double horizontal. cf. temporary A 5, C 5.
4. Double above body. cf. temporary A 4; permanent E 2.
3. Hades re-contacted, cf. temporary A 7, B 3; permanent E 6, G.
2. "Winds" felt (v. of v.) cf. temporary A 2, B 2.
1. "Mist", "a silk robe", "a shadowy form", etc., re-enveiled S.B. double again becoming composite. cf. temporary A 1, B 1; permanent E 1, F.

C. RETURN: STAGE I, REVERSE OF SECOND—VEHICLE OF VITALITY—"DEATH": THE FIRST EN-VEILING OF S.B.
(Read upwards)

SUMMARY OF *EVENTS* IN *PERMANENT* RELEASES (E, F, G, H)
(v. of v. = vehicle of vitality; S.B. = Soul Body)

(Start here and read downwards)

E. RELEASE: STAGE I, THE FIRST—PHYSICAL—DEATH: THE FIRST UN-VEILING OF S.B.
1. "Mist", "a dark shadow" (v. of v.) left body, disconnecting S.B. Released double therefore composite (v. of v. plus S.B.). cf. temporary A 1, B 1, C 1; permanent F, G.
2. Double above body. cf. temporary A 4, C 4.
3. Double often horizontal. cf. temporary A 5, C 5.
4. "Silver cord"-extension. cf. temporary A 6.
5. "Cord" often attached at solar plexus. cf. temporary A 3, C 6; permanent I 2.
6. Hades contacted. cf. temporary A 7, B 3, G.
7. Body died. cf. temporary A 8.

F. RELEASE: STAGE II, THE SECOND — VEHICLE OF VITALITY—"DEATH": THE SECOND UN-VEILING OF S.B.
A. A "veil" or "skin" (v. of v.) left composite double, un-veiling Soul Body; double now simple. Paradise glimpsed. cf. temporary A 1, B 1, C 1; permanent E 1.

(Go to column on right)

H. The discarded (composite) double united with the (largely released) v. of v. of a mediumistic person, passed into the (largely vacated) body of the latter, temporarily possessing it and using it to speak, to write, etc. cf. D.

RETURN: STAGE II, THE REVERSE OF THE FIRST — PHYSICAL — DEATH, BY PROXY!: SECOND EN-VEILING OF S.B.
G. The (permanently released) double either (a) included the v. of v. (usually soon after death) or (b) borrowed "mist", "cloud", "vibrations", "psychic emanations", "vitality", "tenuous matter", "a lace-like substance", etc. from the v. of v. of a mediumistic person. cf. temporary A 1, B 1, C 1; permanent E 1, F, forming a "bridge" for mental and emotional exchanges: neither full Hades nor full Paradise entered. cf. A 7, B 3, C 3, E 6.

RETURN: STAGE I, THE REVERSE OF THE SECOND — VEHICLE OF VITALITY—"DEATH" AND THAT BY PROXY! FIRST EN-VEILING OF SOUL BODY.
(Read upwards)

SUMMARY OF *EXPERIENCES* IN *TEMPORARY* RELEASES
(I, J, K, L) (v. of v. = vehicle of vitality; S.B. = Soul Body)

I. RELEASE: STAGE I, THE FIRST—PHYSICAL — DEATH: THE FIRST UN-VEILING OF S.B.
1. "Tingles", "vibrations", "dizziness", "giddiness" felt (v. of v.). cf. temporary L 1, permanent M 1.
2. "Vibrations" felt at solar plexus (chief exit of v. of v.). cf. temporary A 3, C 6, L 2; permanent E 5.
3. Noises heard in head. cf. temporary L 3, permanent M 7.
4. Non-emotional review of past life (memory-traces in v. of v.). cf. permanent M 7.
5. "Blackout" or "tunnel"-effect (as double separated from body). cf. temporary J 1, L 5; permanent M 2, N 1, O 1.
6. Dual consciousness (while projection is incomplete). cf. M 6.
7. Sensation of rising or falling. cf. temporary L 4; permanent M 3.
8. "Click" heard in head. cf. temporary L 7.
9. S.B. left chiefly via head. cf. permanent M 4.
10. Easy release was like leaving a glove. cf. temporary L 6; permanent M 4.
11. Dim Hades realm (corresponding to v. of v.) contacted, consciousness sub-normal. cf. temporary J 2, K; permanent M 8, N 2, O 2.
12. Indifference to, even disparagement of, body. cf. temporary L 8.
13. Reluctance to re-enter body.

J. RELEASE: STAGE II, THE SECOND — VEHICLE OF VITALITY—"DEATH": THE SECOND UN-VEILING OF S.B.
1. "Blackout" or "tunnel"-effect (v. of v. separating from composite double). cf. temporary I 5, L 5; permanent M 8, N 2, O 2.
2. Dim Hades realm left, bright Paradise glimpsed, consciousness super-normal. cf. temporary I II, K, permanent M 8, N 2, O 2.
3. Emotional review of past life (= "Judgment"). cf. permanent N 3.
(Go to column on right)

(Compare experiences in permanent projections, i.e., at death—M, N, O, P, below)

8. The person was no longer indifferent to, but careful of, body. cf. temporary I 12: consciousness normal.
7. Rapid entry caused "jolt", "click". cf. temporary I 8.
6a. Easy entry glove-like. cf. temporary I 10; permanent M 5.
b. Crash entry like being "sucked back".
5. "Blackout" or "tunnel"-effect (double re-entering body). cf. temporary I 5, J 1; permanent M 2, N 1, O 1.
4. Sensation of falling. cf. temporary I 7; permanent M 3.
3. Noises in head. cf. temporary I 3; permanent M 7.
2. Jolt at solar plexus. cf. temporary A 3, C 6; permanent E 5.
1. "Vibrations" felt. cf. temporary I 1; permanent M 1.

L. RETURN: STAGE II, THE REVERSE OF THE FIRST—PHYSICAL — DEATH: SECOND EN-VEILING OF S.B.
The re-veiling, by the v. of v., of S.B., sometimes with "tunnel"-effect (cf. I 5, M 2), re-constituting a composite double: bright Paradise conditions left, dim Hades conditions entered, consciousness now sub-normal. cf. temporary I II, J 2, M 8, N 2, O 2.

K. RETURN: STAGE I, REVERSE OF SECOND — VEHICLE OF VITALITY—"DEATH": FIRST EN-VEILING OF SOUL BODY

(Read upwards)

SUMMARY OF *EXPERIENCES* IN *PERMANENT* RELEASES
(M, N, O, P) (v. of v. = vehicle of vitality; S.B. = Soul Body)

(Start here and read downwards)
M. RELEASE: STAGE I, THE FIRST — PHYSICAL—DEATH: FIRST UN-VEILING OF SOUL BODY
1. "Dizziness", "giddiness" felt. cf. temporary I 3, L 3.
2. "Blackout" or "tunnel"-effect. cf. temporary I 5, J 1, L 5; permanent N 1, O 1.
3. Sensation of rising or falling. cf. temporary L 4.
4. S.B. left chiefly via head. cf. temporary I 9.
5. Leaving body like leaving glove. cf. temporary I 10, L 6.
6. Dual consciousness. cf. temporary L 6.
7. Non-emotional review. cf. temporary I 6.
8. Hades contacted, consciousness sub-normal. cf. temporary I II, J 2, K; permanent M 8, N 2.
N. RELEASE: STAGE II, THE SECOND-VEHICLE OF VITALITY—"DEATH": SECOND UN-VEILING OF SOUL BODY
1. "Blackout" or "tunnel"-effect. cf. temporary I 5, J 1, L 5; permanent M 2, O 1.
2. Dim Hades left, bright Paradise glimpsed, consciousness· super-normal. cf. temporary I II, L 8; permanent M 8, O 1.
3. An emotional review of past life (= the "Judgment"). cf. temporary J 3.
(Go to column on right)

The permanently-released double (= the ultra physical body of the "dead" man) may enter and temporarily possess the (temporarily vacated) physical body of a mediumistic person, speaking and writing through it: consciousness would be partly normal, partly sub-normal.

P. RETURN: STAGE II, REVERSE OF FIRST — PHYSICAL — DEATH, BY PROXY!: SECOND EN-VEILING OF SOUL BODY
3. Paradise left, Hades entered. cf. temporary I II, J 2, K; permanent M 8, N 2.
2. "Blackout" or "tunnel"-effect ("hollow log"). cf. temporary I 5, J 1, L 5; permanent M 2, N 1.
1. The "semi-physical" substance which is borrowed from the medium's v. of v. enveils S.B. and causes sub-normal consciousness.

O. RETURN: STAGE I, REVERSE OF SECOND — VEHICLE OF VITALITY — "DEATH" BY PROXY!: FIRST EN-VEILING OF SOUL BODY
(Read upwards)

The two Tables given on pp. 171-2, represent summaries of the events and experiences that have been described by people who released a composite double (the release of the "bridge", represented by the vehicle of vitality, necessarily also disconnecting the Soul Body from the physical) and both the projection of a composite double from the body and its re-entrance into it take place in *two stages*. Many have supposed (and stated it as an obvious fact) that all doubles seen are merely images (of physical bodies): but no mental image has ever been described as appearing (and subsequently disappearing) in two stages! These are objective bodies, the vehicle of vitality being both "semi-physical" and "semi-mental" and the Soul Body being "super-physical".

It will now also be clear that in those cases in which only one bodily feature, either the vehicle of vitality or the Soul Body, is released (and this in a single stage), it is objective and not subjective. It is, of course, undoubted that someone occasionally *imagines* that he sees a physical body (and such a phenomenon would be *subjective*): there is much evidence to indicate that many doubles were not imagined—they were objective "semi-" and "super-" physical bodies.

Another point: the Belgian author, Maurice Maeterlinck, observed, "If the revelations of the mystics contain no unconscious reminiscences of what they have read, we find in them so many analogies with the teaching, which later became esoteric, of the great primitive religions, that we should be compelled to believe that . . . *this teaching exists, identical, latent and unchanged, corresponding with some objective and universal Truth*". Citing Maeterlinck's statement in *The Techniques of Astral Projection*[155] we provided an Appendix (I, p.54) in which were tabulated details that occurred in "communications" from the supposed dead: of twenty of these, no less than thirteen were not specifically mentioned by either of the experts in astral projection, namely, Dr. Lancelin in France and Dr. Carrington in U.S.A. Maeterlinck's requirement was fulfilled.

A third and by far the most important point: It is natural that a mortal, a personality, should regard the physical body (and the physical world that he cognises through it) as the touchstone of reality, and regard anything "higher" as unreal, i.e., the Soul with its Soul Body (and the Paradise aura of the earth that corresponds to it), the Over-soul, or Eternal

Self, the Atman of the Hindu, with its True Spiritual Body (and the True "Heaven" that is contacted through It), the Cosmic Christ (the Father-in-manifestation—John i, 1-4), which resembles a vine with the Over-souls of men as its "branches" (John xv, 1, 5) and, finally, the Unmanifested "Father".

But all these—and many other—studies indicate the reverse: God-the-Father is Absolute Reality, the Origin and the End of all else (Rev. i, 8). The reality of Over-souls, of Souls and of personalities is derived from and dependent upon the Unmanifested "Father" who manifests as the Cosmic Christ in the Over-souls of men. Each Over-soul, with a Spiritual Body, manifests through a Soul, with a Soul Body, and each Soul through a physical personality (the "semi-physical", "semi-mental" vehicle of vitality acting as a "bridge").

Hence, those personalities who "wait upon the Lord shall renew their strength"[156]. We mortals do well to "wait" quietly upon God daily (a) on awakening from sleep, (b) about mid-day and (c) prior to entering sleep, always with the attitude, "speak, Lord, thy servant listens!"[157]. This procedure sets up a rhythm which is of inestimable value: it, as well as intellectual development, is of the first importance[158].

So—what, one is asked, is God "like"?: "He" is obviously "like" nothing in the Universe! "He" is indescribable in human terms: "He" can be experienced, but not explained. "He" *is* courage, active good-will or kindness (therefore accepting fully every single personality in the world), truth, beauty, etc. Though described as "love"[159] that word, with our personalities, often means no more than a sentimental fondness. Courage, good-will, truth, beauty, etc.. are not, as we tend to suppose, qualities or attributes of God but "objective" expressions and manifestations of "His" nature and, in so far as any personality thinks, speaks and acts courageously, kindly, truly, beautifully, etc., that personality is expressing and manifesting God. He can do this only through the help of the Cosmic Christ, God-in-manifestation ("As the Father has life-giving power in Himself, so has the Son, by the Father's gift[160]"—"Without Me, you can do nothing[161]). St. Paul realised this ("I can do all things through Christ who strengthens me[162]").

But there often seems to our personalities a hiatus between *the receipt*, by the Soul, of courage, kindness, truth, beauty, etc., and *their appearance in the personality*. This is due to the "blinkering" effect of the relatively dense and sluggish physical body on the relatively subtle Soul Body. Extremely few people have been conscious of having received a single telepathic impression from another person—yet the majority of our most eminent psychologists and parapsychologists have considered that there is good evidence that telepathy is taking place between Souls *all the time*! Similarly, our studies show that it is practically certain that, although we may not "remember" details on "awakening" in the morning, i.e., on re-entering the "blinkers-like", sluggish physical body, all average decent persons (i.e. all whose Soul Bodies are organised by decent living so that they are usable as instruments of consciousness *apart from the physical body*), in addition to receiving telepathic impressions from others, both "alive" and "dead", obtain glimpses of Paradise conditions and their "departed" loved ones therein during periods of deep sleep, i.e., when the Soul Body is almost quite free from both the physical body and its vehicle of vitality. Although details extremely rarely "get through", there is sometimes an unmistakable indication, a peculiar, inexplicable happiness on awakening.

Hence, doubtless, the Master[163] advised, in addition to "*Ask* and it shall be given you[164]", "*Believe that you [Soul] have received . . . and you shall have it*": the personality must have faith and perseverance to bridge the "gap" between the Soul (which *has* received the gift) and the personality (which must become *conscious of* that receipt). As Wordsworth found, "We [Souls] are greater than we [personalities] know". The greatest of American psychologists, William James (*The Varieties of Religious Experience*, Longmans, 1902), was more explicit: he insisted that our "normal" consciousness—that of the physically-embodied personality—is only "a special type of consciousness", that, all about it, "parted from it by the flimsiest of screens [= "veils", "shrouds", i.e., the physical body] there lie potential forms of consciousness entirely different" [= the "supernormal" consciousness that is allowed by the "super-physical" Soul Body and the mystical or spiritual consciousness that is allowed by the transcendent True Spiritual Body]. He realised that we may go through life without suspecting the existence of these "higher" and more significant types of consciousness, the psychic and the Spiritual. "But," he said, "apply the requisite stimulus [= pray, meditate and serve and so "lift", or rather temporarily shed, the "veils"], and, at a touch, they are there complete, definite types of mentality which probably somewhere [in the Paradise and Spiritual Realms respectively] have their field of application". He further pointed out: "They may determine attitudes [e.g., one's disposition to accept psychic and Spiritual truths, to believe in survival in Paradise and in the True Heavens], though they cannot give a map [a simple description expressed in terms of physical space and time—since the physical world has only three dimensions, the Hades world four, the Paradise World probably five and the Spiritual World an infinite number]."

One of the objects of "waiting upon God" is for the personality to become conscious of the life of (a) the Soul and, still "higher" or "deeper" (b) that of the Over-soul or Eternal Self (which is a "branch" of the "Vine"), and thus of the "Father". Integration, "one-ness", "holiness" (=wholeness) follows faithful perseverance in this exercise. But it will be evident that, until the personality becomes aware of the receipt, in the Soul, of the courage, etc. from the "Father" and mediated by the "Son", he must have faith that it has indeed been so received, since the Soul is much greater than and more or less inaccessible to the personality. Hence the Master's words ("Whatever you pray for *in faith* you will receive"—Matt. xxi, 22; "Whatever you [personality] ask for in prayer, *believe that you [Soul] have received it* and it will be yours[165]"). This is not, as might be supposed, an invitation to self-deception (a hypnotic exercise) but to self-knowledge. The personality "proves" the promises made by expressing them in deeds, and noting the results, just as rigorously as a scientist "proves" his hypotheses via the experiments he makes. "Hear what I say and *act upon it*[166]", "Hear the Word of God and *keep* it[167]", "*Do* the will of God and you shall know the doctrine . . .[168]"; "Whoever cares for *his own* safety is 'lost'; but if a man will let himself be 'lost' for my sake, he will find his True (Eternal) Self (=Over-soul)[169]". The ideal is, of course, that occasional awareness of God will become continuous[170]: St. Paul evidently attained this. He said, "The life I [personality] now live is not my life, but the life which Christ lives in me".

As already said, the "semi-physical" vehicle of vitality acts as a "bridge" between the "super-physical" Soul Body and the physical body: it will be clear that angers, fears, etc., "cloud" both the Soul Body which receives courage, etc., from God and the "bridge" via which it is transmitted to the personality. In the words of John Keble ("Sun of my Soul"), these are "clouds" which obscure one's vision. (Given time, they also, of course, eventually appear for all to see in the physical body.)

The "bridge" is adversely affected by tranquilisers, sleeping-drugs, alcohol, etc. It is beneficially affected by steady, rhythmical breathing in which the abdomen, as well as the chest, is gently filled and adequately emptied.

CORRESPONDENCE BETWEEN MICRO-COSM(MAN) AND MACRO-COSM(UNIVERSE)

We have seen that, in addition to (a) the familiar physical body, man is equipped with (b) a "semi-physical" vehicle of vitality, (c) a "super-physical" Soul Body and (d) a transcendent true Spiritual Body: his possible "levels" of consciousness are determined by which body is in use at the time (a) "normal" consciousness, (b) "sub-normal" (c) "super-normal" and (d) Cosmic, Mystical or Spiritual consciousness respectively—see *The Supreme Adventure*[171] and *The Study and Practice of Astral Projection*[172]. Occasionally, in the early stage of the release or projection of a double from the body, when separation is only partial, there is the remarkable phenomenon of dual consciousness (awareness via both the partially-liberated double and the partially-vacated body): this is one of the many facts which are readily understood on the objective body hypothesis but not at all on the imaginary double, the mental image (or the "archetype") hypothesis. The phenomenon also occurs occasionally, during the process of permanent release from the body (see *The Study and Practice of Astral Projection*[173]).

Our physical bodies—calcium, sulphur, phosphorus, oxygen, etc., come from the physical world and eventually return to it. Our ultra-physical bodies doubtless also come from, and return to, ultra-physical worlds (the vehicle of vitality from (and to) the Hades aura of the earth, the Soul Body from (and to) the Paradise aura of the earth and the true Spiritual Body from (and to) the true Heavens).

In South Africa, Professor J. H. M. Whiteman, in his classic work, *The Philosophy of Space and Time*[174], recognised three psychological levels, (a) that which corresponds to the physical, (b) a level which tends towards physical experience [doubtless via the vehicle of vitality and the Soul Body] and (c) "an essential", the "highest" level [= the true Spiritual level].

In U.S.A., Michael M. Hare's *The Multiple Universe*[175]

was reviewed by Martin Ebon[176] as follows: "The concept of a pluralistic universe was developed by William James, and, as Jan Ehrenwald observed, *man is a citizen of many worlds . . .*" This was, of course, said long before in the Scriptures where the vehicle of vitality is mentioned (as "the breath of life[177]") and the Soul Body[178], while the Master assured us, "In my Father's house are many mansions[179]" and promised one of the criminals who was with Him on a cross, "Today you shall be with Me in Paradise" (Luke xxiii, 43) and Who Himself "ascended into Heaven[180]".

Hare considers that each person has "at least two bodies" (doubtless meaning the physical and the Soul Body), one of which has "a counterpart planet" (doubtless meaning the Paradise sphere). This deduction was, of course, claimed as a matter of *first-hand observation* by clairvoyants, astral projectors and "communicators".

EFFECTS OF OUT-OF-THE-BODY EXPERIENCES ON THOSE WHO HAD THEM

(1) *They realised that the Soul Body is man's primary body* (and his physical body only secondary, for thought, feeling, willing, etc.). This applied to Cases herein Nos. 392, 396 and 481 and to earlier Cases Nos. 7, 15, 32, 51, 52, 83, 179, 222, 290, 301, 310, 374, etc.

Phrases used include the following:

"The Real Me occupied a body of a different texture";
"Strive for the Form [Soul Body] which existed before heaven and earth were laid down";
"I realised that my body is not really Me [Soul]";
"The real 'I', the one which thought and acted, looked down on my sleeping self";
"Consciousness [Soul in Soul Body] was apart from it [physical body], something distinct in itself";
"The Real Me is apart from my physical body";
"The Soul can live apart from the body";
"I was outside the body yet I could see and hear";
"To find that, though dead, I still had form [Soul Body], was new to me";
"I can function independently of the body";
"The body is not Me [Soul with Soul Body]";
"The body was not the Real Me";
"I was far more alive and well than when in my body";
"Spirit [Soul in Soul Body] is quite separate";

"The Soul is separate and indestructible";
"I [Soul] am a completely separate entity from it [body]";
"I deliberately got up and walked away from my body";
"Mind [Soul] and matter seem to be separate";
"Consciousness was apart from it [body], something distinct";
"One realises that the body has a life of its own and yet without power to act without the mind";
"There is the corpse in which I lived";
"I was alive and thinking though separated from my body";
"I was outside my body and yet able to see and hear";
"I knew the double is separate [from the body] and indestructible";
"Body and Spirit [Soul] are quite separate";
"I [Soul] am a completely separate entity";
"Now I know that I am a Soul—that I can exist apart from my body".

(2) *They were sure of survival of bodily death.*

This applies to Cases herein Nos. 392, 396 and 481 and to earlier Cases Nos. 1, 2, 12, 15, 17, 20, 27, 56, 67, 72, 74, 76, 117, 139, 144, 158, 160, 170, 171, 179, 185, 188, 189, 195, 217, 293, 304, 309, 324, 346, 352, 376 and 378.

Phrases used include the following:
"The knowledge I gained assured me of a future life";
"I had passed beyond death and will never dread it again";
"The old terror had passed for ever";
"Death is like twilight into sunshine";
"I know that death does not end all";
"Death is the doorway to the life beyond";
"Previous doubts were now swept away";
"I have another [the Soul] Body that will survive the flesh body";
"Death is not what we feared";
"I will never be afraid again about death";
"I am not frightened now";
"If this is death, how wonderful, how easy, how natural!"

These otherwise incredible convictions and conclusions of people who left their physical bodies *temporarily* accord (a) with each other and (b) with the various events ("mist", "cold winds", horizontal position, etc.) and experiences ("blackout", noises in head, etc.) which themselves exhibit the remarkable concordance of occurring both when the body is vacated and when it is re-entered.

Astral projectors are absolutely sure of these effects. People who have not had (or, rather, who do not "remember" having had) projections can obtain, from a study of such testimonies, a very high degree of probability: they yield a virtual, if not absolute, certainty.

But there is other evidence which is also adequately explained on our hypothesis (and on no other)—that which is represented by "communications" from supposed survivors of death. It is now clear that the descriptions which these give of their own *permanent* projections from the body, i.e., deaths of the body, are identical, with regard to both events and experiences, to those of *temporary* excursions.

REVIEW OF TERMS USED

"Astral (bright, luminous, 'star-like') Body": This term is used by different writers with different connotations: some are referring to the "semi-physical" and "semi-mental" vehicle of vitality or vital "body" (via which the physical body is animated, and which "bridges" the "super-physical" Soul Body and the physical body—but which is not, by itself, an instrument of consciousness); others are referring to the Soul Body, man's primary vehicle of consciousness (apart, that is, from the True Spiritual Body which is used by the Eternal Self).

"Double" (of physical body): The released non-physical body is usually outwardly a replica, or double, of the physical. Its composition varies under different conditions and with different people. The temporarily-released "double" of a non-mediumistic person consists of the Soul Body only, i.e., it is simple: that of a mediumistic person, i.e., of a man who has a loose, fluid and extensible vehicle of vitality, is at first composite, comprising (a) the Soul Body which, however, is more or less enshrouded by (b) a significant portion of the vehicle of vitality. Usually, though not invariably, the released composite "double" passes through a second stage—the vehicle of vitality returns to the physical body (to which it properly belongs), leaving the Soul Body in an un-enshrouded condition: the "double" is then simple, as with non-mediumistic people. The permanently-released "double" of a newly-dead man is invariably composite, consisting of (a) the Soul Body which, however, suffers a maximum enshroudment by (b) the whole of the vehicle of vitality. About three days after physical death, this enshrouding "semi-physical" substance is discarded from the composite "double", leaving the Soul Body in its natural (Paradise) World. This process is often called the second "death".

"Etheric (subtle, tenuous, fluid) body" or *"etheric double"*: as for "Astral Body".

"Etheric" double = "semi-physical" vehicle of vitality—all physical objects are said to have their "semi-physical" doubles: hence the immediate "next world", Hades, is very earth-like.

"Hades" = *Sheol*: This state (which is not "hell", the place of torment) corresponds to the "semi-physical" vehicle of

vitality. Immediately after the permanent shedding of the physical body, one enters "Hades", i.e., the "semi-physical" aura of the earth. Man's (usually brief—i.e., three-day) stay in this earth-like environment is due to the fact that his primary body, the Soul Body, is enveiled or enshrouded by his vehicle of vitality. With a man of average spiritual development who dies naturally in old age, the enveilment of the Soul Body causes an after-death "sleep", with dreams, which terminates in about three days (when the vehicle of vitality is shed—at the second "death"). A man of average type who is killed in the prime of life, on the other hand, is at first in a half-waking, half-dreaming condition. True saints pass rapidly through "Hades", unaware of that environment. Gross sinners may remain in "Hades" for a considerable time, for the ideo-plastic conditions facilitate the apparent fulfilment of their earth-directed desires. All men leave "Hades"—the denser part of the total "aura" of the earth, just as the vehicle of vitality is the denser part of man's total "aura"—and contact "Paradise" when they shed the vehicle of vitality, i.e., after the second "death".

"Paradise" = *"Garden of Eden"*: This is "a glorified earth", "the Garden of Eden" of the Old Testament, from which early man was largely excluded as the Soul Body (the "super-physical" aura of man, corresponding to "Paradise", the "super-physical" aura of the earth) became more and more enmeshed in a physical body (corresponding to the physical world). This process, part of "the fall", involved both gain and loss: on the one hand, only by limiting and focussing consciousness could man become individualised and therefore capable of responsibility and Spiritual evolution; on the other hand, he tended to lose direct awareness of both the "Paradise" World and the True Spiritual World with their helpers. This awareness will doubtless be resumed (with the gain of individualisation) as the Soul is resurrected out of dense matter. The "dead", after a period in "Paradise", eventually undergo the third "death", i.e., the shedding of the Soul Body, and can then contact the True "Heavens" of the Scriptures. If qualified by the selfless search for truth and beauty and by selfless service (so that the Spiritual Body has begun to be organised) they are aware of these Transcendent conditions; they live the Eternal Life.

"Remembrance" of out-of-the-body experiences: This is inevitably tardy. Not only is "remembrance" of very rare occurrence, but it is very probable that in very few cases is the whole experience "remembered"—the physical brain

was not involved and shuts them out. Training in sequences may aid "remembrance"—as was realised by Pythagoras who lived several centuries B.C.

"Soul, Psychic or Psychical Body": This is "super-physical" in nature (whereas the vehicle of vitality, by means of which the Soul Body contacts the physical body, is "semi-physical" and "semi-mental"). Called "spiritual body" by St. Paul (I Cor., xv, 35, 44), it corresponds to the "Paradise" realm of the total earth (the "third heaven" of St. Paul) which it interpenetrates. The un-enshrouded Soul Body permits consciousness at "super-normal" or psychic levels, i.e., its activities include telepathy, clairvoyance and foreknowledge. Psychical development by mortals demands concentration, passivity, the cultivation of the image-making faculty and rhythmical breathing; it is not necessarily either spiritual or evil but it can be used as a means of service, in which case it has inestimable Spiritual value.

Survival of bodily death: What we said concerning the details considered in *The Techniques of Astral Projection*, Aquarian Press, 1964, applies also to the details given in the above pages: "Some of our castles (e.g., that at Rochester) were apparently impregnable: they successfully resisted all direct attacks. Yet many fell to indirect approach (Rochester for lack of drains!). The problems of survival has proved almost, if not quite, impregnable to direct attack; yet matters such as those here considered, though constituting evidence of an indirect kind, leave the matter in little, if any doubt." The "super-physical" Soul Body is man's primary body, his physical body being only a temporary condensation or extension of it: when the physical body dies the "semi-physical" bridge, electro-magnetic in nature, accompanies and, for a time, enshrouds, the Soul Body and the person concerned contacts the Hades aura of the earth. In average cases of natural death, however, a "second death" (or "the second half of the first death") takes place: the vehicle of vitality is shed, the Soul Body is un-enshrouded and the Soul contacts the finer, Paradise, aura of the earth—the natural environment of the Soul. (Eventually, if the person's Spiritual nature has developed, after a long period in Paradise, he will shed the Soul Body, i.e., undergo the third "death" and so enter Heaven in the True Spiritual "Body").

True Spiritual, Divine or Celestial "Body": This is a "body" in the sense of being an instrument of consciousness (at Spiritual levels). But it is so tenuous that, unlike the

Soul Body (and the still denser physical body), it has no boundary, no form, since it exists beyond physical space. The Spiritual "Body" interpenetrates both the Soul Body and the physical body. The Soul (and its Body) animates the personality (with its physical body): the Over-Soul or "Spirit" (and the Spiritual "Body") animates the whole man, Soul and personality: it is "within" and "around" him, the Source of all his real growth, power and health.

All true growth and significant activities come from the Unmanifested "Father"; they are mediated by the "Son" (the "Father"-in-manifestation, the Cosmic Christ, the "Vine" of whom the Over-Souls of men are the "Branches"): they pass from this Spiritual, or Divine, level, "down" or "outwards", through the Soul Body and, via the electro-magnetic "bridge", the vehicle of vitality, to the physical body and the personality, and issue as appropriate words and deeds, bringing "the Kingdom of God" to earth.

Vehicle of Vitality: This is the "semi-physical" and "semi-mental", ultra-gaseous or electro-magnetic part of the total physical body: it corresponds to the "Hades" portion of the total earth. When the whole of it leaves the body, the latter dies. Hence, at death, it accompanies the Soul Body, and the immediate after-death double is always composite. The vehicle of vitality is normally shed three days later, much like a physical after-birth. With a few people, this part of the total body tends to be somewhat loose, fluid and extensible, so that (whether they are aware of it or not, and whether they "develop" or not) they tend to be mediumistic and may have experiences which they do not understand. This is the "breath of life" of the Scriptures (Gen. ii, 7). It has three main functions: (1) it transmits vital cosmic forces, gathered by the Soul Body from super-physical realms, to the physical body; (2) it acts as a "semi-physical" "bridge" between the "super-physical" Soul Body and the physical body—without it, Souls could not contact the physical body (and therefore the physical world) and earth-life would be valueless; (3) it, as well as the physical brain, bears a memory-record.

Whenever a significant part of the vehicle of vitality is released from the physical body the latter is necessarily death-like; when, eventually, the whole of it has been released, the body is dead: the "bridge" being completely broken, the Soul Body can no longer affect it or be affected by it.

"There is still much that I could say to you, but the burden would be too great for you to bear. However, when He comes who is the Spirit of Truth, He will guide you into all the Truth"—*Jesus* (John xvi, 12).

"To believe that any past generation held the monopoly of truth, or was able to give it final expression, is not only inconsistent with the teaching of history, but is a flat denial of the Holy Spirit, which was promised to guide us progressively into all truth."—*Dr. Cyril Alington.*

"The proper meaning of 'orthodoxy' is simply 'true' or 'right' opinion. In practical affairs everyone recognises the value of having true opinions. Life itself is a practical affair and we are unlikely to make much of it if we have false opinions concerning the world, our nature, and our relations with God . . . The mistake which 'orthodox' people make is to suppose that they have all the truth and that nothing more can be known".—*Dr. W. R. Matthews.*

"Scientific caution and humility are not enough. A certain boldness also is required, a readiness to grasp a vast range of converging evidence each item of which, standing alone, can lead us nowhere."—*Professor William McDougall.*

"The great controversy which today is dividing the world is over the nature of man."—*Dr. Cyril Garbett,* late Archbishop of York.

"The study of psychical research achieves two things of great value. First, it throws light on what we really are (in contra-distinction to what 'common-sense' urges us to believe what we are). Secondly, it begins to clarify our situation in the Universe by showing that selfhood is not an ephemeral product of the brain, but is linked with the Core of Reality. To realise these things is the first step towards bringing life and immortality to light."—*G. N. M. Tyrrell.*

"Conclusions concerning the psychological data of everyday life are 'proved' by the principle of coherence—they can be considered well-founded if all the known facts are shown to be consistent with each other and if, in addition, they can be woven into a story which will explain society's behaviour."—*Dr. Leslie Way.*

RELEASE	NATURAL Ia	NATURAL Ib	ENFORCED II
person's moral status	high soul body organised	all degrees	all degrees
vehicle of vitality	tight keeps in body	loose projects readily	either type
composition of double	ONE STAGE un-veiled SOUL BODY ↓	FIRST STAGE en-veiling / S.B. / V. of V. ↓ cf. II	ONE STAGE en-veiling / S.B. / V. of V. ↓
experiences	many psychic	few psychic	few psychic
realm	paradise	hades	earth or hades
composition of double	↓ simple throughout	SECOND STAGE un-veiled SOUL BODY ↓	↓ composite throughout
experiences		many psychic cf. I	
realm	↓	paradise ↓	↓
the *return* to the physical body is the reverse of release (explicable only if vehicle of vitality and soul body objective)			
composition of double	↓ un-veiled SOUL BODY ↓	↓ cf. II en-veiling / S.B. / V. of V. ↓	↓ en-veiling / S.B. / V. of V. ↓
body re-entered	in <u>one</u> stage	in <u>two</u> stages	in <u>one</u> stage
frequency	very rare	fairly rare	very rare

LIST OF CASES HEREIN

Case No.
723—A Doctor of Medicine (*in litt.*)
724—Mrs. M. Claxton (*in litt.*)
725—Dr. D. M. A. Leggett (The Need for a New Metaphysic, C.P.S., 1971, p.6)
726—*ibid.*
727—Mrs. M. C. Wilke (*in litt.*)
728—Mary E. Evans (Quart. Review, C.F.P.S.S., 1971, p.16)
729—William Blake (*Light*, xc, 1970, p.188)
730—Richard Jefferies (*The Story of My Heart*, Longmans, 1883, pp. 10, 76)
731—Freda G. H. Laycock (Quart. Review C.F.P.S.S., 68, 1971, p.12)
732—Catherine, M. Washburn Westala, *ibid.*, p.12
733—Harwood Thompson (Seeker at the Gate, C.F.P.S.S., 1970, p.64)
734—*ibid.*, p.65
735—Harwood Thompson, second account, *ibid.*, p.60
736—Dr. Meerloo, *Parapsychological Review*, ii, 1971, p.1
737—Harold Oliver (*Memoirs of the Owen Family*, O.U.P., 1963, p.30)
738—Raymond Bayless (*The Other Side of Death*, University Books Inc., 1971, p.119)
739—Miss S. Ridgway (*in litt.*)
740—Eva Burton ("communicator" of)
741—St. Augustine (C. J. S. Thompson, *The Mystery of Apparitions*, Harold Taylor, 1913)
742—Mrs. I. Guhasy (*in litt.*)
743—Dr. R. W. Ludlow's patient (*Spiritual Frontiers*, iii, 1971, p.20)
744—Mrs. D. King (*in litt.*)
745—Steven Reccia (*in litt.*)
746—Robert Brocato (*in litt.*)
747—W. H. Bradley (*in litt.*)
748—Peter van Muyden (*in litt.*)
749—Robert Monroe (*Journeys out of the Body*, Doubleday, 1970)
750—Kelvin Stevens (*in litt.*)
751—T. Cain (*in litt.*)
752—Eric Laliberté (*in litt.*)
753—Mrs. J. Wade (*in litt.*)
754—Dr. C. G. Jung (*Naturerklarung und Psyche*, Zürich, 1952)
755—Mrs. S. Schoenberger (*in litt.*)
756—Phoebe Payne (& L. J. Bendit) (*The Psychic Sense*, Faber, 1943, p.74)
757—Max Freedom Long (*The Secret Science Behind Miracles*, Kosmon Press, 1948, p.148)
758—J. H. Brown (*Light*, lxviii, 1948, p.126)
759—Mrs. F. W. Shrine (John Myers, *Voices from the Edge of Eternity*, Voice Publications, Box 672, Northside, Calif., 91324—a compilation from (1) *Dying Hours* by A. H. Gottschall, pub. by Gottschall, England, 1888, (2) *Dying Testimonies*, S. B. Shaw, U.S.A., 1898, (3) D. P. Kidder, Carlton & Phillips, N.Y., 1848, *Dying Words*.)
760—Clara Burke (*The Ghosts About Us*, Dorrance & Co., Philadelphia, Pa., 1913)
761—The Revd. A. D. Sandborn's case (from J. B. Palmer, *The Child of God Between Death and the Resurrection*, Palmer, Galveston, Texas).

Case No.
762—Mrs. Julia Roupp (*Guideposts*, reprinted by Meers, 1968)
763—A. P. Terhune (Alice Terhune, *Across the Line*, E. P. Dutton, 1961)
764—Jerold Moger (*in litt.*)
765—A. Davies (*in litt.*)
766—Gordon W. Creighton (*in litt.*)
767—Mrs. Olga Adler (*in litt.*)
768—W. H. Butler (*in litt.*)
769—W. D. Wuttenee, a Cru Indian, Saskatchewan (*in litt.*)
770—Mrs. N. Robinson (*in litt.*)
771—Mrs. Peggy Miller (*in litt.*)
772—Attila von Szalay (*in litt.*)
773—Anne Sinclair (*in litt.*)
774—Thomas M. Johanson (*in litt.*)
775—Harwood Thompson's friend (*in litt.*)
776—Mary Swainson (*Light*, xcii, 1972, p.25)
777—Dr. K. Novotny (cited by Wyatt Rawson, *Light*, xcii, 1972, p.31)
778—Mrs. "I. Beach" (*in litt.*)
779—Mrs. H. Margetts (*in litt.*)
780—J. S. Hindle (*in litt.*)
781—Clifford Thomas (*in litt.*)
782—Mrs. E. Bullinger (*in litt.*)
783—Jane Roberts (*The Seth Material*, Prentice-Hall, 1970, pp. 5, 71, 101)
784—P. E. Cornillier (*The Survival of The Soul*, Kegan Paul, 1921, p.14)
785—Nandor Fodor (*Encyclopedia of Psychic Science*), 1933, p.46)
786—Alex. Erskine (*A Hypnotist's Case Book*, Rider, p.76)
787—H. Willmott (*in litt.*)
788—Miss Victoria Laird (*in litt.*)
789—Brad Steiger's cases (*Minds through Space and Time*), Award Books, 1971)
790—Mrs. J. Alwood (*in litt.*)
791—Mrs. E. Thirlway (*in litt.*)
792—Stanley G. Price (*in litt.*)
793—A. J. Martin (*in litt.*)
794—Mrs. B. F. Leary (*in litt.*)
795—Wanda Sue Parrott (*in litt.*)
796—Mrs. D. E. Munroe (*in litt.*)
797—The Rev. N. A. G. Sieme (*in litt.*)
798—Mrs. M. J. Holland (*in litt.*)
797—Mrs. B. Doty (*in litt.*)
800—Margaret Livermore (*in litt.*)
801—Jimmy E. Ward (*in litt.*)
802—Jerome Paul (*in litt.*)
803—Ida R. Fettleberg (*in litt.*)
804—Linda King (*in litt.*)
805—A. R. Johnston (*in litt.*)
806—Professor Charles T. Tart's marijuana cases (*Nature*, 226, 1970)
807—An electronic engineer (from Professor Tart)
808—A motor-cyclist (ditto)
809—A man who had a fall (ditto)
810—A teacher (ditto)
811—An LSD case (ditto)

Case No.
812—Kargerine Beaton-Troker (*Psychic Experiences,* Vantage Press Inc., 1962)
813—Peter Freuchen (*Arctic Adventure,* H. Wolff Book Manufacturing Co., N.Y., 1935)
814—Dr. Aniela Jaffé's case of re-entry (*Apparitions and Precognition,* University Books Inc., N.Y., U.S.A., 1963, p.144)
815—Dr. Jaffé's case of a released vehicle of vitality (*ibid.,* p.151)
816—Dr. Jaffé's case of pain-avoidance (*ibid.,* p.181)
817—Hannan Swaffer's medium (*My Greatest Story,* W. H. Allen, 1945)
818—James H. Neal (*Ju Ju in My Life,* 1968)
819—C. H. D'Alessio (*in litt.*)
820—Leone (*Parapsychology Review,* i, p.9)
821—Shankracharya (Dr. B. K. Kanthamani, *ibid.,* ii, 1971, p.15
822—Mr. & Mrs. Sage (*in litt.*)
823—Miss Carole Thraum (*in litt.*)
824—L. A. Woodworth (*in litt.*)
825—Mrs. Geraldine Tuke (C.F.P.S.S., 1972, p.20)
826—Mrs. Josephine Lambert (*in litt.*)
827—Mrs. A. Johnson (*in litt.*)
828—A Legal Correspondent (*in litt.*)
829—E. C. Colley (*in litt.*)
830—Alma R. Clarke (*in litt.*)
831—H. Brennan (*Experimental Magic,* 1972)
832—Jean Tunnicliffe (*in litt.*)
833—Kelvin J. Drab (*in litt.*)
834—Mrs. M. Blanton (*in litt.*)
835—W. H. Hudson (*Far Away and Long Ago,* Dent, 1918, p.2)
836—Kathy Roberto (*in litt.*)
837—Experimental investigation by Dr. Karlis Osis, Research Director, A.S.P.R. (*Newsletter,* Nos. 12 & 14, 1972)
838—Drs. R. L. MacMillan & K. W. G. Brown (patient of)

REFERENCES

1. Fodor, N., *Encyclopedia of Psychic Science*, Arthur's Press, 1933, p.100.
2. Grenside, Dorothy, *The Meaning of Dreams*, G. Bell & Sons, 1923, p.35.
3. Battersby, H. Prevost, *Man Outside Himself*, Rider, p.64.
4. *Borderland*, 1890.
5. Gurney, E., and others, *Phantasms of the Living*, Kegan Paul, 1886.
6. de la Mare, *Behold this Dreamer*, Faber & Faber, 1939.
7. *Light*, lxviii, 1948, p.267.
8. *Sydney Telegraph*, Nov. 20, 1924.
9. Kerner, J., *Die, Scherin von Prevost*.
10. Garrett, Mrs. Eileen J., *Adventures in the Super-normal*, Garrett Publications, 1949, p.84.
11. Garrett, Mrs. Eileen J., *Awareness*, Creative Age Press, 1943, p.278.
12. Gerhardi, William, *Resurrection*, Cassell, 1934.
13. *Fate* Magazine: May, 1954.
14. *Light*, lii, 1932, p.298.
15. Harlow, S. Ralph, *A Life After Death*, Gollancz, 1961, p.41.
16. *Journ. S.P.R.*, xlii, 1913, p.126.
17. Muldoon, S. J. (with H. Carrington), *The Projection of the Astral Body*, Rider, 1929.
18. Jefferies, Richard, *The Story of My Life*, Longmans, 1887, pp. 10, 76.
19. Crookall, R., *The Study and Practice of Astral Projection*, Aquarian Press, 1961, p.17. (American Edition, University Books Inc., New York, 1965.)
20. *ibid.*, p.72.
21. *ibid.*, p.121.
22. Richmond, Zoë, *Evidence of Purpose*, G. Bell & Sons, 1938, p.56.
23. Newsletter of Parapsychology Foundation, xi, p.1.
24. Fodor, Nandor, *Encyclopedia of Psychic Science*, Arthurs Press, 1933, p.233.
25. *Bull, Boston S.P.R.*, xi.
26. Owen, Harold, *Memoirs of the Owen Family*, I, O.U.P., 1963, p.30.
27. Bayless, Raymond, *The Other Side of Death*, University Books Inc., N.Y., 1971, p.119.
28. Crookall, R., *The Supreme Adventure*, James Clarke, 1961, pp. 100, 241.
29. Crookall, R., *The Jung-Jaffé View of Out-of-the-body Experiences*, World Fellowship Press, 1970, p.70.
30. Monroe, Robert, *Journeys Out of the Body*, Doubleday Inc., 1970.
31. Ref. No. 25, pp. 101, 137, 142, 148.
32. Crookall, R., *The Mechanisms of Astral Projection*, Darshana International, Moradabad, India, 1968, p.12.
33. *ibid.*, p.93.
34. *ibid.*, p.56.
35. *ibid.*, p.119.
36. *Light*, lxviii, 1948, p.126.
37. Barrett, Sir William, *Death Bed Visions*, Methuen, 1926.
38. Ref. No. 25, p.12.

39. *ibid*, pp. 86-94.
40. *ibid.*, pp. 122, 124.
41. Ref. No. 26, p.70.
42. Ref. No. 16, Cases 1-4, 23, 31, 47, 55. 60, 67, 69, 83, 90, 91, 97, 118.
43. Crookall, R., *More Astral Projections*, Aquarian Press, 1964, Cases 213, 215, 220, 223, 224, 230, 245, 246, 254, 271, 287, 293, 360.
44. Gaythorpe, Mrs. Elizabeth, *Light* lxxxviii, 1968, p.110.
45. Ref. No. 25, p.234.
46. Hyslop, Dr. J., *Contact with the Other World*.
47. Newsletter of the Parapsychology Foundation, xvi, 1969, p.13.
48. Brunton, P., *The Quest of the Overself*, Rider, p.174.
49. Yram, *Practical Astral Projection*, Rider, pp. 40, 180.
50. Cornillier, P. E., *The Survival of the Soul*, Kegan Paul, 1921, p.14.
51. Ref. No. 21, p.46.
52. Erskine, Alex., *A Hypnotist's Case Book*, Rider.
53. Ref. No. 16, Cases No. 20, 32, 38, 49, 60, 68, 72, 73, 74, 78, 85, 90, 95, 100, 102.
54. *ibid.*, Cases No. 44, 70, 85, 99.
55. Ref. No. 39, Cases No. 177, 185, 192, 202, 212, 226, 243, 250, 258, 268, 280, 294, 336, 364, 395.
56. *ibid.*, Cases No. 244, 301.
57. Ref. No. 21, p.244.
58. Ref. No. 29, p.37.
59. *Parapsychology Review*, I, 1970, p.9.
60. Ref. No. 21, p.347.
61. Proc. A.S.P.R., 29, 1970.
62. *Spiritual Frontiers*, 1969, p.9.
63. Presidential Address S.P.R., 1928.
64. Muldoon, S. J. (with H. Carrinton), *The Phenomena of Astral Projection*, Rider, 1951.
65. Kerner, Dr. J., *Die Seherin von Prevorst*, 1929, p.155.
66. de'Espérance, Mme., *Shadow Land*, George Redway, 1897.
67. Ref. No. 26 (Refs. given therein Nos. 189-190).
68. Crookes, Sir William, *Researches in the Phenomena of Spiritualism*, J. Burns, 1874.
69. Macmillan, W. J., *The Reluctant Healer*, Gallancz, 1952, p.153.
70. Ref. No. 61, p.228.
71. W. T. Pole, *Private Dowding*, Watkins, 1919.
72. Ref. No. 45, pp. 35, 58, 60, 170, 171, 211, 123, 296.
73. *Soc. des Sci. Psychiques*, 1914.
74. Ref. No. 21, pp. 113, 251, 256, 407.
75. Durville, H., *Le Fantôme des Vivants*, Paris.
76. Long, Max Freedom, *The Secret Science Behind Miracles*, Kosmon Press, 1948, p.127.
77. Rose, Dr. Ronald, *Living Magic*, Chatto & Windus, 1957.
78. Payne, Phoebe, *The Psychic Sense*, Faber.
79. Garrett, Mrs. Eileen J., *Telepathy*, Creative Age Press.
80. Pole, W. T., *The Thinning of the Veil*, Watkins, 1919.
81. Achorn, Dr. J. W., *Nature's Way to Happiness*.
82. Hudson, W. H., *Far Away and Long Ago*, Dent, 1918, p.201.
83. Davids, Mrs. Rhys, *What is Your Will?* Rider, p.79.
84. W. Wingfield, Kate, *More Guidance from Beyond*, Philip Alan, 1925, p.26.

85. I. Gilbert, Alice, *Philip in the Spheres*, Andrew Dakers, 1948, p.22.
86. *J.A.S.P.R.*, 66, 1972, p.233.
87. Ref. No. 21, pp. 101-105.
88. Maxwell, Dr. J., *Les Phénomenes Physique*, 1903, p.10.
89. Ref. No. 21, p.374.
90. *Proc. S.P.R.*, ix, p.65.
91. Ref. No. 71, p.14.
92. *Psychic News*, Sept. 11, 1937.
93. Gibier, Dr. P., *Analysis of Existing Things*, Paris, 1890.
94. d'Assier, *Posthumous Humanity*, Redway, 1888.
95. Neal, James H., *Ju Ju in My Life*, Harrap, 1966, p.67.
96. Crookall, R., *Out-of-the-body Experiences*, University Books Inc., N.Y., 1970, p.162.
97. Crookall, R., *Events on the Threshold of the After Life*, Darshana International, Moradabad, India, 1968, p.98.
98. *ibid.*, p.34.
99. Davis, Dr. A. J., *Answers to Ever-recurring Questions*, 1868, p.26.
100. Ref. No. 79, p.99.
101. *ibid.*, p.32.
102. Pole, W. T., *Private Dowding*, Watkins, 1919.
103. Fox, Oliver, *Astral Projection*, Rider, pp. 83, 86, 114.
104. Ref. No. 14, p.27.
105. Ref. No. 159, p.213.
106. Howitt, Miss, *Pioneers of the Spiritual Reformation*, 1883.
107. de Morgan, Mrs., *From Spirit to Matter*, 1863.
108. Bird, Malcolm, *My Psychic Adventures*, N.Y., U.S.A.
109. Turvey, V., *The Beginnings of Seership*, Stead, 1909, p.156.
110. Rogers, G., *The Philosophy of Mysterious Rappings*, 1883.
111. Ref. No. 27, p.211.
112. Ref. No. 45, p.308.
113. Ref. No. 60, p.72.
114. Matt. xviii, 19, 20.
115. Heb. x, 25.
116. Ref. No. 29, p.104.
117. Crookall, R., *The Techniques of Astral Projection*, Aquarian Press, 1964, p.58.
118. Ref. No. 16, p.136.
119. Marryat, Florence, *The Spirit World*, 1894.
120. Ref. No. 45, pp. 160, 207, 298, 402, 466.
121. Sherwood, Jane, *The Country Beyond*, Rider, p.63.
122. Ref. No. 25, p.166.
123. *ibid.*, pp. 42, 65, 163, 173.
124. Ref. No. 45, pp. 197, 392, 436, 437.
125. Banks, Frances, *The Frontiers of Revelation*, Parrish, 1962, p.110.
126. Ref. No. 25, p.15.
127. Ref. No. 97, pp. 1, 3, 11, 64.
128. Curtiss, H. A., *Realms of the Living Dead*, Calif., U.S.A., 1917, p.27.
129. Ref. No. 39, p.124.
130. *Light*, xcii, 1972, p.145.
131. *ibid.*, p.40.
132. Ref. No. 25, pp. 14, 15, 19, 21.
133. *ibid.*, pp. 19, 21.
134. *Light*, xc, 1970, p.188.

135. Ref. No. 79, p.63.
136. Crookall, R., *Intimations of Immortality*, James Clarke, 1965, p.23.
137. Vivian, Mrs. G., B.A., *The Curtain Drawn*, Psychic Press, 1961.
138. Ref. No. 115, p.23.
139. Ref. No. 25, pp.72.
140. ibid., pp. 209, 223.
141. "A.B.", *One Step Higher*, The C. W. Daniel Co., 1937, p.381.
142. *Proc. S.P.R.*, xi, 1895, p.93.
143. Thomas, the Rev. C. Drayton, *Life Beyond Death With Evidence*, Collins, 1928, p.174.
144. Barker, Elsa, *Letters from a Living Dead Man*, Rider, 1914, p.108.
145. Heslop, F., *Speaking Across the Border Line*, Charles Taylor, 1912, p.52.
146. Crookall, R., *During Sleep*, Theosophical Publishing House, 1964, pp. 45, 54, 55.
147. Wingfield, Kate, *Guidance from Beyond*, Philip Allan, 1923, pp. 33, 190.
148. Ref. No. 25, pp. 17, 20, 100, 101, 137, 142, 178.
149. *Proc. S.P.R.*, vi, p.117.
150. *Journ. S.P.R.*, xxvi, 1912, p.96.
151. Ref. No. 14, pp. 54-56.
152. Ref. No. 25, p.42.
153. Crookall, R., *The Next World—And The Next*, Theosophical Publishing House, 1966.
154. Fox, Oliver, *Astral Projection*, Rider, N.D.
155. Crookall, R., *The Techniques of Astral Projection*, Aquarian Press, 1961, p.51.
156. Isa. xi, 3.
157. I Sam. iii, 9, 10.
158. John xiii, 17.
159. I John iii, 1, 8, 14, 19.
160. John xv, 5.
161. John xv, 16.
162. John xv, 5.
163. Phil. iv, 13.
164. Matt. xxi, 22; Mark xi, 24.
165. Matt. vii, 7.
166. Mark xi, 24.
167. Luke vi, 47.
168. Luke xl, 28.
169. Matt. vii, 16.
170. Matt. xvi, 25.
171. Gal. ii, 20.
172. Ref. No. 16, pp. 140, 200.
173. Ref. No. 25, pp. 20, 100, 101, 137, 142, 170.
174. Ref. No. 16, pp. 200-202.
175. Whiteman, Prof. J. H. M., *The Philosophy of Space and Time*, pp. 365-6; 411-2.
176. Hare, M. M., *The Multiple Universe*, Julian Press, 1968.
177. *J.A.S.P.R.*, 63, 1969, p.308.
178. Gen. ii, 7; vi, 17.
179. I Cor. xv, 35, 44.
180. John xiv, 2.
181. John iii, 13; Rev. xi, 12.

ACKNOWLEDGMENTS

For permission to make brief extracts from copyright material the writer tenders grateful thanks to the following publishers and authors.

Aquarian Press: R. Crookall, *The Study and Practice of Astral Projection*, 1961, pp. 17, 72, 121; *More Astral Projections*, 1964, p.46.
Arthurs Press: Nandor Fodor, *Encyclopedia of Psychic Science*, 1933, p.233.
A.S.P.R.: 29, 1970; Journ. 63, 1969, p.308.
Bull. Boston S.P.R., xi.
Cassell: William Gerhardi, *Resurrection*, 1934.
Chatto & Windus: Ronald Rose, *Living Magic*, 1957.
Creative Age Press Inc.: Mrs. Eileen J. Garrett, *Awareness*, 1943, p.278.
Darshana International, Moradabad, India: Crookall, R., *The Mechanisms of Astral Projection*, 1966, pp. 12, 56, 93, 119; *Events on the Theshold of the After Life*, 1968, pp. 34, 98.
Doubleday Inc.: Robert Monroe, *Journeys out of the Body*, 1970.
Faber & Faber: Walter de la Mare, *Behold this Dreamer*, 1939.
Garrett Publications Inc.: Mrs. Eileen J. Garrett, *Adventures in the Super-normal*, 1949, p.89.
G. Bell & Sons: Dorothy Grenside, *The Meaning of Dreams*, 1923, p.35: Zoe Richmond, *Evidence of Purpose*, 1938, p.56.
Gollancz: S. Ralth Harlow, *A Life After Death*, 1961, p.41.
Harrap: John H. Neal, *Ju Ju in my Life*, 1966, p.67.
James Clarke: R. Crookall, *The Supreme Adventure*, 1961, pp. 100, 241; *Intimations of Immortality*, 1965, p.23.
Julian Press: M. M. Hare, *The Multiple Universe*, 1968.
Kegan Paul: E. Gurney (etc.), *Phantasms of the Living*, 1886; P. E. Cornillier, *The Survival of the Soul*, 1921, p.14.
Kosmon Press: Max Freedom Long, *The Secret Science Behind Miracles*, 1948, p.127.
Light: iii, 1932, p.398; lxxxviii, 1968, p.110.
Longmans: Richard Jefferies, *The Story of My Life*, 1887, pp. 10, 76.
Methuen: Sir Wm. Barrett, *Death Bed Visions*, 1926.
Newsletter of Parapsychology Foundation, xi, p.1; xvi, p.13.
Parapsychology Review: 1970, p.9.
Oxford University Press: Harold Owen, *Memoirs of the Owen Family*, i, 1963, p.30.
Psychic News: Sept. 11, 1937.
Rider & Co.: H. Prevost Battersby, *Man Outside Himself*, p.64; S. J. Muldoon, *The Projection of the Astral Body*, 1929; *The Phenomena of Astral Projection*, 1951; Yram, *Practical Astral Projection*, pp. 40, 180; A. Erskine, *A Hypnotist's Case Book*; O. Fox, *Astral Projection*, pp. 83, 86, 114.
S.P.R.: *Proc.* ix, p.65; *Journ.* xlii, 1963, p.126; Presidential Address 1928.
Soc. des Sci. Psychiques: 1914.
University Books, N.Y., U.S.A.: Raymond Bayless, *The Other Side of Death*, 1971, p.119.
World Fellowship Press: R. Crookall, *The Jung-Jaffé View of Out-of-the body Experiences*, 1970, p.70.

SUBJECTS INDEX TO CASES HEREIN

Case No.

"Astral shells" (vehicles of vitality discarded at the second "death") 793
"Blackout" (or "tunnel"—as vehicle of vitality leaves body, i.e., first death)   745, 748, 751, 761, 767, 768, 828, 830
"Blackout" (or "tunnel"—as vehicle of vitality leaves composite double, i.e., second "death")   724, 731, 774, 788, 800
Catalepsy (because much of v. of v. has left body)
    739, 742, 763, 765, 768, 778, 793, 801, 802, 813, 824
"Click" ("bang", "plop", "bump", "jolt", "jerk") as v. of v. leaves body 782, 788, 802, 805, 824
"Click" ("bang", "plop", "bump", "jolt", "jerk") as composite double re-enters body   398, 724, 731, 742, 747, 750
"Clothes" worn by released doubles 820
Coldness 802, 823
Difficulty in re-entering physical body 822
Double (whether composite or consisting of Soul Body only) was above physical body   729, 734, 739, 750, 760, 762, 767, 769, 770, 777, 778, 781, 782, 783, 787, 791, 794, 796, 797, 806, 807, 808, 811, 813, 824, 827
Double which was composite (v. of v. plus Soul Body) horizontal when first released at first death   729, 768, 776, 788, 826, 828
Double which was composite (v. of v. plus Soul Body) horizontal prior to re-entering body, i.e., reverse of first death 750, 768, 814, 826
Dual consciousness (of i the double and ii the physical body—and their environments) 751, 801, 802
Dying expected 823, 824
Flying "dreams" (movements of released doubles) 788, 801, 804, 807, 822
"Fog", "mist", etc. (released v. of v. of man, corresponding to the Hades aura of the earth) 788
"Gate", "door", "bridge", "window", etc. (between Hades aura and Paradise aura of earth) 748, 754, 762, 778
Glass (inimical to psychic phenomena) 823
"Glove", "coat", "garment", etc. (suggested when release from body was easy) 771, 774
"Glove", "coat", "garment", etc. (suggested when re-entry into body was easy) 458, 462, 482, 769, 770, 771
Hades sphere ("semi-physical" aura of earth, corresponding to v. of v. of man) 521, 748, 770, 774, 778
Paradise sphere ("super-physical" aura of earth, corresponding to Soul Body of man) 817, 824
Reluctance to return to and re-enter physical body 788, 789, 793, 825, 826, 833, 835
Returns to the body which involved some difficulty 823
Review of past life 833
"Robes" of released doubles (the "clothes" of "spirits")   778, 782, 800, 825, 832
Second "death" (the discarding, by a composite double, of the v. of v.) 724, 731, 774, 824
Sensation of rising (or of falling) as double left body (first death) 753

	Case No.
"Silver cord"-extension (of either v. of v. or Soul Body) seen by deponent	740, 744, 748, 770, 772, 778, 788, 791
"Silver cord"-extension felt but not seen	762, 767, 769, 803
Solar plexus (chief exit of v. of v. from body—hence its "cord" is often attached there)	742, 744, 748, 768
Soul Body ("super-physical" in nature), man's primary body	570, 742, 748, 776
"Spirit lights" (incipient materialisations of discarnate doubles)	744, 745, 747, 768, 778, 802
"Sucked back" (description of released composite double re-entering body)	52, 105, 287, 291, 360, 368, 748, 789
"Suckers" (of vitality)	793
Survival of bodily death	767
"Tingles" (felt as v. of v. quits physical body)	742, 750, 751, 765, 778, 793, 797, 800, 804, 824
"Tunnel"-effect (a prolonged "blackout", i.e., double released slowly from body)	745, 748, 751
"Vibrations" (as v. of v. begins to quit body)	742, 750, 751, 765, 824
"Vibrations" (as v. of v. begins to re-enter body)	789
"Water" (condensed "fog", "mist", etc. see above: v. of v. of man, corresponding to Hades aura of earth)	778
Younger (released double of an aged person tends to revert to youthful appearance)	788